PAKISTAN
The Contours of
State and Society

PAKISTAN
The Contours of
State and Society

Edited by
Soofia Mumtaz
Jean-Luc Racine
Imran Anwar Ali

OXFORD
UNIVERSITY PRESS

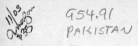

OXFORD

UNIVERSITY PRESS

Great Clarendon Street, Oxford OX2 6DP

Oxford University Press is a department of the University of Oxford.
It furthers the University's objective of excellence in research, scholarship,
and education by publishing worldwide in

Oxford New York

Auckland Bangkok Buenos Aires Cape Town Chennai
Dar es Salaam Delhi Hong Kong Istanbul Karachi Kolkata
Kuala Lumpur Madrid Melbourne Mexico City Mumbai Nairobi
São Paulo Shanghai Taipei Tokyo Toronto

Oxford is a registered trade mark of Oxford University Press
in the UK and in certain other countries

© Oxford University Press 2002

The moral rights of the author have been asserted

First published 2002

ISBN 0 19 579780 9

Typeset in New Century Schoolbook
Printed in Pakistan by
Accurate Printers, Karachi.
Published by
Ameena Saiyid, Oxford University Press
5-Bangalore Town, Sharae Faisal
PO Box 13033, Karachi-75350, Pakistan.

CONTENTS

Editors' Note

This volume is a joint venture of French and Pakistani scholars. The papers it contains were first presented at a conference in Paris on *Fifty Years of Pakistan: Retrospective and Perspectives*. The conference was proposed by Soofia Mumtaz, and co-convened by Jean-Luc Racine. It was hosted by the Foundation, Maison des Sciences de l'Homme (MSH) in June 1998. The meeting provided an uncommon occasion for scholars from France and Pakistan to share their analyses of several topics covering key aspects of Pakistan, an understanding and appreciation of which remain rather inadequate in existing debates. The meeting also served as a prelude to more active scholastic exchange, and sought to facilitate the development of institutional linkages that would enable academics of the two countries to work together on themes of common interest.

A number of the presentations had been updated when they were submitted for publication in this volume. Following the major events that took place after the attacks on the World Trade Centre and the Pentagon in the United States on 11 September 2001, further updates have been provided by some authors. However, since this collection of essays basically addresses the structural dimensions of Pakistan's state and society, the editors have not particularly focused on post 11 September developments. They believe, however, that the contributions collected here provide a useful background for assessing their significance.

The analyses dwell on the major parameters of the historical antecedents, and the political, economic, and social developments that have taken place within the national geographical boundaries, and institutional space, since the creation of Pakistan. The volume thus treats some of the critical sets of relations and processes that have shaped the state and society of Pakistan. A divergence of perspectives and interpretations, and distinctive topical interests are in relative evidence between the French and Pakistani scholars. The discussion emerging therefrom can be turned to creative advantage to serve as a point of departure in future analyses. Multi-disciplinary research in the social sciences can be thus enhanced, and also rendered more complex through a careful screening of empirical evidence.

Three of the articles in this volume have been published earlier. We are grateful to Messrs Royal Book Co., Karachi; and Azad Publications, Lahore; for allowing us to reprint them here. We are also grateful to the Maison des Sciences de l'Homme, the Ministry of Education (Government of Pakistan), and the Embassy of France in Pakistan, and the Pakistan Embassy in France, for facilitating the holding of the conference on which this volume is based.

The editors are of the opinion that an index is not needed in this particular volume as the text is very cohesively structured and the themes are transparent and easy to locate.

Preface:
Understanding Pakistan—
The Impact of Global, Regional,
National, and Local Interactions

The past fifty years have been characterized by some agonising anomalies. The first half of the twentieth century had witnessed the retention of a world system heinous and abhorrent to the majority of the world's population: European imperialism and the continued ascendancy of the North. Yet, even during that egregious half century, a price had to be paid for appropriating the world's resources, for continuing forcibly to occupy external territories, and for subjecting entire societies to the degradation and humiliation of foreign rule. The tensions born out of imperialist competition had propelled European people, their external settler colonies, most notably in North America, and their fellow industrializers on the other side of Asia, in Japan, to tear at each other with a level of ferocity unprecedented in human experience. These denouements comprised the two greatest bloodbaths of human history: the two world wars of the twentieth century.

Following these conflicts, the second half of the century, or for us the past fifty years, witnessed both major continuities and discontinuities. On the one hand, overt European imperialism was rolled back, creating a number of new states or 'nations'. One of these newly emergent states, Pakistan, is the subject of this book. Yet the fortunes of these countries continued to be interpenetrated, and even dominated, by the overbearing economic, political, and cultural weight not only of the old imperializers, but also of the two successor 'superpowers' that sought to continue the ethos of dominance. In parallel, the newly independent states endeavoured to establish, to make, and to remake, their own beings, actions, and histories. The twofold interaction of trends and shifts in the world system at large, as well as the exigencies of internal national and local developments, has governed the pattern of events and transitions in the de-colonised states. Regional realities, or the concerns of national neighbourhoods, have also impacted on the welfare and well-being of these societies. Pakistan itself is a country that presents an intriguing and complex sequence of interactions between local, national, regional, and international structures and processes.

These interactions provide to a large extent the subject matter of this book. The contributions of the various authors are the product of papers presented at a conference of French and Pakistani scholars, held in Paris in June 1998. The occasion was to discuss and review developments in Pakistan during the first fifty years of its existence, and to develop research collaboration in areas of mutual interest. Participants presented studies from their own research work, or areas of current scholarly interest. As the list of contents shows, the chapters and topics fall into place within the more important themes concerning the study of Pakistan's economy and society.

While the chapters in this volume will individually provide a more exhaustive and penetrative analysis of particular themes, we will identify here some of the major parameters within which the sequence of events in Pakistan has unfolded during the past half century. These parameters also embody the articulation of the four interactive layers outlined above: those of the local, national, regional, and international spheres. Let us reverse this sequence, and start by assessing impacts and interactions relating to the wider, or international context.

* * *

Coinciding with the birth of Pakistan were the beginnings of the 'Cold War', the genesis of which was the emergent rivalry between the Soviet and western blocs. Two factors governed Pakistan's response to this growing superpower antagonism. One was the lack of democratic institutions in the country. This institutional weakness had created a decided imbalance in the access to, and appropriation of power and authority in Pakistan, in favour of a dominant triad comprising the military and administrative establishment, and the upper agrarian element. The second factor was the apprehension felt by the fledgling nation towards the perceived aggressiveness, and hostile attitude, of its much larger neighbour, India. Both factors contributed to drawing Pakistan into regional military alliances fostered by the major protagonists of western dominance, under the leadership of the United States. Focused on West Asia and South-East Asia, these pacts, CENTO and SEATO, were designed to contain the threat of communist expansion. From them, Pakistan perhaps hoped to obtain some succour from Indian bellicosity. Even more purposefully, the Pakistani ruling establishment derived western acceptance and support for continuing with its undemocratic ways.

The nexus with the west eventually drew Pakistan into the cauldron of an international genocidal process that has characterized the so-called 'post-imperialist world'. One part of this process was the armed conflict between the western and communist powers, carried out essentially among the hapless people of the South, with the 'cold', or non-lethal war, being reserved for the regions with European populations. The massive human cost of this antagonism was borne, therefore, not by the countries that had perpetrated this conflict, but in arenas of genocide in those very regions that had already suffered from imperialist aggression. The foremost example of these genocidal conflicts was the saturation bombing, chemical warfare, and almost every other form of large scale military homicide, that the western powers meted out to the populations of the ex-French colonies of South-East Asia. For daring to have nationalist aspirations, the populations of Vietnam, Laos, and Cambodia had to suffer several million human casualties, along with social and psychological destruction on an unquantifiable scale. This genocide was committed for the purported western objective of containing communist expansion. In Africa too, entire societies were ravaged through armed struggles and civil wars during the process of de-colonization: conflicts that were instigated and perpetuated to prevent the sceptre of a 'communist' take-over. Similarly, countless deaths occurred in Central and South America, through civil wars and human rights violations, and the repression of civilians by military regimes. All these genocidal activities were inflicted on Southern populations in an effort to contain the enemies of the west, essentially the Soviet empire.

These 'superpower' conflicts eventually reached Pakistan in the shape of the on-going war in Afghanistan since the late 1970s. But this process is also part of the second important factor that has characterized the post-imperialist world. This has been the experience of Muslim countries with the 'world system' since the mid-twentieth century. Beginning with the destruction of Palestine, and the uprooting of the Palestinian people, with the establishment of a Zionist entity, Muslim populations have suffered successive spates of mass mortality. The scale of these has indeed intensified as the twentieth century has drawn to a close, providing a chilling prospect for the fate of Muslim populations and societies in the next century.

Where have these killing fields occurred? The continuing mortality among Palestinian youth and children for challenging Israeli occupation of their land provides the latest chapter in the abhorrent annals of European overseas settlement. The war between Iran and Iraq in the 1980s was another example, foisted as it was on revolutionary Iran, through western instigation, by the regime of Saddam Hussain. The prolongation of this war defied rationality, accompanied as it was by an ever rising death toll. Next was the one-sided war, or virtual massacre, foisted by the west on Iraq itself, inflicted as a punishment for accepting the lure of invading Kuwait. This war caused heavy human losses, again through the sanguinary use of weapons of mass destruction by the United States, Britain, and France. Only an inkling of the kinds of human damage suffered by the

Iraqi people comes from the effects of chemicals and poisons on western troops accidentally exposed to their own weapons. Moreover, after the war, the harsh continuance of sanctions on Iraq has not only decimated the Iraqi social fabric, but is said to have caused over a million deaths. In particular, hundreds of thousands of Iraqi children have died from nutritional deprivation, the unavailability of medicines, and the downturn in the health system.

The people of West Asia have not been the only ones to suffer in this Muslim holocaust. The massacres, rapes, and killings that have occurred in the Balkans, have brought back to Europe its own gory record of the twentieth century. The sufferers in the Balkans were first the Bosnian Muslims, and then the Albanian population of Kosovo. The senior Slavic partner, Russia, has also had a more than ample participation in the Muslim holocaust, with its genocidal war on the civilian population of Chechnya. On an even larger scale, Russia has been an integral player in the war in Afghanistan, at Pakistan's very doorstep. Many of the maladies that currently affect Pakistan originate from the Afghan war. They are, therefore, attributable to Pakistan's involvement with the international domain. More specifically, they arise from the 'superpower' rivalry between the west and the Soviet Union, in which Pakistan got embroiled to its great detriment.

Afghanistan had, in the nineteenth century, been carved out and subsequently retained to act as a buffer between Britain's conquered possessions in South Asia, and those of Russia in Central Asia. This was the so-called 'great game' on the international chessboard, devised by the people of history, for those they imagined being without history. A century later, Afghan neutrality remained a cornerstone in separating Soviet communism from the frontier of the 'free world'. This nexus was threatened, and eventually destroyed, as part of the western strategy to dismantle the Soviet empire. It is no coincidence that the military coup in Pakistan, which overthrew Zulfiqar Ali Bhutto in 1977, took place two years before the Soviet invasion of Afghanistan in 1979. Bhutto, however egregious his failures of leadership, had at least the consciousness to resist American pressure to destabilise the neutrality of Afghanistan, and thereby commence the end game with the Soviet empire. The 'horrible example' that Kissinger threatened to make of Bhutto, did not in all probability relate so much to Pakistan's perceived nuclear designs, as to Bhutto's unwillingness to activate the Afghan front. This task was then assiduously pursued by the clique of military generals that overthrew civilian rule in Pakistan: generals who had been prepared, promoted, and nurtured within the Pakistani army to fulfil strategic western objectives.

The war in Afghanistan claimed more than a million Afghan lives, with several million people being displaced from their homes. Pakistan alone had to support over three million Afghan refugees. Even after the retreat of Soviet forces, the on-going civil war has continued to ravage Afghan society. The emergence of the Taliban, with its rigid ideology, and medieval values, could hardly provide a basis for the long-term sustainability of that country. Pakistani society too, has suffered various distortions, to be discussed further below, and in the subsequent chapters of this book. By contrast, states in Eastern Europe and Central Asia were delivered of the Soviet yoke without shedding a drop of blood. The self-adulatory celebration of east European independence by the west appears even more hypocritical when scant recognition is paid to the process by which it was delivered. These were the heavy human costs, economic dislocations, and social breakdowns suffered primarily by the people of Afghanistan, and secondarily by those of Pakistan. Indeed, the enraged criticism of these societies serves perhaps a function designed to salve the conscience of the genocidal states.

* * *

Another active participant in the current demonization of Pakistan and Afghanistan is the neighbouring country of India. This also brings us to the regional context, the second domain within which our discussion of Pakistan is structured. The causes of the ongoing animosity between Pakistan and

India are by now well known, and the primacy of the Kashmir problem does not require restatement. The large number of civilian casualties in Kashmir makes this another chapter in the recent experience of Muslim populations as victims of genocide. India, over the past half century has continued its intransigence in conceding democratic rights, and the right to freedom, to the Kashmiri people. Encouraged by the lack of international will in curbing its transgressions of human rights, the Indian state has been responsible for the deaths, rape, and torturing of a sizeable proportion of the Kashmiri population. These crimes compare with the similar process of suffering of the Palestinian people, or those of Afghanistan, Chechnya, and the Balkans. Such problems somehow appear much more 'intractable' where the continued repression of Muslim populations is involved. Compare this with the expeditious resolution of the East Timor issue, which occurred within a matter of weeks in 1999.

The problem that Pakistan faces regarding India is, therefore, encapsulated in, and also goes beyond the issue of Kashmir. It lies inherently in the very creation of both India and Pakistan, and concerns the very existence of what can be considered a large empire-type state in this region; and with it, the imbalances in inter-state relations that this phenomenon creates. A large state covering such a major proportion of South Asia, as India does currently, can be regarded as an historical anomaly. Apart from the artificial and foreign imposed configuration of the British Indian empire, which in no way marshalled the subcontinent into a singular entity, South Asia has never had one expansive state. The pre-British polity was that of several regional states, more representative of the normal arrangements of states and territories in South Asian history.

Previously, the Mughal entity, even within the confines of which the different rent yielding units nevertheless retained their quasi-autonomous status, though portrayed as an empire, was really a large, and quite unstable, regional state, mostly confined to the north. Indeed, it actually began to break up irreversibly during its efforts to expand southwards. At some other moments in history, larger regional states have appeared, but only occasionally, and spasmodically.

These, in turn, invariably collapsed as well, leading almost inevitably to fragmentation, rather than further consolidation. By far the most pervasive political arrangements in South Asia have remained the existence of several independent states, rather than one, or even a few overweening entities. Had the subcontinent reverted to the historical pattern of multiple states after independence, many paradoxes that resulted in the aftermath of de-colonisation could have been circumvented.

However, despite the weight of history, the pervasive assumption has been to take the emergence of India in 1947, as somehow normal and 'natural'. Along with this mental construct, the creation of Pakistan is seen as a form of 'separation', or a rather unwelcome division of a single entity. Little thought is given to addressing the inherent subjectivity, and ahistorical protagonism in the idea of 'one' India. On the other hand, there is equally little wisdom in arguments asserting the 'inevitability' of Pakistan. As we know now, some decisions made differently in the climatic moments of British rule could have led to other outcomes.

Addressing a solution to the Kashmir conflict hence, means coming to terms with the numerous anomalies and distortions that emerged in South Asia at the inception of the independence movement itself. Kashmir, in this respect, does not constitute a 'territorial dispute' between Pakistan and India. It symbolises the very contradictions involved in seeking to convert an entire subcontinent of 'state nations' into a single nation state in the aftermath of de-colonisation, in the image of the colonial masters. The move was also paradoxical in so far as the anti-colonial struggle otherwise sought to reject the rationale of the constructs developed during the course of the colonisers' history, as appropriate for the subcontinent. The 'nationalism' propagated by the Congress leadership during the independence movement, on behalf of the entire multinational, multi-religious subcontinental entity, moreover, excluded allusion to the historical events and developments of the last one thousand years of the subcontinent's history. The Muslims of the minority north-Indian provinces, closer to the seat of government, were the first to react to the marginalization of the Muslims implied by such a definition. Sikhs and Christians have since been added to the identities against whom a 'nationalism' defined in terms of *Ram Raj* is asserted. This 'nationalism' continues, furthermore, to be perpetuated, in a surrealist mismatch between words and deeds, in the name of 'secularism'.

The pressure that these anomalies exerted at the largest tier of identities thereby defined during the independence movement, led to the eventual partition of the subcontinent along communal lines. In the absence of the relativity of the earlier context, i.e. Hindu versus Muslim nationalism, the second partition, that which led to the creation of Bangladesh, highlighted, as do the numerous on-going insurgencies in India, the strength of the quasi-autonomous pattern of historical existence in the subcontinent. Kashmir collectively symbolises all these distortions in their very essence. A resolution of the Kashmir conflict, and a 'normalization' of relations between India and Pakistan hence, would require much more realism, and sincerity of purpose, than has thus far been forthcoming.

Yet, having laid the foundation of the 'two nation theory', by defining an 'Indian nationalism' in terms of Hindu symbols, the Indian establishment seeks to lay 'the blame' for partition at the threshold of Pakistan. Its policies, nevertheless, continue to reiterate 'Hindu nationalism' at every instance, both in relations with Pakistan, as well as in the treatment of minorities. The distorted foundation continues to allow further layers of discord to compound. Unless we take into account the recent move towards 're-conversion', little thought is seemingly given by the Indian establishment to the fact that the bulk of the Muslims constitute the indigenous population of the subcontinent, and are recent, albeit devout, converts to Islam. They have, moreover, historically existed either autonomously, or semi-autonomously, within their regional cultural milieu. The territory they occupy as such belongs to them. India cannot covet further expansionism against their wishes. In asserting the Muslim identity of the state vis-à-vis 'Hindu' India, the Pakistani establishment, in turn, increasingly tends to overlook the 150 million Muslim population of India, as compared to 140 million Muslims in Pakistan, of whose rights the early leadership had aspired to be the guarantors: an aspiration difficult to realize within the sovereign confines of another country.

However, as perceptions go, if the Muslims of the subcontinent are perceived by the Indian establishment as 'alien conquerors' who by a twist of historical events find themselves in a reversed equation vis-à-vis the Hindus, and must therefore be 'subdued', or 'punished' for their historical dominance, the cravings of such a mind-set reiterate only too apparently, the 'two nation theory'. The logic of this mental construct had already unfolded in the treatment of the Bengali Muslims by the Bengali Hindus, before the partition of Bengal by the British. The hostility displayed by the latter ensured the staunch support of the Bengali Muslims for Pakistan. The paradoxical nature of these positions can lead but to an impasse of mounting anomalies: if Muslims are 'alien', then partition along communal lines was justified; if they are not, there is no reason for 'secular' India to pursue a policy of perpetual animosity towards them. If the creation of 'nation states' in the aftermath of de-colonisation was 'logical', then the right to exercise national sovereignty by all states is equally sacrosanct.

Human behaviour is too replete with inconsistencies and vagaries to maintain a deterministic approach towards the genesis of Pakistan. Similarly, the equally deterministic paradigm of the 'inevitability' or 'acceptability' of a single Indian 'nation' emerging at the end of the British empire should also be questioned. Clearly, in many quarters this recognition of historical reality has failed to take place. Yet many of the maladjustments and human tragedies of South Asia lie in the devolution, in the mid-twentieth century, of such a large proportion of British possessions to one successor state, which even appropriated for its nationhood the generic term for this region, India. This large state, in turn, has tried to impose a hegemonic relationship on its smaller neighbours. However, Pakistan's refusal to accept an inferior role has not only proved an irritant, but has bedevilled the prospects of regional co-operation in South Asia. Mutual mistrust has led to an arms race that has transferred disproportionate resources to military expenditure. Most importantly, an oversized 'Indian' state has deprived the great majority of its own people of the greater accountability possible with regional nation-states. The continuing and desperate mass poverty in India might well have been alleviated more effectively had South Asia contained several such states. Though average Pakistanis are better off than their Indian counterparts, their material condition could have improved further in the absence of heavy defence expenditure. Thus, the very existence of a large and threatening entity, which in historical terms is an anomaly, increases the level of antagonism and belligerence in the region. This, in turn, has had an adverse effect on the well-being of the South Asian masses, a clear consequence of which is the perpetuation of large scale mass poverty in the region.

If the international and regional structures and processes in which Pakistan has been involved have had highly adverse consequences for its well-being, the situation has by no means been alleviated by internal factors. These are the third and fourth parameters of our analysis, and they relate broadly to the national, and local spheres. Here we by no means intend to enter into any lengthy discussion on these domains, but rather to highlight some of their more telling aspects. Specifically, the role of elites needs to be addressed, as well as the territory of what might loosely be termed 'culture'. We need to assess whether the multitudinous problems that seem to have beset the country, can really be ascribed to such concepts as 'elite failure', and 'cultural malaise'. To some extent both are inter-related, and even inter-dependent. We will take up the former as a national level problematic, and the latter as a set of more localised representations.

* * *

Pakistan's past and present is an epic of the ongoing endurance of the mass of people struggling to survive under adversity. This is a region ecologically little better than a desert, where the level of monsoon rains coming from the east fades away rapidly. This makes summer, or *kharif*, agriculture impracticable. The winter, or *rabi*, crop cannot also reliably depend solely on rainfall. However, the presence of a large groundwater acquifer has traditionally allowed irrigation from wells; and after the advent of electricity, from tubewells. These can have only local applications, and also increase the costs of production. Inundation canals, operating only seasonally, also traditionally accessed limited areas in the vicinity of rivers. It was only with the development, during the past century, of a network of perennial canals, spread over the *doabs*, or interfluves of the Punjab, and in the Indus basin in Sindh, that agriculture on a large scale became possible in this region. The emergent 'hydraulic society' entailed, in turn, extensive in-migration into these sparsely populated areas. The land distribution and settlement processes that ensued, and can be encapsulated under the term 'agricultural colonisation', have created, in Pakistan, the largest contiguous irrigation system in the world. Clearly, survival and sustainability in Pakistan depends fundamentally on the continuous effort of maintaining this hydraulic society. Any major downturn in the irrigation system would undoubtedly lead to a demographic disaster. Meanwhile, the country's population has increased from 35 million in 1947, to 140 million in 2000, with a dangerously high growth rate of three per cent. By 2020 the country's population is projected to reach around 250 million. This is around the level, incomprehensible as it may appear, of the current population of the United States. Human effort alone in Pakistan can stave off the natural consequences of acceding to a harsh environment.

Pakistan's hydraulic society creates its own economic, social, and power imperatives. This is a reality about which analysts choose to remain relatively unaware, lacking perhaps the tools and analytical skills to incorporate this fundamental dimension into their explanations of developments in Pakistan. One problem is that historical understanding and discourse are maintained at a relatively primitive level in this country. The history of the creation of Pakistan, for instance, is confined largely to the same regurgitated and well-worn material comprising banal and repetitive themes concerning 'nationalist' politics. Even these are generally replete with misconceptions and distortions, which are then allowed to proliferate through the textual literature produced for the educational system. For example, even the much publicised address in 1930 by Muhammad Iqbal was by no means the earliest statement demanding a separate Muslim state in South Asia. Iqbal's words echoed, and almost followed word for word, an address made in 1929 by Nawab Sir Zulfiqar Ali Khan. This address was delivered at what was at the time the much more important platform of the All-India Khilafat Committee. It called for the division of South Asia along Muslim and non-Muslim lines, with the creation of a separate Muslim state in the north-western and north-eastern zones.

The misrepresentation of history occurs not by the people, but by the elite, who have appropriated the right to interpret the past. However, this is not the least of the failings of this element in Pakistan. Even before Partition in 1947, the Pakistan region failed to develop a deep-seated nationalist movement, with any properly constituted political organisation, that might have sought popular support from a wider social base. The priorities, and role of the various participants in the eventual genesis of Pakistan, were diverse. The foremost motivation of the initiators of the Pakistan movement, the Muslims of the north-Indian provinces, and Bengal, was primarily: rejection of Hindu dominance. The élite of Sindh and Punjab initially preferred provincial autonomy, in accordance with the Pakistan Resolution, to safeguard their socio-economic interests. Only in the North-West Frontier Province did the 'democratic' nature of social organisation allow a more populist platform to emerge, with the *Khudai Khidmatgars* under Ghaffar Khan. However, the early leadership of Pakistan was concerned with creating conditions that would guarantee the sovereignty of the state and ensure defence against India. Ideological differences between the latter, and the Khudai Khidmatgars resulted in the dismissal of the government of Ghaffar Khan's brother, Dr Khan Sahib, which had been de-legitimized after the populations of the Frontier withdrew their support from Dr Khan Sahib and voted in favour of Pakistan. Henceforth, the 'Red Shirts' have been marginalised by the Pakistani establishment, and regarded as almost seditious by both civilian and military ruling groups.

By 1947, the major Muslim nationalist organization, the Muslim League, had already been heavily infiltrated by larger landlords, to the exclusion of smaller landholders and the middle class, from political leadership. The base was, therefore, established as long as they could retain the support of the upper peasantry, for the continued hold over political and national affairs of a narrow social segment. This comprised none other than the triad strengthened through the emergence of the hydraulic society: the landlords; the civil bureaucracy; and the military hierarchy. As long as the support mechanisms of the upper peasantry held firm, the authoritarian lineages of the Pakistani state could remain embedded and unaltered.

The strategic weakness of the middle class, and of the business element, was accompanied by the exclusion of the rural masses from political participation. This lack of empowerment was to have deleterious effects on the sustainability of Pakistan's political system. The repeated disembowelling of civilian rule, and the desideratum of successive military regimes has been one major outcome. Since its power nodes were never democratic, civilian politics has itself remained personalised, patronage oriented, and de-institutionalised. The building of proper political organisa-tions, with internal democracy, and accountability, and with power flowing from the bottom up, has been beyond the capabilities of self appointed 'politicians'. Consequently, the political spectrum has been suffused with the relatively painless entry of the mafias that dominate almost every sector of this pre-industrial, almost medieval, society. These perhaps are the pragmatic modes preferred by the military, bureaucratic, and agrarian elites, but with consequences that are highly adverse for national stability.

Since 1947, there has emerged a further participant, and stakeholder, in the prevailing protocols of this functional anarchy. Larger scale business has also benefited from these undemocratic processes, through various types of rent-seeking behaviour. This consists of such measures as protective tariffs, rebates and fiscal subsidies, credit at artificially low rates for financing industrial projects, favourable pricing policies, and protected markets. On the basis of these anti-competitive interventions, bigger business has appeared to have thrived, but only through a kind of mercantilist parody of the market economy. With the liberalization of inter-national trade, and in the global environment of competitive market forces, Pakistan's industrialists will need to re-learn modern business in order to avoid disfunctionality. The heavy emphasis on commodity processing, the inability to achieve value addition, the reliance on the mechanisms of corruption rather than performance to achieve goals, and the general failure to move from restrictive family firms to corporate entities, makes the prospect of market success rather remote.

Given these proclivities of the business elite, the smaller scale and informal sectors have, in turn, responded to secure their own segmented territories. They have exploited institutional weaknesses by resisting documentation, and regulatory provisions, and even more tellingly by successfully evading state taxation, thereby leading to major revenue shortfalls. These abbreviations of an ordered society could not, however, be achieved without entering an equally onerous domain of substitute payments and obligations. This was none other than the persistent rental demands of state functionaries, without whose co-operation it would not have been possible to avoid regulation and evade taxation.

These supportive arrangements among the better-off have been reflected in both the continuing exclusion of the mass of people from political empowerment, as well as their continued deprivation of economic resources. The small proportion of annual budgetary allocations for the social sector over the past five decades has left the majority of people illiterate, without basic health and sanitation facilities, and without any tangible improvement in living conditions. They have remained without most of the benefits of modern life, such as access to even rudimentary telecommunications. The resources allocated to the social sector are mostly absorbed by public functionaries, but with very low levels of service delivery in return. Even the substantial amounts of foreign assistance for this sector have circulated within a restricted group of beneficiaries.

The response of the poor to the political economy of exclusion has been almost devastating, evidence of the fact that in the end it is the masses that make history. Deprived of any form of state social security, such as old age and unemployment benefits, and unrestrained, if not actually encouraged by xenophobes, with their reductionist formulas cast in the religious idiom, the poor have multiplied in numbers at an exceptional pace. We have already noted the current and projected figures for Pakistan's population, and its equivalence in another twenty years with the existing demography of the USA, the world's richest nation. The rapid rate of population growth has flattened out the demographic pyramid, quite the reverse of the greater concentration among older age groups in the high-income economies. Already in Pakistan, almost half the population is aged under fifteen. Every year millions will enter the workforce, and within a few years they will enter the reproductive cycle. This quantum increase in numbers can only be dislodged from its highly unattractive Malthusian outcomes through alternative processes that are equally undesirable: some of these could be epidemics, famines, and armed conflicts. The remarkable failure of the manageable and rational way to control population, through family planning measures, provides yet another example of the elite's inability to address priorities. The apocalyptic consequences of this particular oversight might well, however, sweep this disingenuous upper element into some of history's more unpalatable spaces.

Already, the population upsurge has created a situation that is increasingly uncontrollable. If there were any elite strategies for economic development in Pakistan, then prospects of their success have been seriously undermined by the demographic upturn. Public management increasingly lacks the requisite skills and capabilities to operate in the rapidly evolving environment. The denial of mass education to the poor has accentuated the recourse to child labour. This has tilted generational wealth flows decidedly in favour of the parents, thereby acting as a further motivation for larger families, and also the motivation not to send children to school. Thus, the elite's indifference in allocating resources to the social sector, at the right time, is leading towards outcomes that are threatening the very sustainability of society. Consequently, the *mantras* of progress and development, through which the elite seeks legitimacy, now stand in abeyance, and no other paradigm, except perhaps that of religious atavism, appears at hand for the disempowered masses.

Elite failure has manifested itself in various forms. We have already noted the nation-threatening symbiosis between political de-institutionalization on the one hand; and on the other, the continual structured resource transfer to political and business elites, to the civil bureaucracy and public sector management, and to a completely untenable level of military expenditure. To date, no practical effort has been undertaken to stem this haemorrhaging of resources away from public weal. Greater revenue impositions on other socio-economic segments, to underwrite these flows, will further erode the moral economy of the system. This has already been challenged by the growing realization that society's upper element has increasingly tended to draw its income from rents, rather than earn it through productive effort. Sitting now as an incubus on society, its strategy remains palpably to retain the status quo, and to resist any change that might dilute its vested interest. The mechanisms to actualise this strategy have been the lack of transparency and account-ability, and the rejection of genuinely democratic processes, which could have instituted sufficient checks and balances. Additionally, the heavy inflow of foreign assistance, easily diverted by public functionaries, has been a further habit forming input into the rental culture. The mafias that have emerged in the extensive narcotics trade, have increasingly tested the effectiveness of the law enforcement and judicial systems. The pervasive corruption amongst most levels of government officials has been sanctioned through the state's inability to punish these misdemeanours.

These configurations have had major political ramifica-tions. The sheer momentum of distortions has resulted in significantly corrupting the political system. Proper political organizations, with internal democracy and institutionalised methods for the selection of candidates, have failed to emerge in Pakistan. The two largest political parties, as well as most of the smaller ones, have resorted to patronage, nepotism, and monetary payments for the dispensation of tickets for elections. Arbitrary nominations, rather than representative selections, have enabled criminalised elements, or their nominees, to enter the legislatures. Many of these individuals would be convicted felons in any country with a properly functioning legal system. The corruption and avarice of top politicians during the 1990s is already well documented. It was particularly unfortunate for Pakistan that the opportunity for stabilising civilian politics after 1988 was so comprehensively lost by the corruption and venality of the leadership of both the major parties. The criminalization of politics, as so many of the issues discussed here, is by no means unique to Pakistan. These problems are shared, all too commonly, with other technologically lesser developed countries, not least of these is neighbouring India.

* * *

Relating to the role of elites, and indeed encapsulating it, is the more general domain of culture. By this term we mean not simply specific activities, such as the performing, or graphic arts, but rather the 'software' through which a society operates. The term enfolds religious and social values, and the attitudes and mentalities that perforate society. This constitutes the fourth parameter of our analysis of Pakistani state and society. The role of culture, and the proposition of cultural change, is a major component in the process of economic transformation. Where such transitions have occurred, deep-seated adaptations in social values and cultural norms accompanied economic change. The success-fully industrialising nations of western Europe provide rich themes for identifying and understanding this nexus. If the implication is that cultural rigidity, and continuing societal 'backwardness', undermines the prospects of economic transformation, then a society's willingness, or propensity for cultural and social innovation and metamorphosis, becomes an important stimulus for 'progress' and 'modernization'. In the reverse instance, it is perhaps the primacy of the ingredients for economic transformation that in turn engender the corresponding cultural change.

In Pakistan, over the past fifty years, wide differences have emerged in the interpretation of the nature and character of the country's culture. We will discuss these here in terms of three contending themes: 'modernization'; 'Islamization'; and 'indigenization'. While the annals of social analysis are replete with the first two themes, they are relatively reticent on the implications of the third, on which we will, therefore, focus more closely, and which will be taken up here first.

As differentiated from the historical development of culture, in terms of standardised traits, characteristics of language, dietary patterns, and artistic traditions, specific to given geographical areas that vary with variations in population composition and ecological conditions there is, on the ground in Pakistan, an extant culture that has survived, with little seeming change, over several centuries. The caste system, pervasive all over South Asia, also characterized social arrangements in the Pakistan area, especially in the settled agrarian tracts. Tribal societies were also caste-based. Although the internal tribal organisation of the dominant ethnic group, the Pakhtuns and the Baloch in the Frontier and Balochistan for instance, is quite distinct, as is their atavistic carriage of Islam, in that they are not recent converts from Hinduism, the common principle of endogamy for preservation of group identity, and the dependence on hierarchically stratified hereditary occupational groups, and hence their functionality and desirability for the reproduction of the socio-economic system, has ensconced the latter societies in traditional and virtually unchanging structures as well. Continuities and differences with earlier forms of social existence, as a consequence of Muslim inceptions in the subcontinent, and the presence of Islam, therefore, need to be understood with reference to two determining indices: the absence of any radical change in the material base of the societies in question; and the voluntary nature of conversions to Islam. Conversions, moreover, were brought about by the Sufi saints, who ignored orthodox expressions of religion. They did not come about as a consequence of any imperial decree.

The order that served to organise the populations of the subcontinent into a ranked hierarchy of groups, and defined the relations between different categories of groups, evolved according to the manner in which the peculiar division of labour by category was conceived, and came to characterize the practice of a distinctive mode of agricultural production. The presence of Islam diluted the more extreme manifestations of caste, such as the severity of pollution and exclusion. However, since the Sufis who introduced Islam in South Asia placed emphasis on personal piety and love for humanity regardless of communal boundaries (as a stage in the journey towards the state of ultimate union with God, and a more total identity), such a doctrine pre-empted clashes with the belief systems of other communities. In so far as the traditional economic patterns of social survival remained unaltered, so also was the rationale of hierarchical stratification perpetuated. The day to day realities of caste-based interactions thus were extant among all religious groups, including Muslims. Muslim 'caste' hierarchies indeed ran parallel with those of Hinduism, and retained a number of complementarities and similarities with the latter.

Conversion to Islam thus did not mean that Muslims in South Asia transformed their cultural and social persona altogether. However, neither did it mean that they remained identical to their Hindu counterparts. The boundaries of the diverse social strata, after conversion, were devoid of ritual or religious importance. The absence of earlier religious taboos, moreover, sanctioned, in accordance with Islamic practice, the contraction of parallel and cross-cousin marriages. Although 'caste' endogamy, as among Hindu castes, continued to be practised, Muslims and Hindus of the same 'caste' did not inter-marry. The dynamics of the earlier caste structure thus gradually transformed from within, and earlier caste affiliations of Muslim converts assumed a genealogical foundation. The place of a group within the occupational hierarchy furthermore took on a class character.

Religious differences also created differential ideological orientations. Imagined communal affiliations were established with the Muslim world, and associations developed with the places of origin in central and western

Asia, of the diverse Muslim conquerors, the numerous variety
of scholars and visitors to the subcontinent, as well as the
saints who converted the populations to Islam. These
differences created quite wide, if not unbridgeable
philosophical divides in South Asian societies: chasms that
indeed led to the creation of Pakistan itself. Despite these
differences, the absence of any concern with marginalization,
or subjugation to an external non-Muslim authority,
facilitated concordance with indigenous mentalities and
structures, rather than constructing and maintaining
completely distinct ones. A synthesis with their South Asian
identity thus enabled convert Muslims to remain largely
within their customary milieu. Beyond religious observance
and belief, the social and individual behaviours, attitudes,
and mentalities of the bulk of Muslims of South Asia conform
less to the norms of other Muslim populations in contiguous
regions. We may, in this context, consider the inter-
relationship between 'caste', society, and religion in Pakistan.
The structure and function of 'caste' organisation in the
Punjab, the 'bread-basket' of the subcontinent, can be
compared to variations in other provinces.

In their very essence, caste hierarchies are arranged
according to the 'purity' of material and artefacts handled by
hereditary occupational groups. Thus Rajputs, who handled
weapons and implements of military prowess, were more
elevated than Jats, who touched the implements of
agricultural production. Arranged below these were castes
that worked with a host of lesser materials: wood-workers or
tarkhans, iron-workers or *lohars*, pottery workers or
kumhars, leather workers or *chamars*, and so on. At the
lowest extreme of the status chain were those consigned to
handling the least dignified of materials: carcasses and
excreta. These were the most menial castes, or were regarded
as 'outcastes' and 'untouchables'. With the exception of the
last category, which is alien to Islam, and many from which
category embraced Christianity, other social differentiations,
with terminological variations, prevail among Muslims and
non-Muslims alike. As members of different castes converted
to Islam, they retained their caste identity, nomenclature,
and to a large extent, hierarchical positioning. Thus, Muslims

continued to subscribe to their caste origins, whether it was
Rajput, Jat, or service caste status, as did their non-Muslim
counterparts. The structure of inequalities was thereby
perpetuated. However, a re-arrangement of the traditional
elements of organisation gave rise to an authority system of
dominance and submission, in which inequality came to be
related to rights over landed property by virtue of ascribed
status, and the ability thereby to acquire and exercise
political power.

In the Frontier for instance, only the Pashtuns
(descendants of the *Yusufzai* tribes, who were driven out of
the Kabul valley and entered the northern Peshawar plain
as conquerors around 1200 AD) have the right to own land.
Loss of inherited share, as a consequence of sub-division,
extravagance, or other misfortune, can lead to loss of Pashtun
status. Internally, the Pashtun tribal organisation, an
acephalous structure of patrilineal descent, operates on the
principle of equality, although there are now only a few large,
and consequently powerful landowners. The principle of
equality also formed the basis of the practice until the 1930s,
when permanent settlement was imposed, of periodic re-
allotment of land in a rotational system, so as to compensate
for variations in fertility, and ensure uniformity in the type
of land to which members of the descent group had access.
Since status prevents Pashtuns from cultivating the land
themselves, they enter into tenancy contracts, as well as
economic contracts, with different categories of service and
menial groups, for the provision of diverse facilities. Each
Pashtun thus has the freedom to form his own segment,
which practice became the basis of an institutionalised form
of rivalry between contenders to political power and
leadership, specifically partilineal parallel cousins. Each non-
Pashtun, however, is also free to choose his partner in any
contract. He may, moreover alter, or refrain from making
any contract altogether. The status of a Pashtun hence,
depends on his ability, by means of the hospitality he
practices, to build up his following, and become the leader of
a series of localised groups.

The Baloch tribal structure, in contrast, is centralised. The
tribe is either a political unit, the former revenue-yielding

unit, the *tuman*, which was headed by the *tumandar*, or is a politically independent unit, headed by the *sardar*. The latter term, now merely a ceremonial title, applies to former *tumandars* as well. The Baloch practice a mixture of herding and agriculture. They migrated to the area they now occupy (in western Pakistan, eastern Iran, and Southern Afghanistan) as of the eighth century, either from Kerman, or Aleppo in Syria, and are of Arab origin. Initially, the organisation of the Baloch did not subscribe to any principle of common descent. Whomsoever enlisted in a military expedition could gain membership, and became eligible to a share in the spoils. Gradual passage to pastoral production, and a transhumant, and increasingly sedentary life style, gave rise to membership on the basis of patrilineal descent. Baloch 'tribes' thus came to constitute a series of merging segments that owed allegiance to a central chief, below whom were a series of leaders of diverse sections. Land held as common property of the 'tribe' transformed into the private property of the chief, after implementation of the British land settlement policies. Only full members of the chief's family, i.e. those born of a Baloch mother, were given a share in the landed estate. The populations of Balochistan thus fell into the following categories: 'noblemen' or the *sardars* and their patrilineage; ordinary Baloch commoners; and non-Baloch service and menial castes. The latter included traders, cultivators, and serfs. Dependence on their services, similar to the contractual arrangement in the Frontier, permitted the latter groups to join different camps for as long as they chose, and then to move on. In order to preserve their distinguished status, the Baloch avoided social interaction with their subordinate service and menial castes. However, as a consequence of the patronage extended to them, it was also considered 'dishonourable' for a Baloch to dispossess, or threaten to kill anyone living within their 'protective custody'. Many values alien to theoretical Islam thus came to be retained by the Muslims: particularism as opposed to universalism, and social fragmentation, rather than human equality.

Hinduism, however, also had a ritually superior 'holy caste': the Brahmins, the pinnacle, and perpetuators of the caste system. Their caste 'purity' lay in the origin myth of 'Aryan' descent, combined with the fact that they alone could handle the sacred Sanskrit texts and other religious materials, and also reserved the right to conduct religious rituals and ceremonies. Islam has no such equivalent. Muslims in South Asia, however, came to classify their own category of 'holy men' but unlike the Brahmins, none of these were allowed a monopoly over religion, since the realms of the secular and the religious in Islam are not exclusive of each other. Those who were categorised as 'holy' were the *mullahs*; the *Syeds*; and the *Sufis*. The role of the first is institutional. The mullah runs the community mosque, teaches the Quran to children; and performs religious ritual. However, he does so as an employee of the community, or of the state. The latter duties as such are assigned to him because he acquires the expertise to perform them, not because he has the exclusive right to do so by virtue of caste affiliation, or by birth, nor can he thereby exercise authority over those for whom he performs these duties. Only personal piety and charisma can win him a following.

The Syeds pretend to 'sainthood' by claiming descent from the Prophet Mohammed (PBUH). Their status as such is ascribed by birth. Thereby also, they assume the right, in the Brahmanic mode, to interpret theology, an expertise otherwise the prerogative of the judiciary, and the scholars of Islam. The validity of the Syed's claim to 'Syedhood', more frequently than not, is subject to suspicion. However, Syeds may be accorded respect on the basis of their claim to 'holy descent'. Their real influence derives from their ability to exercise political power on the basis of landed property acquired by way of gift, inheritance, purchase, or conquest. For instance, the *siri* land that was set aside for mosques, or offered to 'saints' in the Frontier, was henceforth excluded from Pashtun land. On the basis of land thus acquired, the Syeds, like the Pashtuns, became contenders for political power. Similarly, the Syeds in Sindh, who fled from their homes in central Asia, in the wake of the Mongol invasions in the twelfth and thirteenth centuries, joined the ranks of the Sindhi *waderos*, and the Baloch *waderos* who had seized power from the Sindhi Kalhora kings in the eighteenth century. A poor Syed consequently is treated little better than a beggar. The respect paid to him, by virtue of his claimed descent, is limited to lip service, and the alms he may thereby receive. Sufis are distinct from both these categories. They renounce worldly possessions, and function outside communal organisations. Quite contrary to Islamic practice, and improvising on the Hindu practice of temple *puja*, the homage paid at the graves of the expired Sufis, by Muslims and Hindus alike, bears witness to the continued faith in the mediatory role of the former for divine benediction, even after their death.

Given the numerous cross currents, and syntheses with the South Asian patterns of social existence, the 'indigenous' modes of intra- and inter-group relations among the Muslims of the subcontinent, has been more pervasive than social scientists have cared to test. Caste consciousness converted to class consciousness. Yet it remained embedded within the framework of the former idiom. In practical and psychological terms, the modes of interaction and behaviour in Pakistani society continues to be accordingly defined. Moreover, social groups follow traditional patterns of caste mobility and status assertion to reflect altered circumstances. As different groups have improved their economic position, or changed to more 'respectable' occupations, they have tended to claim a more 'elevated' status. Hence, the proliferation of claimants to such customary upper category status terms as Syed, Shaikh, Khan, Malik, as well as Rajput, and among the rural order, Jat, and Arian.

Partition in 1947 saw the exit from Pakistan of non-Muslim castes, many of which belonged to the upper social strata. The vacuum at the top in the professions, commerce, and even in rural society, was filled largely by the migrants from India in South Punjab and Sindh, and by upwardly mobile Muslim 'castes' elsewhere, thus making the struggle for assertion for upper class status a pervasive and ubiquitous process. On the ground, therefore, in terms of socially significant behaviour, there has occurred a dual process of stratification: one defined by occupational group status; and the other by changing combinations of diverse historically based identity criteria: linguistic, ethnic, or religious faction. Devotion to Islamic ideology notwithstanding, occupational group mobility continues to be wrought with social tension. Group identifications thus are more the product simply of social status claims, which have kept changing over time to resonate the altering fortunes of different groups.

The two other competing ideologies, those of Islamization and modernization, are clearly endeavouring to change the Pakistani persona from its inherent nature, the state in which it has existed for centuries. The first ideology, that of Islamization, essentially derives its justification from the origins of Pakistan as the Muslim majority region of South Asia. The assertion of a politicised demand for the adoption of Islamic laws, the *Shariah*, has already partly succeeded, fuelling apprehensions about Pakistan being launched on the path of the austere far Right. The infusion of religious strictures and constraints into the country's laws, derives more from the threat of violence and disorder, than from electoral or democratic impulses. Religious parties have been consistently routed in Pakistan's elections, yet they have largely achieved their agenda. The sad contrast lies with India, where Hindu fundamentalist parties have achieved majoritarian and mainstream status, and have been voted into power. Yet, India can continue to proclaim normalcy, since religion has not yet permeated law; and also because Hindu fundamentalism has failed to be globally demonised, unlike its Islamic counterpart.

The growth over time of political groupings espousing the cause of converting Pakistan into an Islamic society has, of late, mutated into the emergence of sizeable, and heavily armed militias. Recruitment to these paramilitaries has been spurred on by the call for *jihad*, first in Afghanistan, and then in the oppressed Muslim regions of the Russian empire, and in Kashmir. The proliferation of *madrasas* provides the recruiting ground for these armed activists. The *madrasas* in turn receive their intake from the burgeoning ranks of youth emanating from the rapidly growing population. Controlling these ideological armies, and stemming the nexus between militant schooling and armed and extremist activism, has become a major challenge for the Pakistani state. This phenomena threatens to erode the country's efforts to join the mainstream of international affairs, even though its origins, as noted earlier, might lie in a legitimate sense of grievance over the genocidal treatment of Muslim populations.

However, the Islamic movement in Pakistan is itself divided, not only into the majority Sunni and the Shia communities, but even within the former, into various schools and segments. The factions emanate from several contradictory tangents, with mosques divided between different schools of thought, and with little consensus on the specific attributes of an Islamic society, as also with the preponderance of actual practice vested in customary and tribal law, and with the frequency of Shia-Sunni killings (albeit spurred by foreign interests, including terrorism sponsored by India, among others). Ironically, this atomization of religious belief is not only contrary to the universalism of Islam, but is actually more representative of the traditional spiritual realities of South Asia as a whole. Hinduism itself was never a unified religion, but constituted multiple, and distinct systems of worship, of both greater and lesser gods. It could be postulated that the various schisms and doctrinal sects of Islamic Pakistan reflect this very psyche of fragmentation. Could this be yet another reassertion of the indigenous mind-set, articulated here in the religious sphere, as it is with caste in the social domain?

The third philosophy, that of modernization, is less easy to categorise. There lies the problem not only of defining this term, but also of identifying those segments that espouse it. Then, the various permutations of this ethos, both in content, and over time, need to be elucidated. So too do intellectual foundations and influences, which can be diverse, as well as diffused. The term acquires a wider significance if it enfolds the call not only for material and economic developmentalism, but also for cultural and social transitions towards outcomes other than those represented by extant and incumbent structures. Also of relevance is the debate whether this concept coincides with that of 'westernization', a problematic that itself raises further questions regarding the nature and meaning of the latter term. Thus 'modernization', to an extent even greater than Islamization, does not lend itself to specific connotations, or to singular definitional alignments.

Whatever the pedantic constraints in identifying this notion, we will here discuss 'modernisers' in the context of those who do not wish to have a theocratic state in Pakistan. This element would prefer the laws to be secular, and that individuals in society be governed by their private conscience, and the freedom of choice, rather than be imposed upon by religious ideology. The great *mantra* of this element lies, of course, in the sphere of 'economic development': this is the utopian material goal towards which the modernisers would want to lead society. The lesser, and in Pakistan decidedly weaker, *mantra* lies in advocating greater convergence with a more universalistic culture, essentially of western cultural patterns, which were initially disseminating through colonial rule, and are doing so now through the globalization of the market economy. The objective then is clearly the end of 'feudalism', and 'traditionalism', in both their economic and social manifestations, and their substitution by more modernistic material, and mental structures.

The debates within the modernisers as to the level and degree of change, and its specific forms and directions occurs, therefore, in parallel with the external debate with the theocrats. Over time, can we say that in Pakistan this external dialogue has come to dominate the minds of people, thereby confusing and complicating the discussion on real issues of development and change? Indeed, is there a growing perception that the religious ideologues are gaining inexorable ground, despite their electoral performance, and that returning Pakistan to the mainstream international ethos becomes ever more unachievable? If this is the case, the loss of confidence by the secularists can have wide ranging impacts on business, economy, and society. One manifestation could already be the loss of better quality human resources to external destinations. Even more damaging could be internal consequences: the loss of a sense of purpose and achievement, and ultimately the loss of dynamism, and of the innovational spirit so concertedly avowed by Islam.

Introduction:
The State and the Nation of
Pakistan—A Multifaceted
Assessment

Anniversaries are not celebrated by social scientists the way they are by established authorities, but they offer good opportunities to assess structural legacies and dynamics of change. Fifty years of a young nation are long enough for attempting an evaluation of its past, an appreciation of its present, and—if not an anticipation of its future—an appraisal of its expectations. It was precisely within this historical location—Pakistan at Fifty—that a bilateral seminar held in Paris aimed at offering French and Pakistani perceptions on Pakistan. The scope was multi-disciplinary; the goal, an overview where the historical and ideological foundations of the state, the social fabric of the nation, the economic parameters, the polity configurations, and the regional geopolitics could be assessed.

The seminar was held in 1998, a few days after the nuclear tests were conducted by Pakistan, and the contributions were compiled, then revised in 1999, to form the basis of this book. Most of the chapters of the book offer perceptions which were expressed at that crucial moment between the nuclearization of Pakistan under the elected government of Nawaz Sharif and the military take-over led in October 1999 by General Pervez Musharraf, soon after proclaimed Chief Executive of Pakistan. We have not asked the authors to revise their texts

a second time after the coup, although some authors had
thought improbable the direct return of the Army to the helm
of affairs—an opinion shared by many in mid-1998. While
dealing with their specific topic in the fifty year perspective of
the seminar, the contributors have also offered analyses of the
relationship between military rule, civilian government and
civil society in Pakistan, which shed very precious light on
what is at stake today, and put under significant perspective
the challenges the new regime, and beyond it Pakistan as a
nation, have to address. Reading afresh the manuscript just
after the take-over, I have been convinced of its accrued
relevance. Conceived and prepared in a manner free from the
immediate concern of day to day political developments, the
contents of this volume stand the test of time. They offer also
outsiders' visions. Some of the French (or Swiss as far as
Gilbert Etienne is concerned) authors have a long connection
with Pakistan. Others have been trained on a larger
background, be it the Muslim world west of the Durand Line,
or South Asia before or after Partition. A number of Pakistanis,
including intellectuals, believe that their country is too often
misunderstood. If it is so, this book hopes to offer some
material for a better mutual understanding.

The present introduction will first underline the salient
analyses offered by this volume, in a way respecting its
structure. I shall pay attention successively to the genesis of
Pakistan, to the relationship established between Islam and
its polity, to significant identity challenges, and to the state
of the economy, before addressing the question of democracy,
and regional geopolitical issues. The scope, always, was less
to offer images of Pakistan at fifty, than to analyse long
range trends, structural parameters, significant dynamics.
I take personal responsibility for the presentation of the
authors' contributions offered here. If some brief comments
appear sometimes at the end of each summary, they leave to
the last section of this introduction the task of submitting an
overall appraisal, focused on the decisive question of reform.
Practically all contributors called for reform, and many of
them, explicitly, for political change. A political change did
occur in October 1999, but its interpretation is still a subject
of debate in Pakistan itself. Some analysts would see the

return of the military to the helm of affairs as yet another serious crisis. Others would rather underline that the regular succession of civilian regimes and military ones, since the late 1950s, is less a repetition of crises than a testimony of structural challenges faced by Pakistan, and by many other developing countries. Whichever interpretation one finds valid, the contributions collected in this volume may usefully help to put both the long term evolution and the recent events in perspective. As far as the final section of this introduction is concerned, it offers my personal reading of the seminar, conducted in the light of more recent developments. These perceptions do not engage other contributors nor any institution.

I. Genesis, Historical Process, and Ideological Rationales of Pakistan

Let us start from the beginning: Pakistan before 1947, in other words, the genesis of the new state. The historiography of Pakistan relies mostly on studies focused on the decolonization process, and on what Pakistani authors have labelled as Muslim nationalism.

The lessons of historiography: the perceptions of Partition

The Partition of the former British Raj gave birth to Pakistan, and as such deserves primary attention. Claude Markovits, in his study of some major historical analyses of Partition both in Pakistan and in India, unravels differences and evolutions which result from three distinctive factors: i) established 'national' histories, in Pakistan and in India, have tended to privilege a certain mainstream vision of the event, mostly putting the blame on the other side for the divide which gave birth to the two countries; ii) in the meantime, in both countries, perceptions different from the prevailing 'orthodox' histories have been articulated; iii) the historiography of Partition could not insulate itself from the general evolution of history in (or on) South Asia, and got, therefore, recently enriched with new paradigms.

For Pakistan, Partition is obviously 'foundational for the legitimacy of the state'. It took more than a decade, however, to see the main trends of Pakistani historiography emerge. The first one, observes Markovits, favoured a 'fairly secular' political interpretation of the event, and 'stressed the liberation of the Muslims from political and economic domination of the Hindu majority'. In this minority/majority account, religion was mostly 'an identity marker'. By contrast, the more broadly established second trend was more 'culturalist': 'most Pakistani authors saw the new state as the culmination of the aspirations of Muslim 'modernists' since the time of Sir Syed Ahmad Khan. Jinnah appeared as the embodiment of a modernity finding strength in its Islamic roots'.

In India, to the contrary, the prevailing view saw in Partition 'an outcome which had been the result of an accumulation of human errors rather than of structural factors'. The minority Hindu nationalist historians pointed at 'a deep-seated Muslim conspiracy' against Mother India. The majority left-leaning historians saw in Muslim communalism something different: 'an expression of false consciousness' reflecting 'the class hegemony exercised over the Muslim masses by a narrow elite of landed magnates and big traders who feared the development of a unitary mass movement of Hindu and Muslim peasants and workers'. For both currents, however 'the Pakistan movement and Partition were a diversion from the main struggle against imperialism'.

Pakistani and Indian historians who wrote from the 1960s to the mid-1980s shared at least two common perceptions, despite their wide differences. Firstly, the personal role of Jinnah was seen as decisive in shaping Muslim politics in favour of Pakistan. Secondly, both were very critical of the British, even if for opposing reasons. Most Indian historians saw in the Partition the final legacy of the British 'divide and rule' precept, which tried to weaken the anti-colonial movement, while the Muslim League saw Partition as a means to guarantee power for the Muslim minority. Pakistani historians, on the other hand, underlined the pro-Congress leanings of Lord Mountbatten at the decisive time of the transfer of power. On the whole, asserts Markovits, one had in the 1980s, 'an historiography of the Pakistan movement and of the origins of the Partition, which was a contested one, but no true historiography of Partition', for Partition was not just a matter of states and leaders, another generation of historians started to argue at that time.

Ayesha Jalal's 'iconoclastic study of Jinnah', published in 1985, is still highly debated upon in Pakistan. If Jalal 'put the onus of Partition squarely on the refusal by the Congress, with British implicit support, to make the concessions which could have satisfied Jinnah's demands', she offered also a new image of the Quaid-i-Azam: 'The Jinnah of Jalal was not the supreme politician of earlier accounts, but a man who had gambled and partly failed and had had no choice but to collect his gains in order to avoid complete defeat'. This was a turning point, notes Markovits: 'by lashing out equally at all majors actors' (Indian, Pakistani and British), Jalal helped discredit the approach 'from above' which had dominated the field in the previous period. In the meantime, the rise of new historical trends in India favoured as well a revision of the established perceptions of Partition. With the decline of the Congress and the revival of Hindu nationalism, some Indian historians started to question the significance of Partition for India itself. For Gyan Pandey (1996) for instance, 'it became obvious that Partition cannot be explained only in reference to Muslim nationalism, but that its Other, Hindu nationalism, long hidden behind secularist rhetoric, also played a crucial role in the unfolding of the drama'. Calling for 'a displacement from a state-centred history to a history centred on the actors themselves, those crowds that participated in the massacres as perpetrators as well as victims', Pandey and others echoed the search for a new people's history, advanced for years by the Subalternist school, or turned to new sources (Mushirul Hasan to literature for instance, or Ritu Menon and Kamla Bhasin to women's memories). They reintroduced also the decisive problem of confused identities and violence, which 'national histories' tended to sideline. Historians settled in Pakistan, according to Markovits, have largely neglected these fields, but other historians studying Pakistan have taken these issues into consideration. For instance, Ian Talbot (1996), who focused his attention on 'the popular dimension in the Pakistan Movement and the Partition experience', or Yunus Samad (1995) who saw in the Pakistan Movement 'a constant dialectical interaction' between the divisive ethnicity dimension and 'the notion of a united Muslim nation'.

Besides rethinking the established Indian history, recent publications have helped to reassess the origins of Pakistan, and raised questions not yet resolved today. The relations between ethnic identities and the national project is only one of them. If, as suggests Samad, 'Pakistan was defined by circumstances and not by design', this was bound to raise 'many problems that the country faced after Partition', including the defining issue of Pakistan being or not being an Islamic state. Zia's vision on this point was totally opposed to Jinnah's who proclaimed a few days before Independence 'now that Pakistan has been established (...) religion is a matter within our homes'. Historians have started to raise disturbing questions, both in India and Pakistan, however, concludes Markovits, if 'the history of Pakistani and Indian nationalisms' are solidly established, much remains to be done for constructing the historiography of Partition as such, including its 'two central facts', 'mass violence and mass displacement'. 'Fragmented and contested', the field of historiography remains open to investigation, 'in which the lines of battle are not drawn between Indian historians and Pakistani historians, but within each academic community and even within each individual historian'. One agrees with Markovits: this is not just an academic exercise. If Pakistani and Indian historians take up the challenge, 'one day perhaps a new consensus will emerge on the meanings of the event, which will help cure the wounds rather than allow them to fester'.

The Mughal-British legacies: forgetting the people

Whatever be the decisive importance of Partition, Imran Ali argues that the lineage of the Pakistani state has to be ascertained to a longer history than the Pakistan Movement. How long an history? It is highly debatable to refer to the times of Muhammad bin Qasim or Mahmud Ghazni as the genuine origin of the quest for a Muslim homeland in the region. Much more relevant to the present state of Pakistan is the Mughal Empire in its declining years, and the way the British Empire managed to control, on very different patterns, Punjab and Sindh. Behind the change in nomenclature, can we not recognise in contemporary practices a legacy of the past? 'Instead of courtiers and hereditary magnates there are now caucuses of 'elected' representatives. But can we be sure that the latter are really fulfilling the functions of democratic activity, of the intricate work of committees, law-making and political analysis? Or, do they yet again appear in the capital cities to seek concession and largesse and resource diversion, to consolidate social authority and vie for privilege? (...) Are the larger landowners no longer 'feudal', but so heavily immersed in the market economy as to pioneer that value-added part of the agrarian economy that has or will bring about agricultural capitalism? (...) Is business also a receiving appendage of the state, relying upon subsidies, concessionary loans and write-offs, rather than on the finesse of the market place?'.

In the context of the crisis affecting the Mughal empire in its declining phase, the British experience in Punjab had a decisive impact on the genesis of the socio-economic foundations of Pakistan polity. As Imran Ali underlines, the British 'coopted the militarized upper peasant groups of the Punjab' who had previously eliminated the old Mughal elite and established their supremacy. The process was reinforced by the set-up of the world's largest irrigation system, which 'virtually laid the socio-economic foundations of the Pakistani state, for most of the land was allotted either to large landowners or to army veterans, while the civil bureaucracy exercised 'its control over the management of the irrigation system. Here lay the foundations of the continuing bureaucratic hold over vital nodes of the Pakistani state'. What about 'the losers', the majority of the population belonging to the menial castes and the landless classes? 'Their exclusion under imperialism from the prime economic resource of land ownership, reappeared after 1947 in the serious neglect of social expenditure by the Pakistani State'. This is still largely the present scenario, argues Imran Ali. For the last fifty years or so, the alternative periods of civilian and military rule have preserved the established structure of power and authority. 'The weakness of institutionalized politics has served elite interests', and after adult franchise has been conceded, 'Pakistan has yet to develop proper political organizations, with internal democracy and consensus building processes from the bottom up, the only way 'to provide more democratic representation to a wider social base'. If this is not the case, the erosion 'of the credibility of state institutions' may seriously affect 'the moral economy of the system'. The very poor performance of extremist religious parties in legislative elections contrasts with their 'much apparent prominence over public life'. Still untested, these parties may represent 'an alternative available to the electorate, should it move against the status quo', if a weakened state has to face a major challenge and fails to tackle it. What is a mere hypothesis must, however, draw our attention to the fundamental issue of the relationship established in Pakistan between the State and Islam. The second section of this chapter will address it.

II. Islam and the Pakistani Polity

Conceived as a homeland for the Muslims of India, Pakistan had to face two immediate time-related problems. Some believe that the success of the Pakistan Movement came too fast, as only seven years lapsed between the Lahore Declaration of 1940, which called for a new state, and actual independence in 1947. This problem was accentuated by the demise of the 'Great Leader', the Quaid-i-Azam, Mohammad Ali Jinnah, who passed away in 1948, before the country could give itself a Constitution. The men who took charge after him, the Constituent Assembly, and those who legislated later on have only broadly defined the Islamic nature of the new state, leaving unsettled a decisive issue.

Islam, Constitutions and Law: a policy of compromise?

For understanding Islamization in Pakistan, notes Marc
Gaborieau, one must first set the frame of the relationships
between Islam and politics in the process of state building.
Political life, in this regard, has been structured around two
poles: 'on the one hand religious pressure groups, on the
other, a modernist elite, civilian as well as military, which
kept control of the State apparatus'. When the first
Constitution was promulgated in 1956, religious associations
gave birth to political parties. Two associations of
traditionalist *ulema* offered the 'theological and the political
views of the two main schools of *madrasa* educated clerics':
the Jamiat-ulema-i-Islam, for the Deobandi school, and the
Jamiat-ulema-i-Pakistan for the Barelvi school. 'A legacy of
pre-Partition India', these groups saw a third formation, the
Jamaat-i-Islami, as unorthodox: 'an hybrid of traditional
thought and modernist thinking'. Revivalist and neo-
fundamentalist, the Jamaat-i-Islami, led by Maududi, 'came
to the forefront with a readymade blueprint for Pakistan as
an Islamic state', while the old schools had no political
agenda. The JUI and the JUP, therefore, 'more or less
followed' Maududi's political paradigm: in an Islamic state,
'God would be the only sovereign and legislator'. The
modernist elite had obviously a very different conception of
the sovereign state, influenced by the West. The two forces
had 'neither the same language, nor the same aims', but
relying upon a strategy of outbidding and pressure, 'the
religious groups compelled the modernizing elite to
concessions on the religious nature of the state': the *Shariah*
was made 'the law of the country, at least in principle'.

In the early 1980s, argues Gaborieau, three parameters
defined the Islamization of Pakistani politics: i) Islam is 'an
indispensable ingredient of constitutional, institutional and
political legitimacy; ii) the legitimization results from 'a series
of compromises' between the modernist elite and religious
groups; iii) the trend under Zia was 'in favour of the
fundamentalist religious groups. Jinnah's vision of a
Pakistani state where religion was solely a matter of personal
faith, was, therefore, short-lived. The first Constitution of

1956 defined Pakistan as an Islamic state. Later on, Ayub Khan tried in vain 'to delete the adjective 'Islamic' before 'Republic of Pakistan', 'in the Constitution of 1962. If these concessions by the modernists were a compromise, they were not, Gaborieau asserts, a surrender. The Constitutions of 1956, 1962 and 1973 carefully avoided 'the very word of *Shariah*'. They only said 'that no law should be repugnant with the Koran and the Sunna'. The State, not the *ulema*, have the final say: 'The Islamic tradition was not treated as a system of law taking precedence, but as a set of general principles, to which homage must be paid, but which do not impose specific consequences'. Zia's Revival of the Constitution Order of 1985 resulted in 'the most islamized version of Pakistan's Constitution'. According to Gaborieau, however, the change was 'more cosmetic than substantive'. The same year, the Eight Amendment expanded the powers of the President: the overall compromise was 'in favour of the nation-state, not in favour of the Shariah'. Lately, the failure of the Nawaz Sharif government to have the Shariat Bill passed in the Senate showed that the instrumentalization of Islam was not by itself always conducive to the Islamization of the Constitution.

In the field of Law, argues Gaborieau, the same type of compromise has been observed. The Hudood ordinances promulgated by Ziaul Haq in 1979, followed by the 1986 Act, modified in 1991, were spectacularly regressive: whipping punishment, restrictive law of evidence against Muslim women and non-Muslims, death penalty in case of blasphemy etc. But these regulations do not cover the whole field of legislation. Similarly, the *ulema* sitting in the Shariah benches of the High Court have a limited say in the judicial work, 'still done by State courts established on the British model'. In other words, Zia himself, 'in many ways, instrumentalized the fundamentalist agenda, but did not really put it in operation'. His regime 'was thus one peak in the evolution of the compromise: it was the period in which religious groups got the most favours, but only (or mostly?) 'symbolic ones'.

However, concedes Gaborieau, 'with the Federal Shariah Court, the ulema have a foot in the institutions, and they can exert pressure to further the islamization of the Law'. More importantly perhaps, Gaborieau concludes that the influence of religious groups must not be assessed only through the compromises struck with them in the field of Law. They are also political actors, and as such, future political configurations may or may not favour them. And they are social actors as well: the rise of *madrasas* under Zia, 'has carved for the religious groups, in the field of education, a kind of private domain where they can prosper'.

On the whole, the conception of Islam embodied in constitutional, legislative and judicial texts remaining a matter of debate, the overall relationship between Islam, the state and the nation has to be addressed afresh. For Manzoor Ahmad, this calls for nothing less than a new paradigm.

Islam and Pakistan: the quest for a new paradigm

The key problem for Pakistan, argues Manzoor Ahmad, is the 'great chasm' between the need for a modern state and the conservative ideas 'expressed in traditional religious idiom'. The inability of Muslim intellectuals 'to clarify the concept of a statehood based on Islamic values system' is partly due to the quick emergence of an independent Pakistan, but must be ascribed to medium and long term factors as well. First, Muslim intellectuals failed to appreciate 'the conceptual leap between the objectives of the creation of the Muslim League in 1906 and its later stand in 1940', at Lahore. None, not even Iqbal, could transcend the contradiction existing 'between the universalism of the Islamic approach and its particularization in a single cultural unit'. The problem is not just affecting Pakistan, of course, and Manzoor Ahmad recalls that as a whole 'Muslim intellectualism failed to respond to contemporary challenges'. The sudden death of the Prophet (PBUH), and internal conflicts soon after affected 'the collective mind of the ummah', which subconsciously evolved 'defence mechanisms', two of them being 'a theological structure based on command-obedience pattern', and 'a theological construct which made value parasitic to the will of God', and not intrinsic in itself.

Specific factors aggravated the challenge. Firstly, the land where West Pakistan established itself was 'under the influence of inadequate feudal and tribal leaders' who accepted the idea of a Muslim state because Islam was supposed to respect property: 'they jumped onto the bandwagon of the Muslim League and used the religion as an instrument to arouse the masses emotionally'. Secondly, the demand for Pakistan which emerged from the minority areas was mostly articulated by an urban middle class supporting 'the legalistic and formal approach to religion' advocated by the *ulema*. An anti-intellectual tradition mixed with 'a proclivity for sentimentalism' made many 'incapable of living a rational culture'. True, Syed Ahmed Khan, in the nineteenth century, 'was able to break the deafening silence of Muslim intellectualism existing for the last 500 years', and 'pave the way for developing an alternative construct of Muslim theology'. Iqbal's philosophy argued also that the 'Islamic spirit is free to express itself into new forms'. But these attempts have not provided the consensual basis upon which the nation could be constructed.

Religious parties and other organizations representative of what is labelled as 'urban Islam', by contrast with the popular and less puritan folk Islam, 'have no positive content to their sketchy generalized framework of Islam ideology', when it turns to concrete issues such as the nature of law, human rights, political structure, economic agenda'. Reinforced by social dynamics favouring urbanization, market economy and labour migration, this urban Islam remains 'defensive, polemical', and still retains 'the aura of self sufficiency as a system'. To quote Ahmad, 'the sterility of their thought structure can become manifest only when they themselves or their like get a chance at the governance of a country'. If 'the sense of Muslim nationalism' was mostly, in the pre-Partition days 'parasitic on an opposing factor (the Hindu majority India), 'the rationality of the two-nation theory' itself becomes 'debatable' and in any case offers only a paradigm that 'poses problems in the creation of a modern state embodying Islamic values'. Manzoor Ahmad stresses, therefore, the need for a new paradigm, which has to propose also a new theology. 'In Islam, the conceptual bifurcation of secular and sacred is not admissible'. Three options are, therefore, open. The fundamentalist experience is bound to fail. Out of its failure 'may emerge a critique of the puritanic or reformed Islam'. If this critique promotes a bifurcation of the sacred and the secular, it would offer a recipe for 'a continuous strife'. Neither Iran nor Turkey offer a model.

A third way remains, suggests Ahmad: to deconstruct theology without secularizing Islam, in 'evolving a monistic paradigm where God consciousness serves as a point of reference, and generates a creative process for developing new constructs' able to satisfy the needs of a modern state. Fazlur Rahman had suggested in this regard that the Quran and the *Sunnah* 'provided particular instances of guidance, but in which general principles were implicit'. One has, therefore, to go beyond the classical concept of *ijtehad*, 'where the particular instances served as major premises in a syllogistic type of reasoning': Muslim intellectuals have today to discover the implicit general principles referred to by Rahman, 'and build their own social structures on that basis'. Pakistan, suggests Ahmad, is well equipped for such an attempt, for its two venerated figures, Jinnah and Iqbal, had 'no claim of religious leadership'. Furthermore, its social dynamics are such that they 'will perforce shift the paradigm in such a way that puritanic fundamentalism will be subsumed in a new synthesis'. There is, however, a precondition, which brings us to the point where culture, democracy and ideology meet: 'ground level change can occur only when people participate in a broad universe of discourse which is not available to them now'. This presupposes that Urdu and vernacular languages cease to be monopolized by a one-sided religious discourse. The quest for a new paradigm combining an open Islam and a modern nation has to be carried on in the language of the people.

III. Identity Movements: Religion, Ethnicity and Gender

Obviously, Islam is not just a matter of faith, nor just a major polity issue. The way it is lived, and the way the rulers define it have decisive consequences in the social sphere. This is why the following three chapters dealing with social and identity issues cannot avoid either to address directly the problem of Islamic definition and instrumentalization (Mariam Abou Zahab's study on sectarianism), or to question its instrumentalization in broader contexts than self definition, such as the Mohajir movement (Soofia Mumtaz's case study of Sindh), or the status of women in Pakistan (Nighat Said Khan).

'Pakistan was created on the basis that the Muslims of India had a different identity, yet the question of its identity has never been resolved'. This remark by Nighat Said Khan may well introduce this section, for it has two implications. First, the Islamic identity of the new state was supposed to be overarching, but not necessarily suppressive of other pre-existing identities which, as categories (gender, ethnicity, hierarchies), do exist in any society. Two such cases will be addressed below: gender identities, and ethnic ones, the latter inscribing themselves also in the unbalanced national structure of power which governs both the centre-province asymmetry and inter-provincial relations. The second implication, illustrated by another case-study, is in a way more sensitive: that the Islamic identity itself may be, on religious terms, open to debate and interpretation, leading to sectarian conflict.

Sectarianism as a substitute identity

In her study of sectarian struggles in South Punjab—the area where tensions started in the mid-eighties—Mariam Abou Zahab recalls firstly how the sense of affiliation to Shia or Sunni communities has recently greatly developed: 'sectarian consciousness and some prejudice have always been there but they never prevented coexistence'. What brought the change, which cost no less than 200 lives in 1997 alone? As always, a number of factors, combining structural parameters with contemporary developments. Four decisive elements have to be taken into account. Firstly, Ziaul Haq's Islamization policy. Favouring the Sunnis (and particularly the Deobandi school), it 'brought the theological differences to the fore'. Secondly, the Iranian revolution 'gave a new sense of identity to the Shia community which became more assertive', and opposed, in 1980, the compulsory deduction of *zakat* by the government. Thirdly, the simultaneity of the Shia upsurge in Iran and of Zia's pro-Sunni policy in Pakistan stirred up the existing socio-economic tensions. The impact of the Green Revolution cannot be forgotten. Benefiting as a whole the Pakistan economy, it entailed, however, a local social cost. The modest land reforms pushed big landlords to sell a part of their land to a new middle class of capitalist agriculturers. Both classes engineered the proletarianization of small peasants—particularly tenants—who could not compete with them. In the meantime, the mechanization of agriculture increased unemployment amongst the agricultural labourers. Urbanization accelerated, but not industrialization. Many landlords were Shia. Most of the urban trade was in the hands of immigrants from East Punjab. In this context, the rise of sectarianism 'can be described as a reaction to a growing sense of insecurity and hopelessness resulting from the uneven distribution of resources, and as a revolt of the uprooted and marginalized periphery deprived from access to the political arena'.

The fourth factor was instrumental, but resulted also from the failure of the State to tackle acute poverty and to spread education. 'The mushroom growth of madrasas' cannot be understood outside this context. The problem lies in the type of education such schools provide to students who are sent there by their parents 'to ease their financial burden', and then who find themselves 'completely cut-off from the outside world'. The sectarian *madrasas* blooming 'in a feudal environment where violence is part of the socio-political culture' preach 'the elimination of other sects'; what Khalid Hussain has called 'the jehad within', an internal *jehad* aiming at cleansing the *ummah* itself. But here again the external factors have to be considered, on two accounts: i) in the context of the rivalry between Iran and Iraq, and the competition between Iran and Saudi Arabia, massive funding came from abroad for supporting *madrasas*, ii) the Afghan war not only gave prestige to the *mujahideen*, it developed a gun culture in Pakistan, which found itself submerged suddenly by small arms (the direct result of the US policy that used Pakistan as a front-line state against Soviet forces in Afghanistan). Tens of thousands of young men, graduates from *madrasas* or drop-outs from the Urdu medium system of education, found themselves with 'no skills and relevance to the job market'. 'Full of anger and frustration with the corrupt system', they were ready to listen to charismatic leaders offering them, through religious violence, 'a means of empowerment' and a sacred mission rolled in one.

Mariam Abou Zahab suggests that 'traditional religious parties have no control of the sectarian organizations'. It may be so, but what about the links between extremist religious parties, sectarian *madrasas* affiliated to them, and armed outfits? What about the State responsibility in letting such organizations develop, at the cost of national cohesiveness? 'In the 1970s', notes Abou Zahab, 'ethnicity became a substitute identity but it was branded as treason and violently suppressed'. By contrast, it was the State itself which promoted in the 1980s religious identity, and failed in the 1990s to suppress its extremist degeneration. Perhaps sectarian killings can be stopped. But repression alone will not solve the structural problems which have permitted such a drift, be they acute socio-economic disparities, or the instrumentalization of Islam for political purposes.

The politics of ethnicity: the nation and the federation

The case of Sindh offers another example of politicization of identity. For the Urdu-speaking migrants from northern India and for the Gujarati-speaking entrepreneurs from western India who moved to Pakistan after Partition, their new country was in a way 'the promised land'. Most of these migrants, labelled as Mohajirs, were from an urban background and, notes Soofia Mumtaz, 'expected to play a prominent role in the politics and economy of the country they saw themselves as having struggled to create', much more than the native settlers did. That prospect could not satisfy ethnic Sindhis, who, on the eve of Partition, were hardly a majority in their province where Balochis and Punjabis had settled in significant numbers, with the Punjabis getting, as retired military men, the best irrigated lands. By contrast, limited land reforms did not alter fundamentally the pre-eminence of the feudal landed classes over the poor Sindhi peasantry. Furthermore, the majority Punjabis and the educated Mohajirs quickly established themselves in the central bureaucracy. Later on, the arrival of Afghans refugees in Karachi, and illegal immigration from Bangladesh, Burma and Sri Lanka, accrued the sense of frustration of the native Sindhis.

Zulfikar Ali Bhutto's policy of quotas in provincial services helped them somewhat, but also initiated a sense of competition between unemployed educated Mohajirs and young Sindhis. Two cross-currents developed therefore. On the one hand, Sindhis, mostly of rural stock, felt deprived by the national power structure. The pattern of Centre-Province relationships, the weakness of the political structure (the Muslim League had been poorly organized in Muslim majority provinces), the consequent empowerment of a bureaucracy dominated by Urdu-speaking Mohajirs, the hold of Punjabis on the Army, all concurred to a sense of marginality amongst the Sindhis. On the other hand, in Karachi itself—more and more a non-Sindhi city—the migration flux added to the contrast between the better settled Mohajirs and other communities facing the odds of urban under-development.

The rise of the Mohajir Quomi Movement (MQM) in Sindh has to be understood in this context. True, some 'disenchantment with the promised land', which has not offered them the true leadership they expected, helped the Urdu-speaking Mohajirs to shift 'from a national to an ethnic identity', particularly after the collapse of the One Unit system for West Pakistan, and the revival of provincial politics. The creation of the MQM as a political party in 1984, and its involvement in a Sindhi-Mohajir confrontation are, however, not just the consequence of a local conflict, or a result of a competition between two groups attached to their specific culture (the Mohajirs viewing themselves as the inheritors of the Mughal culture, supposed, by them, to be more

sophisticated than the native Sindhi legacy). National
manipulations are also to be accounted for: Zia's regime used
the MQM to weaken its rival, the Pakistan Peoples Party,
led by the Sindhi Bhutto family.

Soofia Mumtaz may, therefore, wonder if the Sindhi-
Mohajir conflict was not 'an artificial creation', 'more
speculative than real'. This question raises a broader issue
relevant to Pakistan as a whole. Does 'the transformation
from anti-ethnic to pro-ethnic thinking among the Mohajirs
defy the logic of the 'two-nation theory', and the creation of
Pakistan as a separate homeland for the Muslims of India?'.
Mumtaz's argument is two-fold. First, the rise of ethnicity is
to be understood in the context of the Pakistani polity:
ethnicity 'serves to claim a greater share in the power
structure and economic resources of the state, and to register
opposition to the highly centralized, non-representative
nature of state structure, dominated by (civilian and military)
bureaucracies'. Such limitations result from a specific
Pakistani history, marked by 'the absence of any degree of
'stateness' prior to Independence'; by the high centralization
of state authority, built up against external threats—hence
the large defence budget and the political economy of
defence—but also 'vigilant against internal political threats'.
This state pattern, and 'the negligence of the service sectors
and basic needs' which goes along with it, can only accentuate
regional grievances, class differences, and one may add,
identity movements.

These shortcomings of the State, however, do not tell the
whole story, hence the second part of the reasoning. The two-
nation theory, argues Soofia Mumtaz, is not collapsing simply
because other identities manifest themselves. It would
collapse only if Pakistanis 'would accept to be part of the
Indian federation', or if Mohajirs 'would be willing to undo
Partition after the present experience, and return to India'.
This is not the case. Whatever its challenges may be, the
nation is still a goal. 'The severe nature of centre-province
tensions represents a protest against denial of participation,
rather than a refusal of the provinces to participate in the
national political process'. In Sindh, but not in Sindh alone,
concludes Mumtaz 'the perpetuation of a self-seeking non-

representative authority structure, and the accompanying
decay of the political, administrative, and judicial institutions
will continue to multiply internal fissions' affecting the
balance of the federation. For Mumtaz, as for other
contributors, the key to progress is, therefore, a political
renovation, transcending 'the lack of faith' in political leaders
through 'a more representative future', yet to be materialized.

Women's rights and feminism: searching for a new ideology

A more representative future implies a greater recognition of
all sections of the nation. Nighat Said Khan offers us more
than an analysis of what is the status of women in Pakistan
today: she provides a personal insight of what is the dilemma
of those who militate for building a better society through
women's emancipation. The national parameters determining
the legal and constitutional status of women have to be taken
into account. General Ayub Khan 'gave some rights to Muslim
women' through the Muslim Family Laws Ordinance. He
'suppressed fundamentalist religious forces, but he also
suppressed all other dissent'. Z.A. Bhutto, 'liberal and
progressive in terms of women's rights', was, however, 'unable
to withstand the pressure of the Islamic parties'. On the one
hand, he used the mobilization of women both for the success
of the new, socially oriented development programmes
(health, education, population control), and for its electoral
potential. On the other hand, the 1973 Constitution he
promoted 'reinforced Pakistan as an Islamic Republic'. The
Women's Rights Committee Bhutto set up in 1976 suggested
a number of progressive changes in family laws, labour laws,
inheritance of property, divorce and reservations of seats in
assemblies, but not much was implemented before General
Ziaul Haq threw him out in a military coup in 1977.

This was a turning point, for Zia vowed to Islamize the
State, and 'the lynchpin of this process of Islamization was
women'. The celebration of 'the sanctity of *chaddar* and
chardivari'—the veil and the four walls of the house—called
for legislative changes very detrimental to women's status,

be it dress code, sport practices, adultery, marital law or the
Hudood Ordinance of 1979 which specified Islamic
punishments. Against Zia's retrograde decisions, the
Pakistani women's movement gained momentum (the
Women's Action Forum was founded in 1983), and was one of
the most active forces demonstrating against Islamization as
defined by the regime.

Today, however, 'the movement has lost its political
sharpness and energy'. This is partly due to the fact that 'the
women's movement has begun to be defined only by a few
women centred groups, mainly in the urban areas' while in
reality, argues Nighat Said Khan, the ability of women to
'grapple with issues of their own subordination' is often
stronger outside the range of the middle class urban women
who tend to see themselves as more progressive. The
opportunities offered by NGOs engaged in development
softened the tension which stimulated the movement, and
affected its autonomy. In other words, 'the women's
movement has moved from being a movement, to becoming
institutionalized, and becoming a part of the establishment'.

The points raised by Khan, her analysis of the correlation
between the post Cold War unipolar order and the multiple
identities breaking societies 'into smaller and smaller
communities', as well as her comments on the challenges
faced by women's militancy are particularly significant. They
take root in a Pakistani experience, but extend much beyond
the country. They help, henceforth, to recall that Pakistan,
whatever its specificities may be, cannot be dissociated from
much larger configurations. The legacy of Zia is very much
alive and has left Pakistani women 'particularly vulnerable
physically, politically, economically and socially'. This is
precisely why Pakistani women's groups have to reassess
themselves. Not surprisingly, the quest for a theoricization
revival and for the new, more radical ideology Khan calls for,
echoes other women's movements facing the same challenges
in other countries and in different contexts. Khan underlines
particularly the differences between the women's rights
movement, 'a struggle for democracy and equal rights for
women within the liberal feminist tradition', and the feminist
movement, much more radical in its attack against

patriarchy, and seeking 'a more holistic, ideological and a structural transformation of society and a transformation of all relationships including the personal'. Women's rights are not enough: 'we have fought many a struggle to bring women in the mainstream; we have challenged the invisibility of women's contribution to society, we have fought for women's rights to wages and work, for access to education, health, the law and decision making (...), and all to one end: to acknowledge, to reinforce, to give a value to women's works and thereby to give women a place in society, as if this were an end in itself. But (...) we understand that the development of a people is much more than this (...). As women we must start looking for a new vision, an alternative way of developing'.

Khan suggests to search for a new paradigm, 'since feminism is a distinct shift from what has been a universal construct'. Her call is obviously valid beyond the women's case. In Pakistan, and in the world at large, the need of the time is a new development paradigm, regulating the relationship between states, but also between the state and the citizens, respecting both 'the common good' and their individuality. In Pakistan and elsewhere, 'this is a challenge that we must address globally'.

IV. The Political Economy of Pakistan

National construction is not just an ideological experiment and a social process: its economic dimensions are vital, not only for the sake of growth, development and collective well-being, but also because a sluggish economy affects social cohesiveness and political stability. The political economy of Pakistan, unfortunately, has not built upon the 'miracle' of the sixties and seventies, and the national economy, which offered respectable growth rates at one time, is now engulfed in very serious difficulties. The debt trap into which the country has fallen is a matter of grave concern, for it is less the result of a circumstantial crisis than the unavoidable conclusion of structural short-comings.

The long term perspective: a 'culturally-alienated military-dependent state'

Arshad Zaman offers in his chapter a well thought out perspective of fifty years of Pakistan's economic policies. To the classic political history segmentation, he adds another decisive parameter: the calendar of 'relations with sources of foreign assistance'. Most important in this regard was US assistance, in a direct way during the phases of close relationship (1951-62 and 1981-90), and also the IMF-World Bank duet since the early 1980s, when Pakistan got its first extended fund facility from the IMF, complemented by a World Bank structural adjustment loan.

Neither the two partitions (the partition of British India in 1947, and the secession of Bangladesh in 1971), nor the tense relationship with India helped to give prominence to the economy. On the whole, throughout independence, 'the performance of agriculture and the volume of military and economic assistance received have been the proximate determinants of economic performance'. For Arshad, 'the fateful alliance with the USA' built up 'an aid-dependent pattern of development in which fundamental structural reforms were perennially postponed'. The Five-Year Plans, launched with the 'assistance' of the Harvard Advisory Group, were not able to promote self-sustaining growth: the benefits of the Second Plan (1960-65) did not last when the fluctuating interests of Washington led the US to stop aid after the Indo-Pakistan war of 1965.

Whatever the differences between the 'Islamic socialism' of Zulfikar Ali Bhutto, marked by nationalization of major industries and financial institutions but no genuine planning (1971-1977), and the 'Islamic capitalism' of General Zia who undid most of the nationalizations (1977-1988), both the leaders followed the same 'aid mobilization strategy' and 'invoked Islam in an effort to base power in popular values'. In 1979, the Afghan war and the Iranian revolution gave Pakistan a specific geopolitical relevance for Washington, and boosted once again 'aid-dependent development'...till the Soviet forces left Afghanistan. In 1990, United States aid was stopped again when the White House found itself suddenly unable to certify that the Pakistani nuclear programme was strictly peaceful.

The adjustment programmes, in the 1980s and 1990s, also failed to achieve their three goals: i) balance of payments viability; ii) price stability; iii) sustainable growth, for 'macroeconomic stability—which in Pakistan means budgetary stability—', which is 'an essential pre-condition for the success of economic liberalization'. The last phase of the post-'71 economic history of Pakistan, running from 1988 onwards was, to quote Zaman, a time of 'chaotic and damaging liberalization' which brought out 'falling growth and rising inflation and unemployment'. The government's fiscal and monetary policies, as well as the exchange and trade liberalization policies failed, and finally resulted in the late nineties in a 'full blown debt crisis'.

On the whole, concludes Zaman, the combination of the colonial legacy and 'India's consistently hostile posture' compelled Pakistan 'to seek US military and economic assistance, despite the cost it entailed in terms of cultural alienation of the state from the people'. 'With defence considerations paramount, economic policy has continued to take the back seat for most of the last fifty years'. The result is a 'culturally-alienated military dependent state' whose economic vacuum was filled in the 1990s by the IMF-World Bank combine. This has large politico-economic implications, suggests Arshad Zaman in a premonitory way. While the national and expatriated elite 'would like to see the past pattern of post-colonial development continue', the people of Pakistan 'are ready for an indigenous leader who would cut the Gordian knot of external military and economic dependence'. And, Zaman adds: 'No such leader however appears to be on the horizon'. In such a perspective, General Musharraf will also be judged according to the answer he will give to this economic alternative: will his regime serve the elite agenda, or will it cut the Gordian knot?

Pakistan in the late nineties: 'the most dangerous years'?

Gilbert Etienne's paper supplements Arshad Zaman's study well, for it adds to Zaman's fifty years' macro-economic analysis a sectoral approach, more focused on the late nineties. For Etienne, Pakistan faces its 'most dangerous years' on the economic front. The diagnosis is well known: sluggish growth, rising inflation, crushing debt, falling remittances from expatriates working in the Gulf, and fallen foreign exchange reserves. The crisis is, however, not just expressed by macro-economic data. Structural weaknesses are to be acknowledged as well. What Etienne calls 'the economy of leakage' is well documented. The impact of corruption and default loans is aggravated by large scale tax evasion on the one hand, and by the criminalization of a part of the economy, not only massive smuggling and black money, but also 'heroin and arms traffic, both consequences of the endless Afghan wars' on the other. Not to be forgotten, population growth is still very high, and some experts wonder if the country has really gone down from 3.1 per cent annual demographic growth rate in 1981 to 2.6 per cent, as suggested by the much delayed and controversial Census held in 1998.

Etienne, who has long experience of rural surveys in Pakistan, underlines the serious consequences of the neglect of agriculture and irrigation in a country where 52 per cent of the population and 25 per cent of GNP depend on agriculture. Water is the key issue. Badly maintained, the 61,000 km-long irrigation canals, which have been 'a major engine of growth and relative prosperity' now represent 'the major stumbling block for further progress'. Their improvement will require huge investments. The Kalabagh dam, stuck for decades in political controversy and inter-provincial competition, is only a part of the irrigation problem. As a result of the neglect of agriculture, Pakistan had to import millions of tons of wheat. Cotton production is stagnating, while cotton and textiles represent by far a major share (nearly 60 per cent) of Pakistani exports.

More dynamic sectors are noticeable, however. The diversification of agriculture, through milk production, animal husbandry, fish ponds, fruits, testifies to the dynamism of a number of producers. The 'fast track policy' introduced by Benazir Bhutto to reduce shortage of electricity; the liberalization of trade and industries encouraged by Nawaz Sharif, the call for Foreign Direct Investments in power stations, agro-business, pharmaceuticals, etc...aimed at stimulating growth. But the results 'have not been spectacular'. Once again some structural factors explain the failure, at least partially: Pakistan's industry must largely rely upon import for its basic needs (coal, iron ore, oil), and savings and investments have always been too low. But others factors have also had a negative impact: the collapse of law and order in Karachi, the economic capital of Pakistan; controversies about foreign electrical companies; the freeze on foreign currency accounts by the Sharif Government just after the nuclear tests; the economic sanctions attached to the nuclear tests, and the quick degradation of public finances sent negative signals to investors.

In other words, Pakistan has yet to make the best of its assets: a surplus of electricity, a very large irrigated area, a professional class which emerged despite the poor average human development index. The reason is not hard to find: 'at the root of the economic difficulties lie political factors. Vested interests of politicians, feudal landlords, certain businessmen prevent drastic reforms of the fiscal and banking system, the curtailment of all kinds of leakages...A sound financial system going along with more political stability could unleash many dynamic forces. The private sector would invest more in manufacturing. The state would be able to increase public investments and recurrent expenditures in infrastructure, in agriculture, in health and education'. Not surprisingly, therefore, Etienne's conclusion, in tune with Zaman, ends with a call for political change: 'there is a tremendous urge for better governance. A firm and committed leadership ...would be supported with enthusiasm'. Our comment can only be repeated: will the new military regime be able to deliver? Some positive trends underlined by the Government after one year in power (a GDP growth rate of 4.5 per cent, amongst others) remain to be sustained.

V. The Challenge of Democracy: The Lessons of the Past

After the military take-over in October 1999, the dismissed regime of Nawaz Sharif, which had been criticized before its fall, was suddenly almost demonized for its drifts. Many acknowledged, however, that whatever be the responsibilities of Nawaz Sharif's style of government, the problems of Pakistani democracy went much deeper, and were more structural than the concept of mismanagement would suggest. By drawing from the lessons of the past—a recent past for Lafrance, a longer one for Shafqat—the two following chapters define well the challenges faced by the country, if it wishes to develop itself as a vibrant democracy.

Building democracy without democrats? The leadership's responsibility

In his detailed analysis of fifty years of political transformation of Pakistan, Saeed Shafqat assesses 'the forces of resistance and support to democracy'. If democracy is constrained in Pakistan, it is not only due to historical and institutional settings which may have afflicted a country born out of Partition. Foremost is the responsibility of political leaders and elites, who have failed 'to uphold the rule of law': dominant political parties 'have failed to promote pro-democracy environment'. Until the first general election (as late as 1970), the legacy of the colonial administrative structure, 'which established the supremacy of bureaucratic elites' was still alive. Z.A. Bhutto 'sought to establish civilian supremacy over bureaucracy', but also 'to establish his dominance over state institutions', be they military or administrative. Zia and the martial law restored 'the colonial model of politics, where local influentials could be coopted'. The regime de-legitimized not only political leaders, but also politics itself. After 1988, political leadership regained supremacy, but failed again in building up a substantive democracy, for a number of reasons.

The mode of electoral competition, which relies upon patronage for administrative control of resources, is partly responsible for the failure. Democratization (or must we say electoral competition?) 'has led to the development of illiberal tendencies, partisanship, lack of tolerance and distrust in the fairness of an administration' which has been politicized and factionalized to the lowest level. The behavioural pattern of political leadership added to the problem: while professing a democratic creed, the key political leadership indulged in autocratic tendencies. The consequences affected the basic conception of political life, for both Benazir Bhutto and Nawaz Sharif 'have preferred to establish a dominant party system rather than encouraging the growth of a two party system'. The socio-economic profiles of the parliamentarians testify to the limitation of democratic representativeness. From 1988 to 1999, feudal and tribal leaders have always been the most numerous group at the National Assembly (between 50 per cent and 75 per cent of its members). They dominated Benazir Bhutto's cabinets, and sat along with businessmen and professionals in Nawaz Sharif's cabinets, to the constant detriment of the under-represented middle classes. This explains why the 'National Assembly has not been able to develop as an institution that could promote and strengthen democratic norms and practices'.

The Assembly being more a rubber stamp than a genuine forum, and the rule being hostility and confrontation between leading parties rather than bargain and compromise, 'extra-parliamentary tactics' have dominated Pakistani politics. Used as 'instruments of mass mobilization', political parties 'have done little either to democratize their organization or to educate their members to the rules of democracy'. If conflicts cannot be resolved inside Parliament, the change has to come from outside. An alliance between the military and the President 'dislodged elected governments in 1990 and 1993'. Another alliance between the President and the judiciary did the same in 1997. In 1999, the military took over.

Writing before the coup, Saeed Shafqat recalled that 'people have shown vigour and vitality to adopt a democratic parliamentary system and through popular mass movements demonstrated disapproval of military dictatorships'. According to him, 'the passion for democracy continues to resurge, despite ethnic, social, class, religious cleavages, strong authoritarian tendencies and prolonged military rules. There is no gainsaying that cultural and structural conditions weigh heavily against the promotion and plantation of democratic processes and institutions in Pakistan (...). The disappointment is not with democracy as a form of government but with the conduct and behaviour of parliamentarians and political parties who are expected to make democracy work'. This statement inspires hope for the future.

On Pakistan's political parties: networks of solidarity and underground economy

It is precisely upon the role and limitations of political parties that Pierre Lafrance focuses his attention. At first sight, the main polarity of the political spectrum illustrates a major duality, in term of classes and policy. The Pakistan Peoples Party (PPP) of Benazir Bhutto, led by 'an heavily landed gentry' was 'prone to feed the state budget or address the problems of the destitute by taxing the urban rich'. It expected to gain sustainable popular support by 'curbing unemployment and poverty through state intervention'. By contrast, the Pakistan Muslim League (N), whose leaders 'generally belong to the entrepreneurial set', stood for privatization, deregulation, private and foreign investment. The reality is, however, more complex, notes Lafrance, not only because landlords buy shares and businessmen buy land. 'The average parliamentarian is a man of property', so aloof from the populace and from the middle classes that the Pakistan Parliament has sometimes been defined as 'a House of Lords and a Senate', with no House of Commons.

Behind the veil of electoral manifestos, a political set-up has been built up, which encompasses the major parties and their allies. Prone to 'majority absolutism', sustained by a 'culture of leadership and power hoarding' which characterized the PPP since its inception, and 'a tradition of highly controlled freedom' linking the Pakistan Muslim League (Nawaz) PML(N) to Zia's administration, Pakistani democracy appears 'as an aspiration, a longing, but not an actual practice'. Party politics 'failed to pave the way for an open public debate on competing ideas and programme' (just as the National Assembly, as noted by Saeed Shafqat, also failed to do) for a major reason, argues Lafrance: being 'networks of solidarity', parties have a real agenda quite different from their proclaimed objectives. Political parties in Pakistan are not just serving 'natural loyalties' resulting from 'traditional, cultural, religious and ethnic proximities'. They serve also 'functional loyalties', defined as 'privileged relationships with a number of bureaucratic and economic actors'. As solidarity systems, political parties have created a parallel economy which is 'a safety net with regard to the failures and discrepancies' of the more visible economy. Besides land, property and industrial or commercial firms, 'other sources of income' are sought underground, which strengthen 'amazingly' the existing networks: loan defaulting and tax evasion—so heavily denounced by General Musharraf's regime—but also all sorts of trafficking, from smuggling to hoarding commodities and drug trading, not to forget 'oil money from neighbouring Arab countries' benefiting religious parties for the cause of *madrasa* education.

According to Lafrance, these networks of solidarity, built on over-expanding promises and political patronage explain why 'political parties remain so determined to eliminate each other instead of sharing power': clientelism is vital to their sustainability. Must we compare such a situation with the French pre-revolution days, when 'an indebted nobility was disqualified', and soon thrown away by a rising middle class building new political tools better serving its interests? Lafrance, in 1998, visualized no coming revolution in Pakistan, but did perceive two forces which 'could exert enough pressure to impose reforms' and 'challenge the pervasive influence of networks': civil society and the Army. October 1999 provided the answer, when the Army leadership co-opted civil society and elite technocrats for carrying out reforms, at the cost of political parties.

VI. Regional Geopolitics: The Question of National Interests

Contrary to common assertions, countries do not have a foreign policy dictated by their geography. The compulsions of neighbourhood, which obviously cannot be ignored, always offer a choice of possibilities. Selected policies express, therefore, more the weight of political and ideological options than a mere adjustment to unavoidable territorial configurations. In its relations with India and Afghanistan, Pakistan has hence made choices, and has broadly followed two different patterns. While continuity marked most of the tense relations with India, the global significance of the Afghan war offered Pakistan a new opportunity to expand its influence west of the Durand Line. This policy, however, had a price.

The Afghan policy: the price of influence

The Soviet invasion of Afghanistan, which was first seen in Islamabad as a move threatening to Pakistan, offered in fact to General Zia a new credibility, and a number of opportunities. Upgraded as the new frontline state against USSR expansion, Pakistan gained not only from the transit of massive US funding: 'it played a vital part in the definition of the strategy of the mujahideen' on the field, and it even represented them diplomatically, as they were 'not allowed to participate directly in negotiations', recalls Gilles Dorronsoro. Afghanistan, a difficult neighbour for long, was expected to become a client state. When Hekmatyar, associated for many years with the Inter-Services Intelligence (ISI), proved unable to take Jalalabad in 1994, the ISI 'chose the Taliban as their new client'. Islamabad's goal was even broader, in terms of ideology and geopolitics. Firstly, 'for islamist or fundamentalist movements, the Afghan jehad was a unique opportunity to put Islam on the political agenda'— and that fitted Ziaul Haq's vision. Secondly, beyond establishing a friendly government in Kabul, Islamabad sought to obtain, 'in the long term, the de-colonization of

Central Asia'. The ISI tried also to encourage Islamism on the other side of the Amu Daria.

This great design, argues Dorronsoro, backfired for it was based on some misperceptions, and relied upon dangerous strategies. The 'divide and rule policy' followed by Pakistan vis-à-vis various *mujahideen* groups 'prevented the concentration of military or political power', as the Hezb-i Islami of Hekmatyar, the most pro-Pakistan militia, 'did not have enough support in Afghan society to impose itself on other parties'. Although most of the Taliban have been trained in *madrasas* in Pakistan, Islamabad has probably not gained with their accession to power. 'The victory of the Taliban is not a clear cut benefit for Pakistan', contends Dorronsoro. Internally, it has diffused to the country a dangerous arms culture and has increased the risk of destabilization by fundamentalist movements. Bilaterally, 'the Taliban are by no means ISI puppets': they have 'their own agenda in foreign policy and it is a revolutionary one', confronting Western countries, conservative Arab regimes and Central Asian States. Consequently, Pakistan's foreign policy is itself affected. 'The new regime in Afghanistan represents an obstacle to Pakistani projects in Central Asia': Pakistan's influence on ex-Soviet Republics is much less than Islamabad expected when they became independent, and the hypothetical trans-Afghan gas pipeline from Turkmenistan to Pakistan has not been built up. Worse perhaps, are 'the growing difficulties for Pakistan with Western countries and its traditional allies'.

Finally, has the Afghan policy served Pakistan's national interests? Dorronsoro answers no, and argues that it 'could become a classic counter-example of the Realist theory in international relations: the State is not a united actor, but a network of institutions exercising no monopoly over foreign policy, and the very concept of 'national interest' is irrelevant'. Some will disagree with such a formulation, but two decisive questions remain to be answered. Was it wise to push the fundamentalist agenda for geopolitical expectations? Was is safe to expand the politicization of Islam to regional politics? Considering the strong links between the Taliban and the Deobandi movement, it was difficult for the governments of

Benazir Bhutto and Nawaz Sharif to control the 'thousands of Pakistani militants who (were) back in Pakistan after having been trained in Afghanistan', 'since the fundamentalist movements justified themselves by the national cause, the Kashmir issue'.

We are here at the crux of one of the major challenges faced by the post-Afghan war regimes, past and present, for it addresses not only the State policy vis-à-vis armed militancy, but also the intractable question of the Pakistan-India relationship.

Pakistan-India relations: the need for a 'thought revolution'

Because he believes that 'without a 'thought revolution' or a *gelstalt* switch in the way they think about security, no amount of prescription will suffice', Rifaat Hussain chooses to theoricize Pakistan-India relations, rather than enter into the details of their successive conflicts, diplomatic ups and downs or intricacies of the Kashmir imbroglio.

What explains the Pakistan-India rivalry? Four theses have been proposed by various authors. The first one suggests that the confrontation pre-dates 1947, and 'stems from two diametrically opposed philosophies of Hinduism and Islam'. The two-nation theory popularized this ideological contention, which offered the rationale for Partition. The second thesis offers a geopolitical rationale. The hostility between Pakistan and India is seen as resulting from their demographic, strategic and economic asymmetry: 'In the South Asia system, India is the 'hegemonic' power while Pakistan is the challenger resisting Indian domination'. The third thesis offers a psychological explanation. A 'legacy of misperception', born out of an old 'culture of distrust', sustains standard negative images of the Other: many Pakistanis see India 'as unreconciled to Pakistan's independent existence', while many Indians see Pakistan as 'a recalcitrant neighbour' refusing to accommodate itself to the regional balance of power. The last thesis submits that the unresolved issue of Kashmir 'has been the fundamental and continuing cause of tensions' between the two countries. This thesis is obviously not exclusive from the other ones, for Kashmir symbolises the self-definition of each of the two nations (a Muslim homeland for Pakistan, a secular pluri-religious state for India), focalises the geopolitical competition between them, and is the most fertile field nourishing reciprocate distrust and misperceptions.

Where do we go from there? 'With the nuclearization of South Asia' suggests Rifaat Hussain, 'India and Pakistan have been left with no option except to wage peace with each other'. The Lahore Declaration of February 1999 supported in a way this thesis, but the Kargil adventure, a few months later, contradicted it. One may argue extensively about the true meaning of Kargil, and about the expectations shared (or not) by the then Government and by the Army. The episode, certainly, illustrated misperceptions, reinforced distrust and does not facilitate a relationship between the then Chief of Army Staff, now President of Pakistan, and the Indian leadership. But if we believe that peace is better than war—be it an open war or a low intensity one—Rifaat Hussain's theoricization of co-operative security offers genuine guidelines.

While the traditional concept of national security was founded on unilateral interests and national rivalries, the way out, argues Hussain, is co-operative or mutual security, 'multidimensional in scope' (i.e. encompassing not just strategic objectives but also economic, social and environmental goals), 'inclusive rather than exclusive in temperament', open to non-state actors in addition to official ones, and promoting 'co-operation, bargaining and peaceful change' rather than 'coercion, conflict and war'. The memorandum of understanding attached to the 1999 Lahore Declaration encouraged what Hussain calls 'the technical conception' of mutual security, which focuses on the 'danger of inadvertent escalation' of tensions. But we are still far from the 'supportive conception' of mutual security, more encompassing, and still farther from the 'co-operative conception' of mutual security. If the concept of mutual security 'above all, stresses the values of habits of dialogue on a multilateral basis', it will hurt the Indian contention that the Pakistan-Indian tangle has to be solved

bilaterally, whatever could be the role of external powers—
particularly the US—in defining with each party the way to
enhance nuclear security in South Asia. Arms control may
progress in a global frame, but other confidence building
measures, bilateral in nature and content, have suffered a
serious setback after Kargil. Here again, the new Pakistani
regime will have to decide whether to follow the old line or to
be innovative.

The Challenge of Reform

The image of Pakistan emerging from this collective analysis
is rich in questions. Whatever their topic of interest has been,
all authors of this book have, in their own way, called for
change, and I would like to conclude by commenting upon
this need for reform. On 17 October 1999, five days after
taking over power, General Musharraf also called for change.
In his first major address as Chief Executive of Pakistan, he
drew a depressing picture of the state of the nation, which
obviously was supposed to justify the intervention of the
army.[1] One year later, an official document referred again to
'the brink of the social, political and economic abyss' the
country was said to stand close to, but clarified as well that
the Generals acted also for saving the Armed Forces, defined
as 'the only well-regulated and disciplined institution in
Pakistan', from a threatening 'schism' said to be then
instigated by Nawaz Sharif, without providing any more
details about the issues at stake.[2] One may easily discard the
dramatization effect the Army leader chose to rely upon as a
way to enhance the legitimacy, if not the legality, of yet
another coup. Yet many Pakistanis would concede to looking
at their country with a mixture of love and concern.

Rather than speculating on the military and civilian
personalities now in power, or analysing closely their first
steps since the take-over, I will confine my attention to a
point more in tune with the conclusions we may draw from
the seminar contributions. The crux of the problem lies in
the fact that reforms are not only a must, they are also a
challenge, and a tremendous one, for two reasons. Firstly,

change is required on all fronts: political, institutional, economical, sociological, etc. Significant reforms will be hard to implement because they cannot be confined to distinctively separate fields: they are bound to affect interconnected parameters of an overarching system. The weakness of political democracy cannot be understood without paying attention, firstly, to the distribution of power between the social classes and identitarian groups, secondly, to the autocratic tendencies of leaders (including elected ones), and thirdly, to the over-centralization which nurtures provincial frustrations. The economic crisis is largely due to bad governance and political patronage, which are themselves distortions of democratic ideals. The deterioration of law and order results not only from the rise of violent groups relying upon protection from—or intimidation of—political segments: it is also the unfortunate consequence of the political instrumentalization of Islam encouraged for years. At another level, the overall role of the Army expresses both the weakness of the parliamentary democracy and the primordial concern for national security. This legitimate concern, and the power of the military in decision-making processes, account, however, for the oversized defence budget, and hence for the neglect of social and development expenditure. Examples of such correlations could be endless.

Secondly, and perhaps even more importantly, reforms will be challenging because the structural factors of the crisis are decisive, as the retrospect offered by this book shows clearly. In other words, any civilian or military regime willing to make Pakistan 'a sound, solid and cohesive nation' (as Ayub Khan promised) and to provide 'democracy in substance' (as Pervez Musharraf said he would pave the way for) would face not just the need for economic revival and the consequences of recent years of institutional drift: it would have to conduct what would amount to be a national introspection exercise, addressing the very nature of Pakistan, and evaluating its historical legacy. All dilemmas cannot be solved by pragmatic and half-baked, time-saving compromises.

After taking over, Pervez Musharraf said: 'the root causes of all our ills has been the absence of good governance'. But is bad governance really the prime cause? Is it not rather the symptom of a much deeper malaise, the consequence of structural factors which call for more than technical or even institutional improvements? One has to go further than readjusting the institutions and erasing the recent drifts, and to question what made these evolutions possible. One has to address what our contributors have called either 'the need for thought revolution' in regional affairs, the 'quest for a theoricization renewal' in social fields, or the need 'to shift the paradigm' in favour of 'a new synthesis bridging 'the great chasm' between a modern state and the traditional religious idiom.

Pakistan, as most de-colonized countries, had to face the difficult problem of nation-building and state-building, particularly intricate in a pluri-ethnic context. To the standard difficulties faced by newly independent countries, Pakistan added, however, two specific (and correlated) challenges directly connected with Partition, and still unresolved today. The first challenge addresses the nature of the state, and its relationship to Islam. The second one is set by the inability to live in peace with India. These are sensitive issues, because they are generic to the country. And this is why they define what is perhaps the main dilemma it faces. Being sensitive issues, it may be tempting not to address them, in order to avoid matters of possible discord; but being generic, the less they are addressed, the more serious their consequences could be. Sixty-two years after the 1940 Resolution, the key issue is not to wonder if the two-nation theory was valid. Whatever be its difficulties, Pakistan does exist, as a state and as a nation. But the nation's ideology, and its impact on regional policy calls for being reassessed. Has Islam been instrumentalized in a way far different from what the Quaid-i-Azam visualized, a way more and more open to overbidding and radicalization, in order to transcend, under the veil of ideology, the social, economic, ethnic and political tensions that weaken the nation? On the regional scene, Islam has been invoked also in order to justify Pakistan's strategy of intervention in Afghanistan, and in Kashmir as well. Today, such an invocation, perhaps useful internally, serves doubtfully Pakistan's geopolitical interests and its international image.

How to break this vicious circle which entangles Pakistan in regional tensions, and prevents also the articulation of a firm redefinition of utmost national priorities? What line to define, if the Kashmir issue remains pending? Islam and India are seen too often (and sometimes too conveniently) as an insurmountable contradiction, and this legacy of the past impels deeply upon internal dynamics and capacities of reform as well. The overt nuclearization of the subcontinent adds a dangerous dimension to the old difficult relationship. We know, however, that sectarian, ethnic or chauvinist radicalizations, in Pakistan or elsewhere (India included), express 'substitute identities' developed out of socio-economic frustrations, ideological instrumentalizations and short-view political manipulations. To meet such challenges, the type of polity and the objectives the Quaid-i-Azam articulated in his address to the Constituent Assembly on 11 August 1947 seem to offer the best guidelines, provided that they can be adjusted to the growing expectations of a society which has definitely changed during the last fifty years. Consequently, the process of renovation must not be left at the hands of the various elites who have, in the past, brought the country to where it stands today. Intellectuals, recalls Manzoor Ahmad, have a seminal role to play, and all Pakistanis are concerned. In Pakistan, as in many other post-colonial countries, the least challenge is not the empowerment of the citizen.

NOTES

1. 'Pakistan today stands at the crossroads of its destiny—destiny which is in our hands to make or break. Fifty-two years ago, we started with a beacon of hope and today that beacon is no more and we stand in darkness. (...) Today we have reached a stage where our economy has crumbled, our credibility is lost, state institutions lie demolished, provincial disharmony has caused cracks in the federation, and people who were once brothers are now at each others' throat. (...) Is this the democracy our Quaid-i-Azam had envisaged?' General Pervez Musharraf's speech, 17 October 1999, Associated Press of Pakistan.
2. 'One year of the Government: October 1999-October 2000. Report to the Nation', Ministry of Information & Media Development, Islamabad, p. 2.

GENESIS, HISTORICAL PROCESS, AND IDEOLOGICAL RATIONALES OF PAKISTAN

Cross-currents in the Historiography of Partition

This study aims at taking a general look at the historiography of Partition, fifty years after the event. It is particularly concerned with confronting the views of Indian and Pakistani historians, not so much in order to bring out their opposition as to discover commonalities. In other words, it is not an attempt at counterposing an 'Indian' view of Partition as against a 'Pakistani' one, but rather at delineating certain general characteristics of the historians' discourse on Partition, whether they be Indian, Pakistani or of any other nationality.

Dissatisfaction *vis-à-vis* the historiography of Partition as it stands is very often expressed by historians as well as by non-historians. Critics point to the enormous gap between the dryness of the prose of historical narratives and the intensity of the actual sufferings of those who went through the trauma of the event. Hence a new trend of para-historical writings, aiming above all at recovering the voices of the participants, mostly, of course, the victims. While recognizing the importance and relevance of that kind of writing to the emergence of a more balanced and authentic picture of this tragic event, I shall here concentrate, for methodological reasons, on more strictly academic contributions.

Reviewing in 1993 the state of the field in an Introduction to a collection of texts, one of India's best historians of the period, Mushirul Hasan, expressed some dismay at the view which, according to him, had become prevalent in academic circles by the early 1990s that 'Partition could have been averted if the Gandhi-Nehru leadership in the Congress had been magnanimous towards the Muslim League demands, if Mountabatten's predecessors...had shown greater enterprise in devising political initiatives, and if Jinnah had been less intransigent during his dialogues with the representatives of the Crown and the Congress high command'.[1] But such a view was actually a recent one, the outcome of a period of historiographical revision. Ten years before, it was still generally taken for granted that Partition was the inevitable result of deep-seated political rivalries between Jinnah and Congress leaders who had simply been outmanoeuvred by this particularly wily operator. Some saw in this rivalry the reflection of more profound antagonisms between Hindus and Muslims in India, others took a shorter-term view of the event, but all concurred that Jinnah had, from a certain moment in time, a clear view of Pakistan as his objective and they viewed his determination as a crucial factor in the whole chain of events. In the advent of a revised version of the history of Partition, an important landmark was the publication, in 1985, of Ayesha Jalal's book, *The Sole Spokesman: Jinnah, the Muslim League and the Demand for Pakistan*. No single book has probably been as influential in the field of Partition historiography, even though it remains to this day extremely controversial. By challenging existing orthodoxies, it undoubtedly set new parameters for the field. In this work, I shall, therefore, use Jalal's book as a point of demarcation between two historiographical epochs. I shall start with a brief presentation of the historiography of Partition as it evolved prior to the mid-1980s.

The historiography of Partition before 1985

For ten or fifteen years after the tragic events of 1946-48, very little historical work was done, either in India or in Pakistan or abroad. The advent of an historiography of Partition had to wait for the emergence of academic communities with a definite agenda in the two new states, and also for the accumulation of a minimum of documentary evidence. In the 1950s and early 1960s, most of the published literature was of a documentary nature, consisting on the one hand in the compilation of collections of documents, particularly of Muslim League sources, and on the other hand in the accumulation of testimonies of actors (since the archives were still largely closed), mostly of those who were involved in the decision-making process at one level or another. Hence, the multiplication of memoirs by ex-British administrators, Indian and Pakistani ex-ICS officers, Muslim League and Congress politicians, etc, some of which remain of considerable value to this day. The first synthetic accounts were produced in the 1960s, and they aimed mostly at locating the event within the more global context of the history of the two nations which emerged from it. There is no doubt that the status of the event was not the same in India and in Pakistan.

In Pakistan, it was foundational, and the whole question of the legitimacy of the new state was at stake. The Pakistani historiography of Partition was, however, a partial one, since it viewed the problem only from the Muslim point of view. In Pakistan, the history of Partition was largely reduced to a history of the Pakistan movement, and more broadly of Muslim 'separatism' in colonial India. This history was besides heavily biased in favour of Northern and North-Western India and gave Bengal a fairly short shrift, reflecting the dominance of non-Bengali elements in the Pakistani academic community. Non-Muslims, especially the Congress leaders, figured in it but their motivations were never subjected to very deep scrutiny. It was considered self-evident that they had been seeking power for 'the Hindus', and their attitude provided the justification for the growth of Muslim separatism. It would, however, be wrong to talk of the existence of a single 'official' interpretation of the Pakistan movement and Partition in post-1947 Pakistan. At least two different strands of interpretation are discernible in Pakistani historiography. One interpretation is a fairly 'secular' one, which stressed the liberation of Muslims from political and economic domination by the Hindu majority. Religion as such was not given much place in it, beyond that of an identity marker. The emphasis was on the minority status of Muslims in undivided India, and the response of the Muslim leadership to the challenges of that situation.[2] It was an almost purely political interpretation, although it also took into account socio-economic aspects. Another interpretation laid more stress on the role of the Islamic factor in influencing the direction of Muslim politics in the twentieth century.[3] It was a more 'culturalist' interpretation, not without ideological afterthoughts. Whatever their differences regarding the importance of religion in the Pakistan movement, most Pakistani authors saw the new state as the culmination of the aspirations of Muslim 'modernists' since the time of Sir Syed Ahmad Khan. Jinnah appeared as the embodiment of a modernity finding strength in its Islamic roots. That is why the apparent contradictions of the Quaid-i-Azam did not embarrass Pakistani historians. Although Jinnah was on the whole praised and eulogised by them, and writings about him came sometimes close to hagiography, he was, however, not entirely immune from criticism. Thus, in his sensitive study of Muslim separatism, Professor Abdul Hamid did not hesitate to write about Jinnah's attitude to the Cabinet Mission Plan: 'By acquiescing into the Mission Plan, Jinnah had virtually accepted a non-sovereign Pakistan and was prepared to compromise on fundamentals'.[4] Such veiled criticism of Jinnah was rare coming from mainstream Pakistani historians. The latter tended to put the blame for the enormously high human cost of the Partition exclusively on the Congress leaders and on Mountbatten.

In India, where the legitimacy of the state was not similarly at stake, there was no historiography of Partition as such. Muslim separatism and the Pakistan movement were seen as late developments, largely the products of British policies, and they were treated in general accounts of the independence movement as fairly peripheral, a kind of diversion from their central theme of the fight against British imperialism. When detailed attention was paid to the question of Muslim separatism by Indian historians, the dominant theme was that of missed opportunities, of an outcome which had been the result of an accumulation of human errors, rather than of structural factors.[5] That the use by the Congress, including by Gandhi, of Hindu symbols facilitated the mobilization of Muslims by the Muslim League was a point generally missed by Indian authors. There were, however, dissenting voices, mostly outside academics: some Marxists, taking a leaf from CPI ideologue Adikhari's synthesis of Stalin and Jinnah, and influenced by W. Cantwell Smith's views, believed the Pakistan movement was a genuine bourgeois nationalist movement; on the other hand, those who were close to a Hindu nationalist point of view saw in it the continuation of a deep-seated Muslim conspiracy against Hinduism and Mother India. For the left-leaning 'secular' historians who dominated the field in India in the 1970s and 1980s, there was, however, an added element: Muslim communalism, far from being either an authentic bourgeois movement or the mere result of an imperialist conspiracy, was an expression of false consciousness and basically reflected the class hegemony exercised over the Muslim masses by a narrow elite of landed magnates and big traders who feared that the development of a unitary mass movement of Hindu and Muslim peasants and workers would endanger their material interests. Sumit Sarkar, in his authoritative *Modern India*, tended to take this view and to dismiss the League's claim to represent the entire Muslim community.[6] But to these authors also, the Pakistan movement and Partition were a diversion from the main struggle against imperialism. They seemed to think that it was the weakness of the Left in India which had allowed the diversionary forces of communalism to move in.

What I want to stress, however, is that, in spite of wide differences of opinion between Indian and Pakistani historians, and even within the academic communities of each country, a kind of basic consensus could be identified, around a few key points, such as the crucial role given to the dynamics of Muslim politics and to Jinnah's personal intervention.

In 1983, R.J. Moore, an Australian historian, could still write: 'In an age sceptical of the historic role of great men there is universal agreement that Jinnah was central to the Muslim League's emergence after 1937 as the voice of a Muslim nation; to its articulation in March 1940 of the Pakistan demand for separate statehood for the Muslim majority provinces of north-western and eastern India; and to its achievement in August 1947 of the separate but truncated state of Pakistan by the Partition of India'.[7] The emphasis in Pakistan on Jinnah's historical role had nothing surprising about it, but even in Indian accounts he occupied a prominent place. Apart from divergent appreciation on the personality of Jinnah, there was a high degree of consensus on the fact that the creation of Pakistan as a separate state was basically his work, even if the idea of Pakistan was known to be somebody else's brainchild (and here accounts diverged, some singling out Iqbal, others Chaudhuri Rahmat Ali). A Pakistani historian expressed a widely-held view when he stated:

'After March 1940, Jinnah's course became clear. The Muslim League had adopted the conferment of independent status on contiguous Muslim majority areas, i.e., Pakistan, as its goal, and he strove for its achievement with the same tenacity of purpose and single-mindedness with which, some years earlier, he had pursued his dream of Hindu-Muslim unity. All his efforts after that day, his interviews, his speeches, his negotiations, and his strategic moves were inspired by one idea—to achieve this end'.[8]

By contrast with Jinnah's relentless pursuit of a definite goal, all other actors, be they British statesmen or Congress leaders, appeared to have been fumbling, unclear about the objectives they sought. In particular, the role of the Congress was seen as largely reactive. Although Pakistani indictments of Nehru's intransigent attitude towards the Muslim League at the time of the formation of the Congress provincial governments in 1937 were not totally without echoes in India (and received partial confirmation from the publication in 1988 of the expunged passages in Maulana Abul Kalam Azad's memoirs, *India Wins Freedom*, first published in 1958), nobody in India dared yet blame Nehru for the increasing gap which opened up between the Congress and the League after 1937. In Pakistan, a lot of criticism was also directed at Sardar Patel, whose strong hostility to the Muslim League got particular notice. Indian historians were not at ease with the attitude of the Congress leadership in 1947, particularly with the open divide between Gandhi on the one hand, and Nehru and Patel on the other, but by concentrating heavily on Jinnah, they managed to largely avoid the issue.

The part played by the British was one of the most controversial points. Both Pakistani and Indian authors were very critical of British attitudes and policies, but they directed their criticisms at different aspects. Indian authors, taking a long-term view, stressed the fateful consequences of the 'divide and rule' policy followed by the Raj and in particular of the institution of separate electorates in the Morley-Minto reforms of 1909, but did not gloss much over Mountbatten's crucial role in expediting things, while Pakistani historians, wary of recalling the Muslim League's friendly attitude to the British between 1940 and 1946, preferred on the one hand to evoke the role of Muslims in the 1857 uprising and on the other hand to concentrate on the attitude of Mountbatten at the time of Partition and on his undubitable pro-Congress bias.[9] While Mountbatten was generally acknowledged as the midwife of the Partition (Jinnah being its putative father), he nevertheless got a better press in India than in Pakistan, which appears paradoxical, but can be explained in part by the adversarial relationship he had with Jinnah during the last negotiations which led to the actual partition of the Indian Empire. Some also stressed the crucial role played by V.P. Menon, Patel's close adviser, in framing the actual partition plan.

But beyond the endless squabbles about precise responsibilities, there was a deeper consensus between Indian and Pakistani historians about the fact that the division of British India was the result of the growth of a specific political movement amongst the Muslims of the subcontinent. Whether labelled as Muslim 'nationalism' by Pakistani authors, or by Indian authors as 'communalism', 'separatism' being interestingly used both by supporters and adversaries of the movement, the fact is that Muslim political self-assertion was seen as the key factor in the whole chain of events. Divergences existed as to the causes but not as to the fact. Pakistani historians, trying to give substance to the 'two nation theory' formulated by Jinnah, sought to muster all possible evidence on the existence over a long period of a sense of cultural and political separateness among India's

Muslims.[10] Indian historians, less preoccupied with cultural arguments beyond general statements about the existence of a 'composite' culture in the subcontinent, preferred to locate the origins of Muslim 'separatism' in the machinations of a Raj on the decline, a position which was supported by a lot of the evidence available.

Outside the subcontinent, the few historians who dared tackle the Pakistan movement and the Partition, being less preoccupied with matters of state and of political legitimacy, focused particularly on the role played by religion. Some, of whom Paul Brass was the most outspoken, stressed how religion had been instrumentalized by elites, both Hindu and Muslim, to give legitimation to a fight over positions and power, especially in the context of Northern India.[11] Others, while taking more seriously the claim of a struggle for Islam raised by the Muslim League, stressed the existence of a complex combination of factors.[12]

There is no doubt that Pakistani historians gave more importance to the Partition in the overall narrative of South Asian history than Indian historians or historians from outside the subcontinent did. But even Pakistani authors, in their often wide-ranging search for the roots of Muslim separatism, tended to be diverted from a more focused analysis of the event itself in its specificity. In the historiography of Partition as it evolved prior to the mid-1980s, there were thus a certain number of accepted truths which, while giving rise to endless and often acrimonious debates between authors sitting on both sides of the new border, were never really challenged. Maybe the most powerful, although it remained implicit, of these perceived truths was that the fate of millions had been decided by a small group of men, and that at no moment had those millions whose lives had been affected been in a position to really influence events. The most consensual aspect of Partition historiography, which cut across political borders and ideological differences, was the notion that the key to an understanding of the event was largely to be found in the government chambers and the council halls where the powerful had sat and decided the fate of the multitudes. The idea that the history of Partition was above all the history of the millions who had taken part in it and suffered its consequences was rarely considered. A major problem for all authors was how to deal with the terrible kind of violence which had been unleashed in 1946-48. Academic historians are not at ease with phenomena of mass violence, and they often oscillate between cursory description based on official accounts and summary moral condemnation. Because of the persistent silence over the violence, it could be said in the 1980s that one had an historiography of the Pakistan movement and of the origins of the Partition, which was a contested one, but no true historiography of Partition.

Ayesha Jalal and the decline of the high history of Partition

Paradoxically, it was from within this elitist historiography that the most effective challenge came. Although Jalal's preoccupations were strictly with the *haute politique* of the Partition, her iconoclastic study of Jinnah helped nail the coffin on the elitist historiographical project. Jalal located herself firmly in the camp of those who took the view that, in the story of the Pakistan movement, religion had been instrumentalized. She concentrated entirely on Jinnah's political activities, paying little attention to his attitude towards religion, which remains a very controversial subject, particularly in Pakistan, and more generally to the question of his 'Muslimness'. Her considerable critical faculties, supported by a great deal of research in still partly closed archives, helped her make hash, in particular, of the widely-held and somewhat self-evident notion that Partition was Jinnah's original goal. Jalal argued that Jinnah was actually aiming at a federal India in which the League would have shared power with the Congress, and that it was the frustration of that aim which led him to accept Partition as the only way to avoid Hindu domination over the whole of undivided India. Jalal put the onus of Partition squarely on the refusal by the Congress, with British implicit support, to make the concessions which could have satisfied Jinnah's demands.

Jalal's book got a mixed critical response, but it undoubtedly helped change the terms of the debate. Both Pakistani and Indian historians saw some of their most cherished myths challenged. Jinnah, although portrayed rather sympathetically, was shown as having had feet of clay. He had often miscalculated, had relied too much on the British remaining as arbiters, and when faced with the evidence of their decision to depart quickly, had seen his weakness exposed. This had led him, the most constitutionalist of all Indian politicians, to go for 'mass action', an exercise for which he had no skill, and in which he was outmanoeuvred by the wily Suhrawardy, whose intervention at the time of the Great Calcutta killings had had disastrous consequences. Eventually, he had been forced to accept in 1947 the 'moth-eaten' Pakistan, from which East Punjab and West Bengal had been carved out, that he had so contemptuously rejected in July 1944 on the eve of his inconclusive conversations with Gandhi. Jalal's Jinnah was not the supreme politician of earlier accounts, but a man who had gambled and partly failed and had no choice but to collect his gains to avoid complete defeat. He had to constantly battle on three fronts, against regional Muslim leaders pursuing their own agendas, against the Congress leadership, and against the British, in particular the last Viceroy Lord Mountbatten, and in spite of his considerable intellectual powers, had not always proved equal to the task. But, if Jinnah came out somewhat diminished from Jalal's account, as a tragic and pathetic figure, the Congress leaders, including Gandhi, emerged in a frankly unfavourable light. Jalal's view was that they were the ones who had actually chosen partition by their refusal to accept the prospect of a diminished Centre, which alone could have been the basis of a compromise with the Muslim League. By lashing out equally at all the major actors (Mountbatten was not better treated by her), Jalal helped discredit the approach 'from above' which had dominated the field in the previous period.

True, some historians still tried their hand at the genre of 'high' political history and Anita Inder Singh came out with a spirited defence of Congress policy aimed at refuting Jalal's indictment.[13] Others in India, however, took a clue from her critique of Congress policy and mounted a full-scale attack on it.[14] On the other hand, Farzana Shaikh offered the most consistent challenge to Jalal and the instrumentalists in general by shifting the focus to questions of ideology. She argued that, behind Jinnah's demand for a strict parity between the Congress and the League, there was actually a deeper demand for true parity between Muslims and non-Muslims seen as a whole. This demand in its turn was firmly grounded in a tradition of Muslim political thinking which even antedated Sir Syed Ahmad Khan, and in a firm belief that, 'by enabling Muslims to exercise power as the equals of a non-Muslim majority, a more humane society would ensue'.[15] This attempt at recovering the ideological dimension of the Muslim separatist movement remained, however, an isolated effort. On the other hand, a significant work which took a position close to Jalal's and in some way complemented it was Joya Chatterji's study of Bengal.[16] Chatterji showed convincingly that in the East, the actual initiative for Partition came more from the Hindu elite and the rich Marwaris than from specifically Muslim separatist dynamics.

But the main thrust in the historiography of Partition after Jalal has been a shift away from an exclusive preoccupation with *haute politique*. Jalal's book thus had the paradoxical effect of encouraging historians to take a closer look at the event in a perspective of 'history from below', which the Subaltern Studies collective was at the time promoting in India. This led in particular to a new kind of interest in mass violence. In Pakistan itself, however, this new trend does not seem very perceptible yet, and that is why in the third section no recent work produced in Pakistan has been included.

The next section focuses on three recent texts which are, each in its own way, an attempt at displacing the problematic from the level of high politics at an all-India level to that of ground realities, where flesh and blood actors faced real dilemmas and had to solve them, shaping in the process the contours of the two nations which would emerge from the tragedy.

Towards a new historiography of Partition

The shift in the historiography of Partition was due on the one hand to a more general change in the nature of historical discourse in the South Asian field, but it also reflected the advent of new preoccupations closely linked to the growth of what is generally known as 'fundamentalism'. As a new wave of Hindu-Muslim tension affected the subcontinent, culminating in the destruction of the Babri Masjid by so-called Hindu 'fundamentalists', many were led to reflect anew on the tragic events which had led to the division of the subcontinent. If, forty-five years after the Partition, the whole question of Hindu-Muslim relations in the subcontinent remained so loaded with a potential for violence, it showed that the 'surgical operation' performed in 1947 had not really cured the patient. A new look at mass violence in the subcontinent at the time of Partition might offer some clues to the persistence of certain patterns of behaviour in Hindu-Muslim relations. More generally, the violence of the early 1990s helped focus anew the attention of scholars on the human cost of the Partition, not only in terms of the number of victims (no satisfactory count exists, and half a million dead is a generally accepted but largely meaningless figure), but also of the untold sufferings inflicted on millions of human beings by mass displacement, mass violence, mass relocation. Long-forgotten questions, like that of the return of 'abducted' women, suddenly attracted attention again, mostly from Indian feminist authors who criticised the policies followed by the Indian government, which insisted on the repatriation to Pakistan even of women who clearly wanted to stay with their 'new families', a fact which cast, in their eyes, the state as the embodiment of patriarchy.[17]

Gyan Pandey's article, 'Partition and the Politics of History', published in a collective volume in 1996,[18] among other writings by this author on the topic, reflects this historiographical shift: it is an open attack on widely-held Indian views about Partition, in which it figures as a kind of accident in a linear history of the development of an Indian nation. Pandey shows how the trauma of Partition reshaped the Indian nation as much as it created the Pakistani nation, and he explores some of the implications of this basic fact. These are some of the most important points he makes:

he shows that the Partition is not only constitutive of Pakistani national identity, a point which is obvious, but as much of Indian national identity, which is a rarely acknowledged fact. For, if Pakistan defined itself mostly in reaction to India, India in its turn largely redefined itself after 1947 in relation to Pakistan. Post-Partition India was not just the continuation of British India, less the territories which had become Pakistan, it was a new and contested reality over which Partition cast a very large shadow indeed. The impact of Partition on India was not felt only in the two divided provinces of Bengal and the Punjab; Bihar and UP also were very directly affected by the enormous movements of population which took place in 1947-48 and no region of the subcontinent remained totally immune from the turmoil. More generally Partition raised the question of the identity of India: was it to be a Hindu state, as many, not only in the RSS, hoped for, or was it a place where even Muslims could live as free citizens? This question was not settled on 15 August 1947. Many then wanted a mass expulsion of Muslims, which would have made India purely Hindu, and if they did not win the day, it was largely because of the popular revulsion caused by Gandhi's assassination at the hands of a member of the RSS. Therefore, Partition opened a debate on the nature of the Indian state and of Indian society which, more than fifty years after the event, is far from closed. With the benefit of hindsight, it has become obvious that Partition cannot be explained only in reference to Muslim nationalism, but that its Other, Hindu nationalism, long hidden behind 'secularist' rhetoric, also played a crucial role in the unfolding of the drama. Interestingly, Pandey also alludes to the debate which raged at the same time in Pakistan over the nature of the state. He is right to recall Jinnah's basically secularist position, well summed up in a speech pronounced a few days before 14 August, in which he said: 'Now that Pakistan has been established, we will be Hindus, Muslims and Sikhs in our homes. We'll be Pakistani citizens outside. Religion is a matter within our homes. For the rest, we are all Pakistani citizens'. In the last fifty years, the question whether Pakistan is or is not an Islamic state has also remained unresolved.

He pleads for an approach of the event which would not place it in too much of a short-term perspective, such as 1946-48. His suggestion that the origins of Partition go back to 1937 has nothing original about it and is accepted by most authors; however his proposal to extend the study to 1956, the moment when the process of family reunification which followed the disorders came to an end, deserves notice, in view of the attention recently paid to the problem of the 'abducted' women and children.

He stresses the contingency and indeterminacy of the new border, not only on the ground (with the Radcliffe Award on the exact delineation of the Punjab border announced only on 17 August), but even more in the mind of the people. For, to the vast majority, neither India nor Pakistan had any particular meaning; they only saw the rending of the fabric of their lives, as the new line cut through family, lineage, clan affiliations to impose 'religion' as the only determining criterion of identity. In view of this, the decision to migrate from one state to another was not an easy one to make. In the Punjab, the people had no choice, but elsewhere they often agonized for months, even for years, before making the move, and some did cross borders more than once. For, in spite of the simplistic equation of Muslim = Pakistan, and Hindu = India, to millions there was nothing evident about the question whether one was Indian or Pakistani. As Pandey writes: 'Let us not try to fix this history as though from the moment of the announcement of Partition on 3 June 1947, it was clear to all minorities that they had to move then, that the Muslims, Hindus and Sikhs were their enemies, and that their nation was somewhere else. The process whereby these 'truths' are established is long drawn out and uncertain'.[19]

Pandey's main point is that the history of the Partition does not fit easily within these well structured and strongly teleological narratives that national histories tend to be. He calls for a displacement from a state-centred history to a history centred on the actors themselves, those crowds that participated in the massacres as perpetrators as well as victims. This call to a history of the Partition from below remains, however, largely at the level of intentions, since it is not supported by a serious methodological reflection on sources and their nature. Pandey seems to think that literature holds the key, that it is in works of fiction that the true human drama of Partition finds expression, but this leaves aside the question of the specific position occupied in the field by the writers of fiction, which cannot be passed over lightly.

Pandey's text can be seen as representative of the shift in the attitude of some radical Indian historians around the Subaltern Studies collective towards the study of Partition, but it would be naive to assume that his point of view is widely accepted beyond those radical circles. On the contrary, within a political context characterized by the rise of Hindu nationalism, one can witness the resurgence of a discourse on Partition which sees it as symbolic of the decadence of Hindu India for which a redress must be found. This discourse is still marginal in academic circles, but its existence must be noted.

No similar shift is discernible in Pakistani academic writings on Partition. That is why a Pakistani point of view will be presented here on the basis of the work of two authors based in the United Kingdom, one of whom is British and the other Pakistani.

Ian Talbot's volume of essays published in 1996, *Freedom's Cry*,[20] attempts to apply to the history of the Muslim League and the Pakistan movement the perspective of a 'history from below', by focusing in particular, in a first section which appears under the broad title of 'Popular Participation in the Pakistan Struggle', on three little-studied aspects: the role of the crowd in the movement, the role of the Muslim National Guards, and the question of popular participation in the context of the politics of the Punjab in 1944-46. In his introduction to those essays, Talbot aims at distancing himself from current Pakistani historiography and its almost obsessive focus on the words and deeds of Jinnah. He writes: 'Jinnah did not...single-handedly create Pakistan. His negotiating skills would have counted for nothing, if ordinary Muslims had not been roused in their hundreds or thousands by his call for a homeland in which they could throw out the Hindu yoke.'[21]

In the first piece, about the role of the crowd, Talbot attempts to come to grips with the problem of mass violence at the time of Partition. This is a welcome effort, although the author is somewhat hampered by his theoretical eclecticism, his attempt at combining Sandria Freitag's Habermasian approach on collective action and the 'public arena' and Elias Canetti's much more conventional typology of crowd movements. His focus is not specifically on violent crowd actions, since he also examines processions, especially those which accompanied Jinnah's tours across India at the time of the 1946 elections and *hartals*. But the most interesting section of the paper is the one devoted to the analysis of a certain number of little-known urban riots in the North West Frontier Province. He notes that in these riots, where the local Hindu and Sikh population of the towns was the target of attacks from largely tribal Pashtuns, property rather than persons was singled out, a contrast with the case of anti-Muslim riots in India where the rioters sought to kill rather than to loot. Perhaps not too much should be made of this contrast: after all the Muslims who were attacked by Hindu crowds in India were generally poor people with very little property. The specific patterns of violence in those riots are, however, the subject of an interesting discussion by Talbot. Although he does not come out with a single explanation, he emphasizes Muslim sensitivity to what he calls 'the wrongful use of material objects in worship', which led to systematic destruction of Hindu places of worship and idols. But he is aware of the limitations of an explanation in terms of iconoclasm, and tends also to stress the importance of considerations of 'honour' as well as of territory. In spite of his careful look at these riots, Talbot's analysis of their meaning remains partial. Nor is their 'popular' character very clearly established, as there is evidence of widespread participation in them by prosperous traders and professionals.

The 'popular dimension' does not come out very clearly either from the study of the role of the Muslim National Guards, who appear to have been drawn largely from the lower middle-classes. Talbot himself acknowledges that the impact of the Guards remained limited to a North Indian urban milieu. He stresses that a Muslim volunteer movement never took root in the rural areas of the Punjab, Sindh or the North West Frontier, where the major role of intermediation was played by the *pirs* and their wide networks of *murids*.

A third essay on 'Popular Participation in the Pakistan Struggle' takes a close look at Muslim politics in Western Punjab in 1944-46, and more particularly at the 1946 provincial elections which were a moment of such crucial importance in the emergence of Pakistan. Talbot wants to show that pressure from 'below' played a role in producing a shift in the attitude of the Muslim landed elite from the Unionist Party to the Muslim League. This pressure was largely articulated through the *pir-muridi* relationship. Talbot sees as the key to the League success in the 1946 elections 'the ability to link the Pakistan idea with popular aspirations and to anchor this message within the substratum of local rural Islam'.[22] On the question of popular Islam and the way the League attempted to channelize it, David Gilmartin has produced very interesting analyses,[23] on which Talbot could have drawn more.

Although they partly fail in their declared aim of establishing the Pakistan movement as a grassroots movement, these essays nevertheless develop interesting insights into the regional dynamics of the Partition in the North-west of the subcontinent. In the second part of the book, entitled 'The Human Face of Partition', Talbot draws on literary texts and journalistic pieces to bring out the sum of personal tragedies that the Partition represented. These essays are well-written and interesting, but they do not seriously address the methodological problem posed by the use of literary materials for the purpose of historical analysis.

Yunus Samad's book, *A Nation in Turmoil*, published in 1995,[24] chooses another path to challenge the orthodoxies of Pakistani nationalism by focusing on the dimension of ethnicity which was present in the Pakistan movement in a constant dialectical interaction with the notion of a united Muslim nation. Taking a fairly long-term view of Partition, across the two decades 1937-1958, it brings out the basic contradictions in the Pakistani national project, which are still unresolved forty years later. Samad focuses particularly on the underlying tensions within the Muslim League and the Pakistan movement between centralism and regionalism. This was an aspect which had been given importance by Jalal, but she had focused almost exclusively on the rivalry between Jinnah and the provincial leaders of the League, to the detriment of a more in-depth analysis of the problem. What Samad's work brings out clearly is that the contradiction between the centralizing aims of the League leadership and the aspirations of the provincial elites, which got largely suppressed in the brief moment of political unity which presided over the birth of Pakistan in 1945-47, came into the open anew after 1947 and tore at the foundations of the new state, leading to the emergence of Ayub's dictatorship with which the book closes.

Samad thus sums up the dilemma of Pakistan at the time of independence: 'Pakistan was defined by circumstances and not by design, and this fact was behind the many problems that the country faced after partition. There was no single interpretation of Pakistan held either by Jinnah or the Muslim majority provinces, the League had no significant party structure, and there were strong regional and ethnic forces located in the provinces. All these were to become the source of major problems after independence'.[25]

Although it is focused on one aspect of Partition, Samad's book is a timely reminder that the study of popular participation in the Pakistan movement cannot ignore either the ethnic-regional or the class dimension, in as much as the weight of dominant groups in rural society was considerable at the local level and influenced to a large degree provincial and national politics.

Samad's work shows that a politically-centred approach to the history of Partition retains validity, provided the level of analysis chosen is not only the central level, and lower echelons of the polity are fully taken into account. Partition is also a political process, and the study of it cannot ignore politics totally to concentrate only on the personal sufferings and tragedies of actors as mediated through fictional works. Apart from the more general methodological problems implied, the selection of works of fiction would always in any case be subjective and necessarily partial. All in all, this would be the negation of the possibility of any meaningful history, and that is why such extreme views, even when voiced by prominent historians like Gyan Pandey, have to be firmly rejected.

More than fifty years after the event, can it be said that there is an historiography of Partition, as distinct from the historiography of Pakistani and Indian nationalism, which are solidly established fields, although not always intellectually very rewarding? This is a debatable point. Mass violence and mass displacement, which are the two central facts of Partition, have not yet really found their place in historical discourse. A lot remains to be found in archives which could throw new light on these two aspects, even if oral testimonies and literary sources already provide a lot of vital evidence. It must be said also that the existing historiography of Partition is mostly a Punjabi one; relatively little work has been done on Sindh and Bengal, two areas also vitally affected. The aim of this presentation is not, however, to derive firm conclusions about the directions the historiography of Partition is heading for or should be heading for. It seeks rather to delineate a historiographical field, which is at the same time fragmented and contested, but in which the lines of battle are not drawn between Indian historians and Pakistani historians, but within each academic community, and even within each individual historian. Partition, like the Holocaust, is one of those traumatic events that undoubtedly throw a challenge to history as an academic discipline. How to recover the sufferings of millions of human beings and incorporate them within a discourse which, by its very nature, is of a generalizing kind? Some answer by proposing to altogether throw to the winds the historical discipline, finding its tools inadequate to the task. This position is respectable, but not acceptable. Academic historians, in India, in Pakistan and elsewhere, must continue to take up the challenge. They must direct the focus of their enquiries towards the real actors, those millions whose lives were indelibly stamped by their participation in the tragedy. This will also offer a way towards a rapprochement between Pakistani and Indian historians. One day perhaps a new consensus will emerge on the meaning of the event, which will help cure the wounds rather than allow them to fester.

NOTES

1. M. Hasan, 'Introduction', in M. Hasan (ed.), *India's Partition. Process, Strategy and Mobilization*, Delhi, 1993 (1st ed.), pp. 1-43, p. 2.
2. See for instance Khalid bin Sayeed, *Pakistan: the formative phase*, London, 1968.
3. See Waheed-uz-Zaman, *Towards Pakistan*, Lahore, 1963; and I.H. Qureshi, *The Struggle for Pakistan*, Karachi, 1965.
4. A. Hamid, *Muslim Separatism in India: A Brief Survey 1858-1947*, Lahore, 1967, p. 237.
5. See in particular Ram Gopal, *Indian Muslims. A Political History (1858-1947)*, Bombay, 1959 (1st ed.).
6. S. Sarkar, *Modern India 1885-1947*, Delhi, 1983, p. 427: 'The League won its demand for Pakistan without its claim to represent the majority of Musims being really tested, either in fully democratic elections or...in sustained mass movements...'.
7. R.J. Moore, 'Jinnah and the Pakistan demand', *Modern Asian Studies*, vol.17, no. 4 (1983), pp. 529-561.
8. M.S. Ikram, *Modern Muslim India and the Birth of Pakistan*, Lahore, 1997, 7th ed. (1st ed., 1965), p. 385.
9. Thus Abdul Hamid, op. cit., p. 245, closes his account with the following lines: 'It is clear that Mountbatten had understood India's good exactly as Congress leaders had understood it'.
10. See I.H. Qureshi, *The Muslim Community of the Indo-Pakistan Subcontinent*, The Hague, 1962.
11. P. Brass, *Language, Religion and Politics in North India*, Cambridge, 1974.
12. See in particular F. Robinson, 'Islam and Muslim Separatism', in D. Taylor and M. Yapp (eds), *Political Identity in South Asia*, London, 1979, pp. 78-112.
13. A. Inder Singh, *The Origins of the Partition of India 1936-1947*, Delhi, 1987.
14. See in particular H.M. Seervai, *Partition of India. Legend and Reality*, Bombay, 1989.
15. F. Shaikh, *Community and Consensus in Islam. Muslim representation in Colonial India*, Cambridge, 1989, p. 213.
16. J. Chatterji, *Bengal divided. Hindu communalism and partition*, Cambridge, 1995.
17. See, inter alia, R. Menon and K. Bhasin, 'Abducted Women, the State and Questions of Honour: Three Perspectives on the Recovery Operation in Post-Partition India', in K. Jayawardena and M. De Alwis (eds), *Embodied Violence. Communalising*

Women's Sexuality in South Asia, London & New Jersey, 1996, pp. 1-31.

18. G. Pandey, 'Partition and the Politics of History', in M. Dutta, F. Agnes and N. Adarkar (eds), *The Nation, the State and Indian Identity*, Calcutta, 1996, pp. 1-26.

19. Pandey, ibid., p. 10.

20. I. Talbot, *Freedom's Cry*. (The Popular Dimension in the Pakistan Movement) and (Partition Experience in North-West India), Karachi, 1996.

21. Ibid., p. 10.

22. Ibid., p. 97.

23. See D. Gilmartin, Empire and Islam. Punjab and the Making of Pakistan, Berkeley, 1988, and subsequent articles.

24. Y. Samad, *A Nation in Turmoil. Nationalism and Ethnicity in Pakistan*, 1937-1958, Delhi, 1995.

25. Ibid., p. 118.

Past and Present:
The Making of the
State in Pakistan

Investigating the antecedents and present structure of the
state in Pakistan creates, at the outset, methodological
problems concerning the scope and extent of such an exercise.
Within the necessarily constrained confines of the present
study, it would neither be viable nor possible to give a
detailed account or description of the 'evolution of the state'
in this region. Rather, it will be our effort here to identify
the various themes, issues and structures that could
contribute profitably to an understanding of this problematic.
The emergence of Pakistan in 1947 marked a clear break
from the past, with de-colonization from the British Indian
empire constituting the creation of two states, the other being
India. This bifurcation of the British raj, with its attendant
controversies regarding the desirability of the outcome, can
thus be viewed as a watershed in our analysis. From then
on, the more direct sinews of the Pakistani state can be
traced. However, this moment cannot be the starting point of
such an analysis, for it loses much of its character and
significance if it fails to be placed within a larger historical
perspective.

The question then arises as to how far back in time should
the lineages of the Pakistani state be situated. For many
Pakistani historians, the genesis of the idea of a separate
homeland for the Muslims of South Asia, which for them
Pakistan apparently represents, lies at the very inception of

Muslim interventions in this region. Analysis would thus be initiated from a period a millennium earlier, from the incursions of Mahmud Ghazni and later Muhammad Ghauri, or from even further back, with the forays of the Arabs under Muhammad bin Qasim in Sindh in the eighth century. Indian historiography, on the other hand, would tend to reject such long-standing linkages. It would prefer to see Pakistan as more the product of a greatly shortened line of causation, even one restricted to the climactic years of British rule, towards the mid-twentieth century. This study will not be concerned with the relative veracity of these differing interpretations, since they essentially fail to address some of the seminal issues concerning this subject. The simple presence of Muslims, or even Muslim-ruled states, in this region, throws scant light on how to analyse the making of the state in Pakistan. Nor is this task particularly propitiated by the contrary notion that Pakistan was almost the accidental consequence of negotiating difficulties among politicians at the time of de-colonization.

To trace continuities from the past, it is important, at the very least, to discuss the nature of the Mughal state. This provides an insight into the symptoms and dynamics of power, and their impact on economy and society, in a longer-standing arena of polity under indigenous rule, before such structures were refracted through the overlay of colonial control. Making comparisons with this earlier period, and identifying parallels, similarities and dissimilarities, might well provide an instructive mirror for understanding current values, identities, roles and processes. Moreover, the Mughal empire in its declining years, and the political formations that emerged between the collapse of central authority and the assumption of power by the British, have had more than a tangential impact on the way in which power is distributed in Pakistan itself. The transitions during the eighteenth century in the north-western parts of the erstwhile Mughal empire did, in turn, have a major impact on the strategies of control, incorporation and exclusion followed by the British during their tenure in this region. These policies, and the structures which they helped evolve, then exercised a decisive influence on the contemporary political economy of the

Pakistani state. Thus, analysing continuities from the past, even the not so recent past, can hopefully prove integral to a construction of the state in Pakistan. This longer-term perspective, so often ignored by analysts of the Pakistani state, might well provide a more balanced, as well as a deeper, understanding of this subject. It would thereby counter the more ahistorical diagnoses preferred by social scientists, based essentially on the assumption of fundamental discontinuities around the mid-twentieth century.

To return to the Mughals, there is one highly significant caveat in assessing this period, which also impacts intrinsically on the way in which current state structures in South Asia are imagined. For the same reason, states prior to the Mughal empire perhaps provide a scenario that is more representative of South Asian realities, and indeed of 'normalcy', at least in the context of historical incidence. The problem lies with the very word 'empire'. Historically, the large state in South Asia is very clearly an aberration (and may we thence assume an abnormality?). Throughout its history there have been only a handful of attempts at creating states extensive enough either to be called empires, or to go much beyond the provincial boundaries existing in present-day India and Pakistan. Smaller and localised polities, and at best regional kingdoms, have been more the norm in South Asia. Empire-type states have only existed briefly and spasmodically, and they have come up after very wide intervals of time. They have also been highly transitory. Very soon after they have attained a sizeable extent, not by any means covering all of South Asia or even significant portions of it, they have invariably tended to decline rapidly; and before long to disappear completely. Even with the Mughals, collapse followed soon after the attempt to expand beyond northern India. And the Vijaynagar empire, which could at least claim longevity, was really no more than a large regional state, confined to southern India.

If because of its size the Mughal empire was atypical, it now appears less so because shortly after its collapse it was succeeded by yet another large state, the British Indian empire. Significantly, this latest reconfiguration appeared under foreign fiat, and had little connection with indigenous needs or capabilities. Indeed, had this foreign intervention not occurred, the post-Mughal phenomenon of the re-emergence of smaller regional states would in all probability have perpetuated itself, even to the present day. Such a situation would have been far more balanced than the existing one, of a large and over-sized state exerting hegemonic and even life-threatening pressures on the smaller states of South Asia. The access to democratic rights, to greater autonomy in decision-making, as well as better prospects for economic development and the alleviation of mass poverty, might well have been more attainable targets. Presently, smaller states like Pakistan need to allocate major proportions of available resources to defence spending, in the hope of trying to ensure their very survival. At least, the perceived Indian threat provides the military in these states with the justification for absorbing sizeable expenditures, which could otherwise have been utilised for social development. These polarities have stemmed from the assumption that the successor to the colonial empire should be yet another empire-like entity, that of India. They have had decisive influences on the shaping of the state in Pakistan: an issue to which we will return presently.

The conceptualization of the Mughal state itself has varied between different types of historians. At the cost of simplification, if we take traditional historiography to comprise three schools of interpretation, interesting dichotomies appear in the analysis of the Mughal state. British 'imperialist' historians constantly harped on the negative factors of Mughal rule. The rulers were generally cruel, insensitive to the needs of the people, given to fratricide, addicted to lethal intoxicants, overly pleasure loving, harsh in the levy and exaction of revenue, treacherous in their politics, and so on. By implication, the British in India had none of these egregious habits or characteristics: they were morally upright, personally honest, sensitive to the welfare of the people, and fair and modest in their revenue demands. Hindu historians have stressed the advantages gained by Akbar in incorporating Hindu magnates, intermarrying with Hindu princesses and even

experimenting with religious syncretism. By accommodating
to the sensitivities of the majority, Akbar progressed towards
being a genuine Indian ruler; and he thereby assured the
prolonged tenure of the Mughal dynasty. Aurangzeb, on the
other hand, lost this vital acquiescence of the majority
through his purported policies of religious intolerance and
proselytism. And the third school, that of the Muslim
historians, is divided by their secular or religious persuasion.
The former have tended to agree more with their Hindu
counterparts, while the latter have ascribed to Akbar's
liberalism the beginnings of the decay of Muslim power,
which Aurangzeb's more correct ideological approach tried
belatedly to rectify. Clearly, each of these schools has used
history as a means for self-justification.

While these interpretations are of little help in tracing
continuities and parallels, other aspects of the Mughal power
structure, economy and society, can be of greater relevance.
For one, there is the notion of the Mughal empire as a
'conquest state', in which the basic urges of the ruling groups
had little to do with the more abstract values of humanitaria-
nism or welfare. Rather, they were governed by the more
palpable need for revenue, rent and the surplus from the
productive classes, in whatever form that happened to be
generated. With time, there occurred an increasing burden
on the productive elements, to support expanding upper social
layers of agrarian and rent-receiving intermediaries, state
functionaries, military and para-military levies with varying
levels of resource demands, and the hordes of hangers-on
that were attached to this military-administrative-feudal
structure. This economic burden was further fuelled by
conspicuous consumption and unsustainable lifestyles,
stretching from the royal court and the larger magnates to
the more petty functionaries and rent receivers. There was
also heavy expenditure on monuments of all kinds, for both
the living and the dead. These projects certainly increased
demand in the construction sector, but they entailed onerous
capital outlays on essentially unproductive investments.
Urban construction and the expansion of cities were clearly
linked to the growth of a vibrant secondary sector, but this

also indicated that little returned to the rural economy that eventually had to underwrite these expenditures.

The Mughal economy as a whole did not lack impressive features. For a pre-industrial society, clear strengths lay in the aggregate output of material goods, the extensive range of arable and livestock resources, the quality and diversity of manufactured products, and the skill and dexterity of artisans and craftsmen. The ability to convey large volumes of commodities, even on medium and long distance routes, the logistical infrastructure for this transport system, and the sophistication and scale of mercantile transactions, clearly placed the Mughal empire at least at par with, if not well above, contemporary Europe. However, unlike the latter, the commercial sector remained subordinate to an entrenched state structure into which it could only be minimally co-opted, and that too at best at its highest merchant-financier levels. It thereby failed to gain the autonomy and the self-assurance that enabled its European counterparts to move, from much more humble beginnings, towards capitalism and eventually industrialization. The stifling lack of innovation in manufacturing techniques, and the lowly position of actual producers, further characterized the Mughal economy. The continued dominance over society of the upper agrarian hierarchy and state functionaries retarded the prospects of systemic change. Such shortcomings have led to raising negative questions about the potentialities and capabilities for capitalist development in South Asia. Of course, the role of colonial interventions in creating structural retardation cannot be discounted. But the question of the capabilities of the indigenous system still needs to be raised.

Can parallels be drawn between conditions in Mughal times and the nature of the Pakistani state? Does the latter display a qualitative shift in its ethos, or are the 'basic urges' of the two essentially similar? Is the state in Pakistan best discussed through a chronological treatment of its evolution, under some assumption of linearity? Or, do comparisons and structural parallels with earlier periods, or for that matter with other environments, provide a keener insight and more genuine understanding of the real workings of the system? Of course, the nomenclature has changed extensively. Instead of the central and provincial *darbars*, with their factions and ethnic alignments, there are now legislative assemblies, comprising political parties. Instead of courtiers and hereditary magnates there are now caucuses of 'elected' representatives. But can we be sure that the latter are really fulfilling the functions of democratic activity, of the intricate work of committees, law-making and policy analysis? Or, do they yet again appear in the capital cities to seek concession and largesse and resource diversion, to consolidate social authority and vie for privilege?

Other institutional workings can be similarly queried. The state functionaries appear to be more professionalised, operating within functional public departments, with organizational structures signifying a contemporaneous ordering of things. However, is the pervasive incidence of corruption simply a mechanism of monetary exchange, or does it also represent a more primordial obeisance to social power and caste consciousness? The military, too, comprises distinct careers, without the earlier formal integration with civil power. Yet, there has been consistent osmosis between the two, both in the long years of military rule and in the constant influence over civilian decision-making. And, are the larger landowners no longer 'feudal', but so heavily immersed in the market economy as to pioneer that value-added part of the agrarian economy that has or will bring about agricultural capitalism? Finally, the upper end of the business community appears in the vanguard of modernization, with the use of technology, management and modern finance. Or, as the recent revelations of massive defaults in project loans have illustrated, is business also a rent-receiving appendage to the state, relying on subsidies, concessionary loans and write-offs, rather than on the finesse of the marketplace? One may query whether the appearance and semblance of things are equal to the substance of things; whether indeed modern terminology is not simply the encryption of hoary traditionalism.

The Mughal empire in its decline phase can be seen to throw up further questions relevant to the analysis of contemporary Pakistan. Research has now shown that the downturn in the fortunes of the empire had strong economic undercurrents. During a couple of centuries of 'stability', the rent dependent classes had burgeoned in size, with consequent enhancements in their demands on productive resources. They had also become increasingly unmanageable by the centre, turning appointments into hereditary fiefs, and given to impeding the flow of revenue. The retaliation to these elite disfunctionalities was the growing resistance of landholding groups to revenue and rental exaction. In the Punjab, the western part of which came within Pakistan, the resistance developed during the first half of the eighteenth century into outright rebellion, spearheaded by peasant landholding groups. Many of these recalcitrants sought cohesion by adopting the Sikh faith, which, from its earlier, quietist Khatri trading caste origins, now changed its character into a militant and violent movement of protest against Mughal rule. By the mid-eighteenth century, the Sikh *misls*, or warbands, and other Muslim and Hindu peasant confederacies, had succeeded in removing Mughal control over the Punjab. The peasant rebellion went even further: it also almost completely neutralised, and even physically eliminated, the old Mughal elite in this region. The dominant, landholding village castes established their autonomy, freed from superior claimants. Several peasant leaders also became large landholders, and some were even recognised as princely states by the British.

These violent transitions had major long term consequences on the political economy of the region. They could also serve as a model for astute managers of any subsequent state, regarding the real sources of destabilization of state authority. These lessons were well understood by the British. On entry in the Punjab, in the mid-nineteenth century, they were confronted by a situation very different from their experiences during their expansion elsewhere in South Asia. Except perhaps in the territories overrun by the Marathas, the British had to contend with regional states ruled by independent 'kings'. These were none other than the descendants of Mughal viceroys and provincial governors, who had asserted their independence as Mughal power waned. Presumably, under these potentates the agrarian hierarchy was in essence preserved. No social change of the

Punjab type had occurred there yet: the old elites were still incumbent. The task of 'rationalising' society was then left to the British. The Permanent Settlement of Bengal of 1797 was one such instance of expeditious social turnover. Further west, too, they set about constraining the old incumbencies, through revenue pressures and revenue diversions, thus becoming competing claimants to the agrarian surplus. The ensuing tensions eventually led to the armed conflict of 1857-58, in which the British succeeded in pruning large elements of the old elite.

The British experience in the Punjab was very different. They read correctly that the alienation of the landed peasantry had spelt disaster for the Mughal state; and they formulated their strategy accordingly. They co-opted the militarised upper peasant groups of the Punjab to fight, and eventually prevail, in the armed struggle of 1857-58. Thence, these groups were recruited in growing numbers into the British Indian army, till the Punjab alone came to provide over half this force. These levies were used first in the Anglo-Afghan wars, and later in British imperialism's conflicts all over the globe, including both world wars. The lower, service or 'menial' castes were excluded from recruitment, except for the human exigencies of the world wars. Meanwhile, families of larger landholders were co-opted through inclusion into the middling military ranks. The historical basis for the pre-eminence of the military in Pakistan was already in place under imperialism.

A comparison with Sindh is illustrative here. What, one may ask, were the consequences of this province's failing to witness the upper peasant hegemony that had wrenched a new order in the Punjab in the eighteenth century. In Sindh, the control of the large landlord element continued from Mughal into colonial times. The British did displace some ruling families, but by and large they were content to settle with landlord intermediaries. The Sindhi peasantry remained subordinated to landlord dominance in the new state of Pakistan. Not having removed the incubus of feudalism, it failed to share the dynamic experiences of its Punjabi counterpart, in military service, in the new agrarian frontier, as we shall see, and in an international diaspora. Even within

Pakistan, the serf-like relationships in rural Sindh have prevented an underskilled rural population from benefitting from economic opportunities and developmental transitions. Witness, for example, the phenomenal growth of the city of Karachi at its doorstep, a process whose benefits have gone predominantly to immigrants coming from Indian territory and from the upcountry Punjab and Frontier provinces.

By far the most important development in the Pakistan area during British rule was the opening up of a 'hydraulic society' in the Indus basin. The flat, alluvial plains of the Indus river and its tributaries were too arid for *barani*, or rain fed, agriculture, of the type enabled by monsoonal rains further east. Traditional irrigation systems could only command tracts contiguous to the rivers, leaving vast areas uncultivated. From the 1880s, the British began to construct a network of perennial canals to colonise the new lands with settlers from more populous tracts, and those with whom they wished to cement political alliances. These canal tracts formed not only the largest irrigation system in the world, but also became the backbone of the Pakistani economy: without them the country would not be able to sustain more than a fraction of its present population. Indeed, the land settlement policies pursued by the British virtually laid the socio-economic foundations of the Pakistani state. Without entering into the details of these colonization schemes, their salient features need to be highlighted.

The strategic impact of agricultural colonization was the further consolidation of those who were already dominant. The major proportion of land, and in some schemes as much as eighty percent, was allotted in smallholdings of up to fifty acres. Almost exclusively, and through deliberate policy, the recipients of land belonged to the 'agricultural castes'. These were already incumbent landholders, belonging to the village upper social layers, who had earlier rebelled against Mughal rule, and whom the British had already co-opted through military services. They were also the castes responsible for paying land revenue, the income source on which the fiscal viability of British rule depended. In return, the British had recognised the 'proprietary rights' of these castes over village lands, itself a major concession. Moreover, in a remarkable piece of conservative legislation in the Punjab, and in the Punjab alone, the colonial authority adopted the Alienation of Lands Act, in 1901. This forbade members of 'non-agricultural castes' from purchasing land belonging to the agricultural castes. This attempted to cushion the latter from losing lands through the debt mechanism and mortgage foreclosure, and generally from the disruptive effects of the market economy. Constraining the social market for land was an overtly political measure, diametrically opposed to trends in Britain itself, where new, more profit and investment oriented landowners had expedited agricultural change.

Agricultural colonization had several other repercussions on the state structure. A significant amount of land was allotted to the larger landowners, further entrenching this class in society. This also provided the basis for its continued resilience in post-1947 Pakistan. Extensive areas were also reserved for a number of military functions, such as horse-breeding tenures; and land grants to soldier pensioners, and to war veterans after the two world wars. No other province in British India could even remotely match the Punjab in providing such tangible means for rewarding military service. The powers of the civil bureaucracy were also enhanced through its control over the management of the irrigation system. Here lay the foundations of the continuing bureaucratic hold over vital nodes of the Pakistani state. Commercial groups could also purchase canal irrigated land at auctions, while their major gains lay in the rapid growth of commodity trade and the emergence of agro-processing. Since this class happened to be predominantly non-Muslim, any benefits to society from an emerging 'bourgeois' ethos were emaciated by its emigration to Indian territory at Partition in 1947.

While accounting for the gainers from colonial rule, can we also identify those who might have been the losers? The ones explicitly excluded from the granting of land were those who were already landless. In village society, these sections belonged to the service castes, or 'menials' and 'kamins' as they were officially categorised. In numbers, however, they easily composed a majority of the rural population. They could migrate to the canal tracts and continue to offer labour services, without which anyway the rural economy would be untenable. But the administration was extremely conscientious in ensuring that they would not obtain occupancy or proprietary rights to agricultural land. Their exclusion, under imperialism, from the prime economic resource of land ownership, reappeared after 1947 in the serious neglect of social expenditure by the Pakistani state. This diversion of resources is reflected in adverse indicators for primary education, basic health, sanitation, water supply and such, as indeed in the elite's hesitation to institutionalise democracy.

Let us, therefore, take stock of the Pakistani state around the time of its formal inception in the mid-twentieth century. Comparisons with India could be useful here. Indian nationalism, and more specifically the strategies of the Indian National Congress, gained much strength from wresting away from the British the support of the upper peasantry, especially in the Hindu-majority provinces. This development crystallised with the results of the 1936 elections; and was a consequence of the agrarian crises that simmered through the economic depression of the 1930s. More pro-British landlord interests lost ground; and these were further depleted after 1947, when the Congress rewarded its upper peasant support base with land reforms. Alliances with business and the urban middle classes provided a national platform for the Congress, in a state that could only have been imagined because of the control of a single imperialist power over the entire subcontinent.

The emergence of Pakistan is traditionally seen within the context of 'separatism', from a purportedly cohesive whole, called 'India'. Its creation has been viewed as accidental, unnecessary or unfortunate. By contrast, Muslims have mostly tended to see it as the culmination of a separate identity in South Asia, which could be best retained by the formation of a distinct nation. They have viewed the emergence of Pakistan as a response to the highly threatening posture of 'Indian nationalism', in wanting to gain control of the British Indian empire in its entirety. Clearly, the notion of a renewed empire-state was bound to create cleavages along any of the fault lines of South Asian society: religious, ethnic, regional, linguistic or social. Britain's hurried withdrawal left the field clear for the Congress to assume power over this expansive empire-state, but not before the religious factor could achieve, in the form of Pakistan, at least a partial regional solution. Later, the further division of Pakistan into two states, in 1971, created even more genuine national entities. The juggernaut of the Indian empire-state, on the other hand, could well over time prove unworkable; and it would eventually collapse, with South Asia returning to the more typical and realistic structure of regional formations.

For Pakistan itself, the question arises whether the sources of political power witnessed much continuity from the earlier period. In contrast to India, the larger landowners in Pakistan have continued to enjoy greater political prominence; and they have resisted effective land reforms to date. Their pre-1947 strengthening, through canal irrigated land grants, was also reflected in their success in retaining the electoral support of the enfranchised upper peasantry. This structure has not been essentially modified in the subsequent half century. The lack of voting activity after 1947 failed to provide electoral indicators, virtually upto 1970. However, the 'basic democracy' system, introduced during the Ayub Khan regime in the 1960s, was clearly intended to re-establish the political participation of the upper peasantry. Even the nationalization policies of the Pakistan Peoples Party government of the 1970s helped the agrarian hierarchy, in that it thwarted an emerging large-scale business element, which might have challenged the entrenched order. The more rapid industrialization of the 1960s, accompanied by greater wealth concentration and the emergence of business 'monopoly houses', could in the longer run have diluted the power of upper agrarian groups.

A large part of the nationalization programme was in agricultural inputs, agro-processing, and in distribution of agricultural commodities. Such industries as tractors, agricultural implements and edible oils were nationalised. Procurement and distribution of the major foodgrain, wheat, as well as other crops, and export trade in the major cash crops, cotton and rice, were brought under state parastatals.

As private sector investment receded, the public sector took up investments in several agro-industries, such as fertilisers and farm mechanization. Moreover, there followed a further move by Zulfiqar Ali Bhutto to nationalise the smaller scale, intermediate agro-processing sector comprising flour and oil mills and cotton ginneries. In effect, managerial personnel, presumably more compliant towards landowners' interests, were substituted for entrepreneurs, in these forward linkages in the agricultural value chain. These smaller scale enterprises were de-nationalised soon after the military coup of 1977; but privatization of larger scale industry only commenced in the 1990s.

Thus, through the alternating periods of civilian and military rule in Pakistan's fifty year history, the structure of power and authority in Pakistan have remained relatively stable. Even in an environment where adult franchise was conceded, the long years without the exercise of electoral choice were to the advantage of entrenched interests, since the rural and urban masses were denied a political platform. The weakness of institutionalised politics has also served elite interests. Since the return of civilian democracy, after the end of military rule in 1988, two major political parties have been in contention, the Muslim League and the Pakistan Peoples Party. Both have been dominated by top and middle leadership cadres that have followed highly personalised agendas. Individuals who are caste nominees, or who now have cash flows from the likes of contraband trade and illicit earnings, have predominantly obtained party nominations for legislative elections. Pakistan has yet to develop proper political organizations, with internal democracy and consensus building processes from the bottom up. This would truly provide more democratic representation to a wider social base.

Clearly, the current situation is not at present one of alienation of the upper agrarian groups from the state. This is indicated by the continually dismal performance in legislative elections of religious radical organizations, also known as the extremist or fundamentalist segment. While these groups have assumed much apparent prominence over public life, they have been unsuccessful in gaining even one per cent of legislative seats, despite several opportunities in the past decade. This does remain an alternative available to the electorate, should it move against the status quo. However, it is one that has yet to be exercised. This eventuality remains hypothetical, but it could be a response to a major crisis facing the Pakistani state, or to a loss of credibility by the state establishment.

Such a scenario could develop from a number of tensions, not least being one already referred to, namely the rapid de-institutionalization of the state. This has involved the progressive de-structuring of procedures and protocols, the replacement of systems with personalised processes, and the retention in an increasingly complex environment of patron-client mentalities. Major and serious downturns in the efficiency and integrity of almost all branches of the public service have threatened to erode the credibility of state institutions. If and when such agencies as the civil bureaucracy, the police, the revenue service, and others, are perceived by the people as their adversaries, and indeed as detrimental to national sustainability, then the moral economy of the system will begin to be challenged. Situations could then emerge where understanding the lessons of history and the strategies of the past could become of paramount importance.

Bibliography

Ali, Imran Anwar. 1975. *Punjab Politics in the Decade before Partition*. Research Monograph Series, no. 8. Lahore: South Asian Institute, University of Punjab.

———. 1976. "Relations between the Muslim League and the Punjab National Unionist Party, 1935-47." *South Asia. Journal of the South Asian Studies Association of Australia and New Zealand*, No. 6.

———. "The Punjab Canal Colonies, 1885-1940." 1980. Ph.D. Thesis, Australian National University.

———. "Malign Growth? Agricultural Colonization and the Roots of Backwardness in the Punjab." *Past and Present* 114 (February 1987): 110.

———. *The Punjab under Imperialism, 1885-1947*. 1989. Princeton: Princeton University Press, 1988. South Asia edition of this book New Delhi: Oxford University Press 1989.

_____. "The Punjab and the Retardation of Nationalism." 1991. In *The Political Inheritance of Pakistan*, ed. D.A. Low, London: Macmillan.

_____. *Equity, Exclusion and Liberalization: Pakistan and the Threats to National Sustainability*. SEPHIS Conference on 'Equity, Exclusion and Liberalization: a Debate among Historians'. Zanzibar, September 1996.

_____. "Telecommunications Development in Pakistan." 1997. In *Telecommunications in Western Asia and the Middle East*, ed. Eli M. Noam. New York and Oxford: Oxford University Press.

_____. "Canal Colonization and Socio-Economic Change." 1997. In *Five Punjabi Centuries: Polity, Economy, Society and Culture, c. 1500-1990*, ed. Indu Banga. New Delhi: Vedams.

_____. *Past and Present: The Formation of the State in Pakistan*. Paper presented at Conference on Pakistan. Maison des Sciences De'l Homme, Paris, June 1998.

_____. "Business and Power in Pakistan." 2001. In *Power and Civil Society in Pakistan*, ed. Anita Weiss and Zulfiqar Gilani. Karachi: Oxford University Press.

ISLAM AND THE PAKISTANI POLITY

Religion in the Pakistani Polity

In order to explain the purpose of my study, I will start with a paper I wrote almost two decades ago, for Olivier Carre's book, on 'the political roles of Islam in Pakistan'.[1] In Pakistan—with the policy of Islamization which progressively accelerated from the Constitutional debate (1948-1956) to the rule of General Zia (1977-1988), Islam played a variety of roles; according to a classification propounded by M. Khalid Masud,[2] I may enumerate them as follows: they were

---

The topic of 'religion in the Pakistani polity' was chosen in order to discuss, with the Pakistani scholars who participated in the colloquium, some of the work which has been done in Paris about Pakistan. The research alluded to here was started in the 1970s in a seminar on political Islam organized by Olivier Carré in the Institute of Political Studies. Two books came out of this venture: the first called *Islam and the State in the World Today* (Carré 1982/1987) of which there has been, I believe, a Pakistani edition; and the second, *Islamic Radicalisms* (Carré & Dumont 1986). The work was continued at the EHESS (Ecole des Hautes Etudes en Sciences Sociales) in a pluri-disciplinary research team on the 'Peripheral Muslim World' and more particularly in my seminar on Indo-Pakistani Islam (Gaborieau 1990). Several Pakistani scholars, invited as associated professors, joined in our work, notably M. Khalid Masud of the Islamic Research Institute, Ahmad Hasan Dani, Akbar S. Ahmed and Muhammad Qasim Zaman: they participated either in a collective volume on Islam and Society in South Asia (Gaborieau 1986b), or in a conference on Islam in South and South-East Asia organized by professor Denys Lombard and myself in 1986, or—in the case of Muhammad Qasim Zaman—in the present conference. A new impetus has finally been set by the creation of a research team on Pakistan, jointly headed by Christophe Jaffrelot and myself under the double patronage of the Centre for the Study of International Relations and the Centre for the Study of India and South Asia; this team produced a collective work entitled *Pakistan* (Jaffrelot 2000) in which the topic treated here was revisited (Gaborieau 2000).

attempts at Islamizing the State, at Islamizing the Law, at
Islamizing political life, at Islamizing the economic and
banking system, at Islamizing knowledge... Attempts which
met with varying degrees of success.

In this paper I will focus on the first two, concentrating on
the place of Islam in the Constitution and in the legal system,
the two domains in which Islamization has been most
conspicuous, if not effectively successful. But, since the
process of Islamization is not understandable without some
knowledge of the operation of political forces, I will start
with the Islamization of politics.

The questions I will ask are derived from my 1982/1987
paper in which I made the following three assessments:
1. In Pakistan, Islam is an indispensable ingredient of
   constitutional, institutional and political legitimacy.
2. The legitimization process is produced by a series of
   compromises between a modernist elite and a variety of
   religious groups.
3. The trend of the evolution was then (in the late 1970s and
   early 1980s) in favour of the fundamentalist religious
   groups at the expense of the modernists.

The central interrogation in the present paper is the
following: do these statements hold true two decades later?
In order to give an answer concerning the three assessments,
I have first to make a sketch of the political arena in Pakistan
to assess the identity and the dynamics of the groups between
which compromises are effectuated.

Islamization of the political field in Pakistan

A characteristic feature of political life of Pakistan has always
been the polarity between, on the one hand, religious pressure
groups, and on the other, a modernist elite, civilian as well
as military, which kept control of the State apparatus.[3]

The religious groups are specific to the Pakistan context.
They are religious associations turned, after 1956, into
political parties. These religious associations themselves were
of two different kinds. On the one hand there were two
associations of traditionalist *ulema*; a legacy of pre-Partition

India, but re-organized in view of the creation of Pakistan, they represented the theological and political views of the two main schools of *madrasa* educated clerics: the JUI (Jamiatul-ulema-i-Islam) representing the Deobandi School; and the JUP (Jamiatul-ulema-i-Pakistan), the Barelvi school.

On the other hand, there was a *sui generis* neo-fundamentalist religious group, the JI (Jamaat-i Islami); it was an hybrid of traditional thought and modernist thinking.[4] It was shaped into a revivalist, not to say messianic, movement under the leadership of Sayyid Abu'l-A'la Maududi who, at the time of Partition, thought of himself as the *mujaddid*, the Renovator of Islam, or perhaps even, the *Mahdi*.[5]

From the very beginnings of Pakistan, there was a very curious relationship between the *ulema* and Maududi. The former saw the latter as sectarian, unorthodox; but, as they had no political agenda for the new State created under the name of Pakistan in 1947, they, in fact, followed the lead of Maududi: he had come to the forefront with a ready-made blueprint for Pakistan as an Islamic State, where God would be the only Sovereign and Legislator.[6] So from now on I can, without too much simplification, set as a principle that religious groups more or less followed the agenda of the JI.

Opposing these religious groups with their agenda of an Islamic State, were not so much groups or parties than an elite which had a double inheritance: it was trained in the British way in the Civil service or in the Army; it embodied a different conception of the State. Following a model borrowed from the West, it emphasized the sovereignty of the State which should have the last say, and would promulgate Laws framed by legislative assemblies elected from the people.

There was little common ground between the two sides, if any. There could be no real negotiation because they had neither the same language, nor the same aims.

The transactions could generally be characterized as outbidding: by putting the stakes higher and higher, the religious groups compelled the modernizing elites to concessions on the religious nature of the State. This outbidding often went through demonstrations, or even riots, the first example of which were the anti-Ahmadiyya (also

Ahmadis) riots of 1953.[7] Later, it was through such outbidding that first Zulfikar Ali Bhutto and then General Ziaul Haq were enticed to make the major concession of making *shari'a* the Law of the country, at least in principle; and of devising measures against the Ahmadis who were proclaimed a non-Muslim minority.[8]

Keeping this political background in mind, I come back now to the three assessments made in the beginning, and see if they hold true after two decades.

A stable agreement: the Islamic nature of the State

The first compromise was about the religious nature of the State. Pakistan was proclaimed in 1956, in the first Constitution, to be an Islamic State. Is this to remain so? From time to time some people entertain the hope that one may come back on this point. Thus, in a recent Pakistani publication which was echoed in a French one,[9] the well known (but one time censored) statement of Jinnah in the first Constituent Assembly was recalled:

'In the course of time Hindus would cease to be Hindus and Muslims would cease to be Muslims, not in the religious sense, because that is personal faith, but in the political sense as citizens of the State'.[10]

But this seems to be a vain hope. Again and again the religious character of the State has been reaffirmed; for instance when, at the time of the promulgation of the 1962 Constitution, Ayub Khan tried to delete the adjective 'Islamic' before 'Republic of Pakistan', he was compelled to reintroduce it, because of the uproar provoked by his decision. Such a commitment to the Islamic character of the State is understandable because Islam is the *raison d'être* of Pakistan: any Pakistani citizen, however liberal and secular in his outlook, is attached to his religious identity. And any political move or ideology which would not have the sanction of Islam, however formulated, would not gain acceptance. Islam, therefore, is a necessary ingredient of political legitimacy. The Islamic character of the State was best formulated in the Objectives Resolution[11] which were first put as a preamble to the Constitutions of 1956, 1962 and 1973, and finally inserted in the Constitution as an integral part of it by General Zia in 1985.[12]

Proclaiming the religious character of the State has implications for the status of the minorities.[13] By promoting the Muslim community and making only Muslims eligible for certain high posts, the Islamic State institutes two categories of citizens: Muslims of the various recognized sects (Sunnis, Twelver Shia, Ismailis...) on the one hand; and on the other, religious minorities deemed to be non-Muslim. At the time of Partition the main minorities were Hindus, Christians and Parsis; Ahmadis were added in 1974 after a vote of the Parliament declared them to be non-Muslim;[14] there have been demands that the Zikris of Balochistan (an off-shoot of the Mahdawis) also be declared non-Muslim. The official list of non-Mulims, in the 1985 Revival of the Constitution Order (art. 51), is the following: 'Christians, Hindus, Sikhs, Buddhists, Parsis and Ahmadis'.[15] They suffer several legal disabilities: they are not eligible for the posts of President and Prime Minister; they have separate electorates; and, since the Shariat Ordinances of Zia in 1979, their testimony in the courts does not have an equal value with that of Muslims. Discrimination remain minimal. But, because the religious minorities are also demographically weak (around 5 per cent of the population, including the Ahmadis), they become vulnerable.

However, such discrimination is a corollary of any kind of religious State. For instance, in Nepal, which remains a Hindu kingdom even after the new 1990 Constitution, the religious minorities, i.e., Muslims and Christians, suffer disabilities.[16]

It seems, therefore, that Pakistan is bound to remain a religious State; and that, as a corollary, there will remain some discrimination between Muslims and non-Muslims, even if the nature and the extent of discrimination may again vary, as it varied between 1947 and 1985.

Shifting compromises on Constitution and Law

Since the demand of the religious groups to have Pakistan proclaimed an Islamic State was conceded, does it mean that all their demands were satisfied, and that they had the last say? It has been long emphasized that this was not the case.[17] I will demonstrate this fact in the light of the Constitution and the Law of Pakistan.

As mentioned above, at the beginning of the Constitutional debate Maududi came forward with an articulate blueprint for an Islamic State.[18] It was most forcefully summed up in the 'four demands' made by Maududi in 1948: he insisted, in particular, that the *shari'a* would be 'the basic Law of the land' and that the 'State will have no authority to transgress the limits imposed by Islam'.[19] But the texts of the three Constitutions of 1956, 1962 and 1973, show that they fall very short of these demands. The very word *shari'a* is carefully avoided: it is only said that no law should be repugnant to the Quran and the *Sunna*. Furthermore, no operative mechanism was devised to bring existing legislation in conformity with the divine Law, for the Consultative Council on Islamic Ideology set up for this purpose had no power and was given a purely advisory role.

According to the Pakistani Constitutions, the final decisions are taken by the elected assemblies and by the President. It is the State, not the *shari'a* as expounded by the *ulema*, which has the final say. The modernists were thus the main beneficiaries of the Constitutional debate. The Islamic tradition was not treated as a system of Law taking precedence, but as a set of general principles, to which homage must be paid, but which do not impose specific consequences. Western political ideals, on the other hand, occupy the most important place in the Constitutions. The latter were clearly the result of compromises which weighed heavily in favour of the modernists.

Did the situation change when, under the regime of General Ziaul Haq, the Constitution was amended in 1985 by the Revival of the Constitution order?[20] The aim of this order was to Islamize the Constitution of Pakistan; it led to 'the most islamized version of Pakistan's Constitution'.[21] Yet, on scrutiny, the Islamic change is more cosmetic than substantive: renaming Parliament *Majlis-i Shura,* a phrase dear to the Islamists, was clearly a cosmetic operation. But, on the other hand, the Eighth Amendment promulgated the same year (Order no. 14 of 1985), which gave the President vast additional powers, may be construed as yet another concession to the Western version of the nation State, conceived this time not as democratic, but as authoritarian. I are still in the realm of a compromise in favour of the nation State, not in favour of the *shari'a.*

If the Constitutions remained a compromise, was not the much publicized Islamization of the Law in Pakistan effectuated under the Zia regime a really substantive change? Indeed, the acts and ordinances promulgated between the first ordinances in 1979,[22] and the Enforcement of Shariat Act of 1991[23] are spectacular.

But here again this new legislation has to be appreciated in reference to the whole body of Pakistani Law and in reference to the persons who drafted and applied the new Islamic Law.[24] It has long been remarked that the scope of this new legislation was limited to a few aspects of civil and criminal Law: personal Law, fiscal and financial legislation and questions of procedure are outside its domain.[25] A recent analyst has come to a similar conclusion after examining the content and operation of the Hudood Ordinances promulgated in 1979.[26] To sum up his analysis, the harder *hadd* punishments (involving death for fornication or amputation for theft) having not been put into use, the existing Laws were modified mainly on three points: the application of the milder punishment of *ta'zir* (whipping) in a limited number of cases; the modification of the Law of Evidence as far as Muslim women and non-Muslims are concerned; and thirdly the 1986 Act, modified in 1991, punishing with death derogatory remarks against the Prophet Muhammad (PBUH). For the rest, i.e., in the great majority of the cases, the Penal Code, the Evidence Act and the Procedure Code, which were drafted by the British in the second half of the nineteenth century, remain in operation.

A similar remark may be made also as to the agencies through which the new legislation was passed. The

traditional experts in Islamic Law, the *ulema*, have had a
limited say in all these matters. Ordinances and Laws were
either promulgated by the President, or voted by the
Parliament, who are the two authorities of the State who
have a say. The *ulema* sat only in the Shariat Benches of the
High Courts which were established in 1981, and were
replaced in 1986 by a Federal Shariat Court; in the latter
court only three *ulema* sit as against five judges. All are
appointed and dismissed at the discretion of the executive.
They can only examine and decide if certain provisions of the
Law (but not all) are repugnant to the injunctions of Islam.[27]
All judicial work is still done by State courts established on
the British model: the traditional Islamic judge, the *qazi*,
who has been suppressed since the British conquest, has not
been reinstated.

In matters of Law, as in matters of Constitution, I am,
therefore, still in the domain of compromise: the balance is
still heavily in favour of the modernizing elite which manages
the State and the judicial apparatus. The realm of
substantive Islamic Law and of the traditional experts has
still been very circumscribed. The Islamization of the Law
has been spectacular, but has remained symbolic.

But with the Federal Shariat Court, the *ulema* have a foot
in the institutions; and they can exert pressure to further
the Islamization of the Law; a case recently noticed is their
role in imposing the death penalty for derogatory remarks
made against the Prophet (PBUH).[28]

One may, however, underline how difficult it is for
Pakistani policy makers to go further on the way of
Islamization. After the nuclear tests of May 1998, followed
by an aggravated economic crisis and a growing criticism of
the government in power, Prime Minister Nawaz Sharif, the
leader of the Muslim League, did try to find rejuvenated
support by playing the Islamic card: he called, in September
1998, a large convention of *ulema* for reinforcing the *shari'a*
as a legal reference, fourteen years after Zia's attempt in
this direction. The opposition immediately denounced the new
Shariat Bill as an instrumentalization of Islam, used for
masking what was called the growing authoritarianism of
the Prime Minister. If later the National Assembly voted in

favour of the Shariat Bill submitted by the Government, it
was clear that the Senate would reject it, and the Act was
not forwarded to the senators. Once again, the ambiguity
surrounding the role of religion in the Pakistan polity was
clearly exposed.

Outbidding comes to an end?

I now, as a conclusion, come to the third question: in which
direction did the compromise between the religious groups
and the modernist elite evolve? With the peak marked by the
beginning of the Zia regime twenty years ago, the balance
seemed to tilt more and more in favour of the religious
groups. Is this still true?

With the Zia Regime now fourteen years behind us, I can
make assessments. In the light of the foregoing analysis
I may first reflect that, even between 1977 and 1988, the
religious groups got only minimal concessions. In fact, in
many ways General Zia instrumentalized the fundamentalist
agenda, but did not really put it into operation. The lesson
was not lost on the JI, which had set hopes on General Zia
and participated in his first government: it soon withdrew
from the government.[29] At the end of his life, Maududi
(d.1979) was disillusioned; he is reported to have said: 'When
historians will write of the Jamaat, they will say that it was
yet another *tajdid* (renewal) movement that rose and failed'.[30]

The Zia regime was thus one peak in the evolution of the
compromise: it was the period in which religious groups got
the most favours, but only symbolic ones. The tide has turned
back and their influence on the State apparatus seems to be
decreasing.

But does it mean that the influence of the religious groups
may continue to decrease? I may once again recall that they
have a foot in the State apparatus through the Federal
Shariat Court and other advisory institutions. They may
continue to exert pressure for further Islamization: but their
weight will depend on the evolution of the political situation,
a question outside the scope of this paper.

Another result of the Zia regime, through the encouragements for *madrasa* education, is to have carved for the religious groups, in the field of education, a kind of private domain where they can prosper.[31] Here is another avenue, outside the State apparatus, where they can exert increasing pressure for the Islamization of the society. But this again is outside the scope of this paper.

NOTES

1. Gaborieau 1982/1987.
2. Masud 1997.
3. Binder 1961; Ziring, Braibanti and Wriggens 1977; Ziring 1980; Nasr 1994; Talbot 1998; more references in Long 1998, pp. 31-166.
4. Gaborieau 1986a; Nasr 1994.
5. Maududi 1940/1960; Nasr 1996.
6. Maududi 1967; Binder 1961, pp. 70-108; Adams 1966 and 1983; Ahmed 1987, pp. 93-116; Nasr 1996, pp. 80-106.
7. Binder 1961, pp. 259-296.
8. Nasr 1994, pp. 170-188.
9. National Commission on History and Culture 1995, p. 36, quoted in Monnot 1997, p. 470.
10. Jinnah 1989, p. 17; see also Binder 1961, p. 100.
11. Binder 1961, pp. 142-154.
12. Mehdi 1994, pp. 104-105.
13. Ahmed 1987, pp. 179-181; Nasr 1996, pp. 99-102; Gaborieau 1999.
14. Friedmann 1989, pp. 40-43.
15. Mehdi 1994, p. 106.
16. Gaborieau 1994 and 1999.
17. Gaborieau 1982/1987, pp. 185-189.
18. Maududi 1967; Binder 1961, pp. 70-108; Adams 1983; Gaborieau 1986, pp. 39-51.
19. Binder 1961, p. 103.
20. Mehdi 1994, pp. 103-107.
21. Mehdi 1994, p. 104.
22. Mehdi 1994, pp. 109-156.
23. Amjad Ali 1992.
24. Gaborieau 1982/1987.
25. Gaborieau 1982/1987, p. 191.
26. Mehdi 1994: chapter 3.

27. Mehdi 1994, pp. 213-215.
28. Amendment of the 1986 act in 1991, see Monnot 1997, p. 466.
29. Nasr 1994, pp. 188-205.
30. Nasr 1996, p. 45.
31. Malik 1996.

Bibliography

Adams, Charles J. 1966. "The Ideology of Mawlana Mawdudi." In *South Asian Religion and Politics,* ed. Donald E. Smith, 371-397. Princeton: Princeton University Press.
_____. "Mawdudi and the Islamic State." In *Voices of Resurgent Islam,* ed. John L. Esposito, 1983. 99-133. New York, Oxford University Press.
Ahmed, Ishtiaq. 1987. *The Concept of an Islamic State. An Analysis of the Ideological Controversy in Pakistan.* London: Frances Pinter Publishers.
Binder, Leonard. 1961. *Religion and Politics in Pakistan.* Berkeley: University of California Press.
Amjad-Ali, Christine, 1992. *The Legislative History of the Shariah Act,* Rawalpindi: Christian Study Centre.
Carre, Olivier, ed. 1982. *L'islam et l'Etat dans le monde aujourd'hui.* Paris: Presses Universitaires de France, (English translation, *Islam and the State in the World Today.* 1987. Delhi: Manohar).
_____. In collaboration with Paul Dumont, 1985-1986. *Radicalismes islamiques,* 2 vol. Paris: L'Harmattan.
Friedmann, Yohanan. 1989. *Prophecy Continuous. Aspects of Ahmadi Thought and its Medieval Background.* Berkeley: University of California Press.
Gaborieau, Marc. 1982. "Roles politiques de l'islam au Pakistan." In Carre, ed., op.cit, 189-203.
_____. 1986a. "Le néo-fondamentalisme au Pakistan: Maududi et la Jama'at-I Islami" in Olivier Carre and Paul Dumont, ed. op.cit, 1985-1986, vol. 2. 33-76.
_____. ed. 1986b. *Islam et société en Asie du Sud.* Paris: Ecole des Hautes Etudes en Sciences Sociales.
_____. 1990. "Séminaire général" and "L'islam Indo-Pakistanais: bilan des activités (1982-1990)", *Lettre d'information. La transmission du savoir dans le monde musulman périphérique,* Paris, Ecole des Hautes Etudes en Sciences sociales, (E.H.E.S.S.) no. 10. 2-17.
_____. 1994. "Une affaire d'Etat au Népal depuis deux siècles. Le prosélytisme chrétien et musulman." *Archives de sciences sociales*

des religions, vol. 87, 1994, pp. 57-72 (Revised English translation: 'Proselytism and the State: The Historical Case of Nepal', in David E. Guinn, Christopher Barrigar & Katherine K. Young, eds. 1999. *Religion and Law in the Global Village*, McGill Studies in Religion, no. 5. Atlanta (Georgia): Scholars Press. 203-219.

———. 1999. "La tolérance des religions dominées dans." Inde traditionnelle: ses prolongements modernes au Népal et au Pakistan', in Guy Saupin, Remy Fabre & Marcel Launay, eds., *La tolérance. Colloque international de Nantes, mai 1998. Quatrième centenaire de l'édit de Nantes,* Presses universitaires de Rennes/Université de Nantes, 1999, 451-461.

———. 2000 "Islam et politique." in Christophe Jaffrelot, ed. *Le Pakistan.* Paris: Fayard. 399-422.

Jaffrelot, Christophe, ed. 2000. *Le Pakistan.* Paris: Fayard

———. Jinnah, Muhammad Ali. 1989. *Speeches as Governor General of Pakistan, 1947-1948,* Lahore.

Long, Roger D. 1998. *The Founding of Pakistan. An Annotated Bibliography.* Lanham (Maryland) & London: Scarecrow Press.

Malik, Jamal. 1996. *Colonizing Islam. Dissolution of Traditional Institutions in Pakistan.* Delhi: Manohar.

Masud, Muhammad Khalid. "Islamization in Pakistan." Unpublished lecture in Paris, E.H.E.S.S., November 1997.

Maududi, Sayyid Abul A'la. 1963. *A Short History of the Revivalist Movement in Islam,* translated by Al-Ash'ari, Lahore, Islamic Publications, from the 5th rev. ed., Lahore 1960 (1st Urdu ed. 1941 under the title *Tajdid o ihya-i din*).

———. *The Islamic Law and Constitution,* 1967. Translated by Khurshid Ahmad, 3rd revised ed., Lahore: Islamic Publications (first published 1955).

Mehdi, Rubya. 1994. *The Islamization of the Law in Pakistan.* London: Curzon Press.

Monnot, Guy. 1997. "Pakistan. Troisième génération." *Mélanges de l'Institut Dominicain d'Etudes Orientales,* no. 23, 463-470.

Nasr, Seyyed Vali Reza. 1994. *The Vanguard of the Islamic Revolution. The Jama'at-I Islami of Pakistan.* Berkeley: University of California Press/ London: I.B. Tauris.

———. 1996. *Mawdudi and the Making of Islamic Revivalism.* New York: Oxford University Press.

The Cultural History of Pakistan. Islamabad: National Commission on History and Culture. 1995.

Talbot, Ian. 1998. *Pakistan. A Modern History.* London: C. Hurst & Company.

Ziring, Lawrence. 1980. *Pakistan: The Enigma of Political Development*. Folkstone: Dawson & Sons.

Ziring, Lawrence, Braibanti, Ralph, and Wriggens, Howard. 1977. *Pakistan: The Long View*. Durham: Duke University Press.

Pakistan: *Aporia* of its Kind

Pakistan is now being defined as an ideological state. Over a period of time this platitude has been repeated so often that it is now considered as a self-evident truth. The continuous aggressive advocacy of this idea has overshadowed all attempts at objective analysis especially in the Pakistani academia. It serves the political ambitions of certain groups as well as of the ruling elite of Pakistan. In the absence of serious intellectual efforts, the concept of Pakistan remains an *aporia*. In what follows, an attempt has been made to analyse the inherent ambiguities of the idea.

Pakistan's creation was allegedly based on the two nation theory, i.e., Hindus and Muslims who lived in India were two distinct, different, and at times, antagonistic cultural entities. Although it is a moot point that only two nations lived in India, by whatever definition of nations, there is no doubt that the two largest groups were those of the Hindus and the Muslims. These two cultural entities in India had a historical and civilizational backdrop, an identity and a self-image of their own, having a different set of characteristics, yet, in the context of Indian politics each one's identity and unity was parasitic on the other. Left alone, Muslims and Hindus were subdivided into nationalities, sects and ethnic and linguistics groupings.

The idea of the creation of a separate state for the Muslims of India took time to grow as is evident from the history of the struggle for freedom in India. The Muslim League, the party which was responsible for the creation of Pakistan, was envisaged at the time of its formation in 1906, as a party that sought to promote feelings of loyalty to the British

Government and protect the political rights and interests of Indian Muslims.[1] It took the League thirty-four years to crystallize the idea of separate state/states mainly because experience taught them that they could not trust the Hindu leadership in an undivided India for the protection and preservation of their culture, despite the secular and humanistic stance of the Indian National Congress and Gandhi. It was in March 1940 that the Lahore (or Pakistan) Resolution was passed. The sense of insecurity amongst the Muslims was intense in areas where they were in a minority, with the exception of Muslim Bengal which had experienced similar insecurity before it was partitioned as a separate province in 1905 by Lord Curzon, and later when the partition was annulled. The Muslim majority areas were under the influence of feudal and tribal leaders. Although the Muslims of the minority provinces could not clearly answer the question as to how a separate state/states, which were supposed to be established in Muslim majority areas, could protect the Muslims in minority areas, or in what sense they would be able to preserve their cultural and religious identity, yet it was in these provinces that the Muslim League was more organized and deep-rooted. A later League Resolution, despite showing an awareness of the problem, depicts the thorough inadequacy of Muslim leaders in comprehending the situation fully when it says that 'adequate, effective and mandatory safeguards shall be specifically provided in the constitution for them and other minorities for the protection of their religious, cultural, economic, political, administrative and other rights and interests in consultation with them'.[2] The mandatory part of the resolution is vacuous. At most, it is an expression of a wish or hope that minority cultures would be protected in the two states.

But the point at issue is not only a lack of understanding of political realities either at the time of passing this resolution, nor a lack of foresight of the events that might unfold themselves in the coming fifty years or so. The point is that the Muslim intellectual at that time failed to appreciate the fact that there occurred a conceptual leap between the objectives of the creation of the Muslim League

in 1906, and its later stand in 1940. Though political parties
do change their stance to cope with the changing realities of
life, this change resulted in a paradoxical situation. Those
who mainly demanded the creation of Pakistan were those
who were not going to get it. Those who belonged to the
majority provinces, except for Muslim Bengal, were not yet
convinced of the necessity for such a step. In none of the
majority provinces of the western region had the Muslim
vote been effectively organized until well into the 1940s. In
Punjab, the Muslim League could make significant headway
only in the 1946 elections, where prior to that time the
Unionist Party, a coalition of Muslims, Hindus and Sikhs
had ruled the province for years. Not much different were
the cases of other Muslim majority provinces in the western
region. It was only when the feudal and tribal leaders realized
that their future in an undivided India would be unsafe that
they jumped onto the bandwagon of the Muslim League and
used religion as an instrument to arouse the masses
emotionally to side with the demand for Pakistan. It took
only seven years and five months between the demand for
Pakistan and the coming of the state into existence, probably
the shortest in the history of struggle movements against
any colonial rule. The duration was too short and the
implications of demanding a state on the basis of religious
culture, i.e., Islam, were too involving and profound to allow
Muslim intellectualism enough time to clarify and crystallize
the concept of a state based on the Islamic value system.
There was a great chasm between the modernistic idea of a
state based on Islamic culture, and that of conservatives
whose ideas were expressed in traditional religious idiom
and despite sectarian variations in details were easily and
readily understood and accepted by the Muslim masses.[3]

Those who know the history of the struggle for Pakistan
know very well that it was as late as 1930 that a positive
content based on ideology was expressed and incorporated
into the struggle for Muslim independence by Iqbal in his
Presidential address at the Allahabad session of the All India
Muslim League. His proposal for creating an entity, within
or outside the British Empire, in the Indian subcontinent,
approximately corresponds with what is now known as

Pakistan. But neither Iqbal nor Muslim intellectualism could satisfactorily resolve the tensions that exist between the universalism of the Islamic approach and its particularization in a single cultural unit. Hence, Pakistan found itself with no clear cut definition of a nation, no clear concept as to what type of state it was going to be and no firm policy profile for its development. Everything, including the basic organization of the government had to be done *de novo*. It is astounding how the state survived against so many odds which it had to face during the first few years of its creation, and it goes to the credit of the people and their will to survive that Pakistan did not collapse as was wished by its adversaries. However, despite the early goodwill of the people, the conceptual confusion and the lack of a robust intellectual culture deprived the nation of a workable constitutional structure and good governance.

The conceptual confusion soon ensued a debate as to the type of state Pakistan was going to be, i.e., Islamic as interpreted and construed by the conservatives supported by the uneducated but easily excitable public, or a modern state as envisaged by Jinnah in particular and other League leaders in general. The Jamaat-i-Islami, a small but well organized political party of the middle class even declared the state as being un-Islamic and prohibited its members from joining government service, as it was considered to be aiding and abetting an 'evil state' (*taghut*). They demanded that the state declare itself to be an Islamic state and launched a campaign, organized demonstrations and printed millions of postcards to be sent to the Constituent Assembly for this purpose. Maududi's argument was that such a declaration was tantamount to a confession of faith by an individual who intends to become a Muslim. The latter actions would have to conform to the avowal of faith made earlier. No one questioned at that time the legitimacy of this argument and accepted it as a self-evident truth, though it was based on three questionable notions; (*a*) that actions are always the outcome of intentions, (*b*) that the state is analogous to human individuals, which can be converted to Islam by an act of avowal thus legalizing the relationship of the citizens and the state, and (*c*) that the state established at Madina during the days of the Prophet (PBUH) was an Islamic state in the sense the theologians now construe it to be. These notions, even if not patently wrong, needed a lot of explaining and conceptual clarification. The motivation of the religious leaders may not be doubted, but their intellectual bankruptcy and utter ignorance of the nuances of a state existing in the twentieth century bamboozled them into the seductive belief that Islam, as delineated a thousand years ago, has a complete answer to all life problems including economic, political and legal structures, and would somehow bring back to life an ideal social welfare state as presumably existed during the early days of Islam.

The demand for making Pakistan an Islamic state was more popular in West Pakistan than in the eastern wing. The reasons are obvious. The western wing of Pakistan was dominated by a feudal and tribal structure with huge land holdings owned by a few landlords. Somehow or the other, Islam, as interpreted by the conservative theologians in West Pakistan, was supportive of this cultural milieu. They considered land ownership an inalienable Islamic right and under no authority was it considered permissible to take it away from them. One of the top leaders of the Jamaat-i-Islami, Maududi, wrote a book *Masala Milkiat-e-Zameen* (The Issue of Land Ownership) in 1950, in which he justified, according to the Quran and *Sunnah* (the two basic sources of Islamic Law and religion) that the right of land ownership is inviolable.[4] The book was written to ward off the socialist thinking that was gaining ground mostly in East Pakistan, as also in West Pakistan's educated middle class and in labour unions. Islam apparently posed no danger to the ruling elite. It actually helped to maintain a status quo and did not call for either drastic economic or land reforms. The ruling elite believed that the Islamist could be appeased by approving the 'Objectives Resolution' by the Constituent Assembly; by declaring Friday as the weekly holiday; and by declaring Qadianis to be non-Muslim etc. None of these measures challenged the status quo of the feudal political leadership or helped solve the real economic and social issues that beset Pakistan.

The intellectual scene today is not only as confused as it was during the early years of the creation of Pakistan but has worsened at the ground level by the presence of violent groups which are prone to use *argumentum ad-baculum*. The reason is that all sections of society which are at variance with each other are incapable of accepting a rational culture. Pakistan as it geographically exists today has been either anti-intellectual or non-rational for ages. The people have a proclivity for sentimentalism, can be quickly provoked and have a mental set-up that cannot sustain a long and involving rational argument. Unfortunately, all this is not happening only at public or mass level, but also in the institutions of higher learning, at universities, in scholarly seminars, religious discussions, in newspapers and in books. In the university departments, genuine scholars in the areas of History, Philosophy, Sociology, Anthropology and Economics are conspicuous by their absence. Pakistani universities are hardly producing any research worth its name in the fields of Humanities and the Social Sciences. Positive sciences are not doing any better and are stuck to a particular paradigm of research. Intellectual culture has not taken root in the universities and with commercialization of education whatever remnants of disinterested scholarship were left are eroding fast. No one even feels the need and necessity to develop these areas and it serves the ruling elite as well; as robust intellectualism tends to become an agent for change in society.

Why has Muslim intellectualism failed to respond to contemporary challenges in the Islamic world in general and in Pakistan in particular? More fundamentally, why has Muslim intellectualism been moving within the parameters they set for themselves in the tenth century AD? It would be worth its while to determine the causes for the development of a particular paradigm for Muslim intellectualism.

Muslim society at its nascent stage had to suffer from a number of severe jolts, the first being the almost sudden death of the Prophet. Given the religious aura and authority of Prophet Mohammad (PBUH), and the unwitting but latent faith of the community in the continuity of Prophet Mohammad's (PBUH) existence, it was a shock for the people

to realize that he was no more amongst them.[5] Soon after,
within a span of fifty years the community had to deal with
internal conflict, two civil wars and possible total
disintegration.[6]

The dread of disintegration seemed to have seized the
collective mind of the *ummah* and it subconsciously resulted
in the evolution of a number of defence mechanisms. For
example, firstly the community organized itself around a
strong centre which gradually gave way to kingship, despite
the fact that Arab society at that time was not authoritarian
but highly individualistic. Secondly, they opted for and
developed a theological structure based on a command-
obedience pattern. The primary commander being God, Who,
according to this theology was transcendent and exclusive to
the world whereas the secondary commander being the
authority holding political power (*ululamer minkum*). The
metaphysical support for such a position was provided by a
theological construct which made value parasitic on the Will
of God. X is good because God wills it to be good, otherwise,
nothing has an intrinsic value in itself. When this theological
structure is applied to law making, God becomes the eternal
lawmaker and no piece of legislature, thus made, can ever be
modified or changed. Law then, it seems, is not made for
social good, rather social good is a product of law. If a piece
of legislature fails to produce social good the fault cannot lie
with the law itself, but with the ill intentions of those who
apply it. Such fallacies, which the religious arguments, in
general, suffer from are commonly used both at the pulpit
and in the universities.

One of the consequences of this intellectual paradigm is
that law becomes supercilious to any moral or social appraisal
and anyone who dares to suggest it is threatened by
ex-communication or with dire consequences.

That Muslim intellectual history offered at least three
alternative paradigms i.e., rational, mystic, and scholastic,
yet the community chose the last is not surprising.
Rationalism calls for responsibility and humankind is prone
to shun it. Human beings, by nature find comfort and ease in
simply obeying orders and following authority.[7] In addition
to the natural propensity of people for obeying orders, the

socio-political conditions of the time when theology was taking shape demanded an authoritarian model. It was accepted both by the people and by the jurists. This model of law-making later became so ingrained in Muslim minds that it now seems like a self-evident truth, equivalent in all respects with religion *per se*. That this construct of religion is one of the several theological cum metaphysical structures was lost sight of. This mode of thinking became second nature to the Muslim mind and any criticism against it posed a threat to the very core of its religious being. That a person can be deeply religious or even a Muslim, without concurring with a particular theological cum metaphysical structure is taken to be a contradiction in terms.

In South Asia, Islam was established initially in the form of small settlements in the coastal areas. Later, as an empire it came face to face with another strong civilization, i.e., Indian, rooted in the cultural ethos of Hinduism. The two civilizations, i.e., Islam and Hinduism remained in juxtaposition to each other, neither of them pliant enough to be absorbed by the other nor strong enough to annihilate the other. They marginally influenced each other on the plane of customs, rites, rituals and socio-cultural behaviour. Muslims jealously guarded their monotheistic identity, whereas Hindus were always wary of the alien Muslim rule. Under such circumstances it was but natural that the Muslim community in India felt vulnerable and insecure and tried to cling to the letter of the law and emphasized formal expressions of religion rather than the inner content. The reform movements of Ahmad Sirhindi (1564-1624) or Shah Waliullah (1703-62) are indicative of the attempts to guard against the collective dread that the *ummah* suffered. When religious support was solicited for the Pakistan movement, it was provided by the *ulema* with their legalistic and formal approach to religion and supported by the trading bourgeoisie and the urban middle class Muslims of the subcontinent. Once Islam got itself associated with the creation of Pakistan, little did the leaders realize the sort of *aporia* it was going to present for the development of a modern Muslim state. This is the general perspective of the creation of Pakistan, which shows that Muslim intellectualism failed to grasp fully that:

a. Muslim nationalism in India was parasitic on an opposing factor, i.e., Hindu/Indian/Bharati nationalism.

b. The demand for a state based on Islam cannot be reconciled with the universal aspect of Islam.

c. The limited support for the demand for Pakistan came mainly from the urban theological Islam of the subcontinent.

d. This Islam represents a particular theological structure where God is wholly transcendent and external to the world.

e. The illiterate masses were emotionally motivated by the idea of a glorious past.

f. This paradigm poses problems in the creation of a modern state embodying Islamic values, as Jinnah envisaged.

It is not presumed here that history always follows cold logic, or that the division of India could have been avoided. India had hardly been a united kingdom and given the existential situation it would have divided into a number of units. But with a longer educational background, greater intellectual vigour and more time to play their part, the Muslim leadership could have influenced the flow of events more positively and might have worked out a better thought-out plan for the governance of independent Muslim state/states which in any case were to emerge sooner or later. But rationalism and the vision of an independent democratic Indian peninsula were difficult to come by during the hectic days of the Second World War. Nevertheless, for today, a better understanding and an analysis of the contemporary situation can help to shape the future. Given Pakistan, as it is, consisting of a geographical unit approximating to the vision of Iqbal, with its socio-political and religious dimensions, the crucial question is, from here to where? Can a conceptual analysis of the situation help us to adopt a course of action which is conducive to future development of the country?

Let us avow at the outset that religion, in whatever form, does play an important role in the life of the people of Pakistan. Any attempt to banish it from their lives would be doomed to failure. Religion, despite its failures and misuses,

is one of the most important and cogent transcendental
reference points which provide a ground for altruistic values.
Devoid of this transcendent reference, human beings are
prone to succumb to egoism or utilitarianism at best. It is
also one of the strongest motivational forces which can impel
people for doing good even at maximum personal cost. It is
also true that in Islam a conceptual bifurcation of secular
and sacred is not admissible. Islam operates only under the
category of an all-pervasive sacredness and the only
distinctions admissible are of virtue and vice or good and
bad. In a sense, Islam sanctifies the so-called secular acts
subject to their intention of aiming at what is commonly
accepted as good, and yet, paradoxically Islam de-sanctifies
those human actions which are normally considered purely
religious. All religious rituals and rites professedly aim at
the social good, improving the quality of human life and the
betterment of society. Religion becomes an all-pervasive
consciousness from which actions flow as if out of necessity
and not because of command, either external or internal. In
other words, the category of secular is already subsumed
under the sacred or vice-versa. Human actions transcend both
these categories and become religio-neutral. This might be
one of the reasons that Islam has been so secularization-
resistant, whereas the three other great religions, i.e.,
Christianity, Hinduism and Confucianism have been more or
less secularized.[8] The fault of the modern apologetics of Islam
is that they implicitly admit the duality of the secular and
the sacred and then try to coerce the two categories into one
under a theological construct based on the command-
obedience pattern. The tensions between the two in this
paradigm can never be resolved. The better approach should
have been to start with only one category (spiritual) and
later admit a bifurcation of functions of the same under an
all-pervasive religious consciousness. The authenticity of an
action thus is not derived from the fact that it obeys certain
laws, but that it ensues from an authentic source and hence
can create laws of its own.[9]

It may appear far-fetched, but if there is going to be a
paradigm shift in the understanding of religion, it is going to
be provided by the Muslim intellectualism of the South Asian

region. There are reasons for these conjectures. Some of which are:

1. Amongst the Muslim countries which are comparatively more developed are those which have adopted one of the two alternative paradigms available, i.e., secular and sacred. Turkey has adopted the secular mode and tries to enforce it with state power, like an ideology. The countervailing modality is showing greater acceptance in the masses and a conflict in the two modalities would be counterproductive for any rationally acceptable definition of the purpose and justification of the state. Unless a justifiable paradigm is developed which can subsume the religious consciousness and fulfill requirements for the development and functioning of a modern state, the total resourcefulness and strength of a community cannot be galvanized for appropriate social action. The other country i.e. Iran, has accepted the paradigm of divine rule through the *Imam*, who is now in occultation, and during the interregnum, the juris consults would interpret the divine intentionalities. True, this idea is much closer to the will of the people but can degenerate into the theocracy of a church. The basic contradictions within society would remain unresolved. Adopting either of these alternatives would mean riding on the horns of a dilemma unless the Muslims of South Asia resolve it in a new conceptual perspective.

2. Despite the strong hold of the conservative religious paradigm and an introvert collective psyche it was here that, while retaining religion, a new critical method was developed by Syed Ahmad Khan (1817-1898) for understanding and interpreting religion. Syed Ahmad went far beyond his predecessors in other parts of the Muslim world, and was able to break the deadening silence of Muslim intellectualism existing for the last 500 years. In his efforts to apply science to religion, which robs religion of its very nature and appeal, he paved the way for developing an alternative construct of Muslim theology. It was through his efforts that, despite stiff opposition from conservative Islam, a window was opened

for Indian Muslims to the western world, a phenomenon which was unique in the history of Muslim intellectualism in the subcontinent. No one ever before, even when they had opportunities during Mughal reign, had ever thought of benefiting from the Portuguese or the British who were making inroads in India with new knowledge and technology.[10] Later, Iqbal became another exception who, educated in the western traditions, named his collection of lectures delivered at Madras the *Reconstruction of Religious Thought in Islam*, and opened up the possibility of reconstructing Islamic thought that was palatable to conservative Indian Muslim intellectualism. Though Iqbal very carefully worded the explication of his thought, he did not dare to bring about the full implications of his idea of *ijtehad*. Yet, he termed it the *Principle of Movement in Islam*, which was very significant. Within the overall perspective of his philosophy, the Islamic spirit is in a process of continuous creation and is free to express itself in new forms not necessarily identical with the previous. No other attempt has been made to develop a new hermeneutics of Islam based on a non-scholastic or non-Aristotelian logic except that of Iqbal. Both these attempts are important steps towards developing a new paradigm and both have their origin in South Asia.

3. In Pakistan (and in other Muslim countries as well) there is occurring an important demographic change, i.e., the shift of populations from the rural to the urban areas. Moreover, the communication revolution is affecting the rural population in a very significant way. These changes are producing two very important consequences. Firstly, the feudal hold on a significant sector of the population is lessening. Those who migrate or are exposed to modernity in an urban situation no longer remain bonded voters to feudal lords who stand for elections. This change has been visible through successive elections in Pakistan. It may take a couple of decades until an over-riding qualitative change occurs in the ruling classes of the country. Secondly, and even more significantly, factors like urbanization, political centralization, market economy, labour migration etc, have been eroding the

social bases of what Gellner calls Low Islam or Folk Islam and converting the masses to High Islam or Reformed Islam. Reformed Islam confers a genuine shared identity and a kind of ratification of the social ascension of Muslim populations, and converts them from rustic or folk state to a puritanic, self assertive and ego augmentative state. This conversion also strengthens urban values and provides a countervailing force against feudal culture. It is not surprising that for the first time in Pakistan, all the significant political and semi-political parties denounce feudalism and consider the acquisition of vast areas of land by the feudal lords as un-Islamic. Jamaat-i-Islami's new *Amir*, as against his predecessors, now considers feudalism as one of the evils besetting the country, and Dr Israr Ahmad[11] advocates that lands in Pakistan are not *ushri* (land that belongs to a person and on which he pays a tax) but *khiraji* (lands acquired as a result of conquests and belonging to the state).

4. Reformed or Urban Islam is well-entrenched in urban areas in Pakistan as well as in other Muslim countries. Partly due to anti-colonialism and partly due to its very nature Urban Islam is defensive, polemical, and distrustful of western ideologies and philosophies. It still retains the aura of self-sufficiency as a system, and ascribes the failures of governance and lack of development to persons or to international conspiracies. Since they have not done well in elections in most Muslim countries, it is easier for them to shift the blame to others. Ziaul Haq, who was supported by the Muslim reformist in general, had more efficacy than a normally elected assembly, and who purportedly wanted to establish the rule of Islam in Pakistan, was later rebuked by the Islamists because instead of effecting a perceptible betterment of social and individual values, the public morality deteriorated and political culture degraded. In countries like Algeria, High Islam was not allowed to play its part politically and hence could retain the *argumentum ad-hominem* in blaming others for the failure of governance in a Muslim country.

5. Urban Islam has a wide range of grades at one end of which is a highly conservative, puritanic, dogmatic and formalistic position supported by polemics with an aura of ideology. Incidentally, the populace belonging to this set has not substantively increased in percentile. In Pakistan, its range has been 2-3 per cent. On the other end, Urban Islam touches the borders of Folk Islam where a saint or a *mullah* plays a pivotal role in ritual performances but does not control the whole life of the individual as in Folk Islam. The individual here is oriented towards a cause, a principle, or an authority controlling the group via ethnic, political and economic factors. This is one of the reasons that, other things being equal, they do vote for those whom they consider more religious, yet religiosity is not a single motivational factor of their behaviour.

6. The so-called Urban Islam has yet to realize that they have no positive content to their sketchy generalized framework of Islamic ideology. They have basic difficulties in clearly defining the (*a*) nature of law (*b*) human rights (*c*) political structure (*d*) the role of God as Sovereign in juridical behaviour (*e*) economic agenda unequivocally enunciated and aims and objectives of economic activity of the people in a Muslim state, and (*f*) a clear view of what is permanent and what is changeable in Islamic religion and Muslim theology. The sterility of their thought structure can become manifest only when they themselves or their like get a chance at governance of a country. Out of their failure may emerge a critique of puritanic or reformed Islam either resulting in a bifurcation of human behaviour into secular or sacred or in a more robust conceptual effort, for evolving a monistic paradigm where God consciousness serves as a limiting concept or a point of reference, and generates a creative process for developing new constructs. In the former case, i.e., the bifurcation of the sacred and secular, the two antipodes will be in continuous strife, the sacred insisting on more and more puritanism and fundamentalism, and the secular on a liberal society and indulgent morality.

7. It seems that the social dynamics in Pakistan will perforce shift the paradigm in such a way that puritanic fundamentalism will be subsumed in a new synthesis. It will be achieved through a deconstruction of theology without secularizing Islamic religion. Islamic intellectualism has a historical tradition of similar nature (rationalist) though it has not been dominant. The overwhelming influence of deductive logic in the development of Muslim law and dogma left little room for alternative theological structures to develop in the past. The politico-social set up, which was oriented towards authoritarian forms of government, was not conducive for critical appraisals of the forms of government. Muslim political theorists and intellectuals were content to enunciate the qualities of good rulers or at the most advise them how to provide for good governance. The idea that the people have a right to depose a bad ruler or elect a new one through public franchise could not find any ground in the political philosophy of Islam. Right of dissent was allowed but with pre-conditions amounting to nullifing rather than encouraging the idea. It is only in the twentieth century and that too under the influence of modern western thought that Islamic political thought has changed its language and has started using the concepts of human rights, freedom, franchise etc. The legitimacy of organized political parties, and the development of a social welfare state are now accepted as normal ideas not antithetical to Islam.

The contemporary western and secular world considers this change in the language of Islam as political Islam and presumes it to be a foe of its own civilization. A thesis even suggests that future clashes would be between civilizations and the immediate contestant in the field against western civilization is Islam.[12] This is a misreading of the cyclic changes that have been occuring in the Islamic world right from the very beginning.[13] Twentieth century influences on Islam have opened up a society which was closed and inward looking for the last millennium. It is but natural that for every step taken for reconstructing Islamic thought there is a backward reaction.

The significance of religious language of contemporary Urban Islam is that it is non-spiritual, non-mythological and mostly secular and ideological. The oft-repeated phrase, popularized by Maududi's writings, firstly in South Asia and later universalized in the Middle East is that 'Islam is not merely a religion but a system of life'. In Pakistan, which is a professed Islamic state, the demand of religious parties is to introduce the economic and political system of Islam, whatever that may be. The implicit contradiction between the nature of religion and that of an ideology has not become apparent, i.e. that religions are *intentional* in their origin whereas ideologies are *propositional* and can be true or false. What is now required of this changed perception of religion is to let it discover its own deficiencies and eventually, without becoming secular it could become, in a sense, 'non religious' religious. The category of religion would then become redundant yet God consciousness may still play a part to put limits to social and individual moral behaviour. So long as Islam as an ideology remains untested, its hold as an infallible truth will not be diminished. It has got to be 'seen' that the 'ideological formulations' of religion as they are at the moment, are not sufficient for bringing about a good change in society, otherwise the need for deconstruction and a *de nouveau* reconstruction would not be felt.

Pakistan, where both Jinnah and Iqbal are venerated and where both of them laid no claim to religious leadership looks like the most apt place for developing a paradigm in which both religious and secular categories are subsumed. However, this understanding has to reach the masses and to do that has to use the vernacular means of communication. At present there is an utter lack of communication between the modern and the traditional, and language is keeping them apart. The religious discourse in Urdu, the national language of Pakistan is overwhelmingly one-sided, whereas those who have access to English are exposed to a broader discourse with a different logic. The ground level change can occur only when people participate in a broad universe of discourse which is not available to them now. Pakistan's prospects lie

in developing this paradigm for the urban literates in their
own vernacular.

NOTES

1. See, Philips, C.S., (Ed.) *The Evolution of India and Pakistan*
   1856-1947, London, 1962, p. 194.
2. Qureishi, I.H., *The Struggle for Pakistan*, Karachi, 1965,
   pp. 134-48.
3. Ahmad, Manzoor, 'Islamic Response to Contemporary Western
   Thought', *Islam in South Asia'*, Ed. Jullundhri, R.A., Lahore,
   19℮5, pp. 1-30.
4. 'Islam has not put any restrictions on property rights of land of
   any kind in respect of quantity or quality of any type. The
   ownership of anything legally and rightfully acquired can be
   retained without any restriction and limitation if all legal rights
   and duties laid by *Shariah* are duly paid. Money, livestock,
   articles of daily use, houses, means of transportation, in short
   there is nothing on which any limit on legal ownership is
   imposed'. Maududi, Syed Abul Ala, *Masala Milkiat-e-Zamin*,
   P.78 1969 (translation).
5. The shock of his death was so great that Hazrat Umar (RA)
   refused to believe that the Prophet (PBUH) was dead and declared
   that 'the apostle will return as Moses returned [from the Mount]
   and will cut off the hands and feet of men who allege that the
   apostle is dead'. It was only when Hazrat Abu Bakr (RA) recited
   the verse, 'Muhammad is nothing but an apostle. Apostles have
   passed away before him. Can it be that if he were to die or be
   killed you would turn back on your heels? He who turns back
   does no harm to God and God will reward the grateful?' (3:136)
   Hazrat Umar (RA) said 'By God, when I heard Hazrat Abu Bakr
   (RA) recite these words I was dumbfounded so that my legs
   would not bear me and I fell to the ground knowing that the
   apostle was indeed dead. See for details Mohammad Ibn Ishaq's
   Sirat Rasul Allah, trans. Guillaume A. OUP 1987.
6. The Prophet's (PBUH) death created a crisis; so much so that his
   succession was settled on the very day he died, even before his
   burial. To avoid in-fights between various tribes, the community
   needed an immediate leader to face any major threat to its
   survival. Very soon new challenges appeared in the form of
   apostasy (*ridda*) campaigns. See Shaban, M.A, *Islamic History
   AD 600-750*, CUP, pp. 16-27.

7. See, Fromm E., *Escape from Freedom*, Avon Books, NY 1965. Erich Fromm analyses the illness of contemporary civilization as witnessed by its willingness to submit to totalitarian rules. The cause is to be found in the minds of all men with often appalling results.

8. Gellner, E., *Post Modernism Reason and Religion*, London, 1992, pp. 11-22.

9. Ahmad Manzoor, 'The Concept of God', *Al-Ma'arif*, Vol. 27, Lahore 1994, pp. 29-83.

10. Kibria, G. 'The Backwardness of Pakistan', *Irtiqa*, Vol. 20, Karachi, 1998, pp. 120-164.

11. Formerly a member of Jamat-i-Islami, now has his own organization called 'Tanzeem Islami'.

12. Huntington, S.P., 'The Clash of Civilizations' *Foreign Affairs*, 1993.

13. There is a widespread belief amongst Muslims that after each hundred years a reformer is born to bring back the purity of religion and near the end of the world will come the final saviour.

PART THREE

IDENTITY MOVEMENTS: RELIGION, ETHNICITY AND GENDER

Sectarianism as a Substitute Identity: Sunnis and Shias in Central and South Punjab

Conflicts over identity are a major source of internal tensions in South Asia. Identities are defined in terms of boundaries, that is in reference to another group, to the 'Other'. The main contradiction of Pakistan—a modern secular state founded on religious sentiments—has not been resolved.[1] Pakistan has never been a nation-state; highly fragmented, it has failed in integrating the people into a nation by making their Pakistani identity their most treasured possession. People had to find other identities whether ethnic group, caste, language, *biradari*[2] or sect. The political vacuum created in the Zia era was filled by the emergence of ethnic and sectarian organizations.[3] In the 1970s, ethnicity became a substitute identity but it was branded as treason and violently suppressed. The environment in the 1980s was religious; religious identity was fostered by the state and official sanction was given to the religious organizations during the Afghan war in the name of Islam.

Sectarianism in Pakistan

Sectarianism which is, in Pakistan, a Deobandi-Shia[4] rather than a Sunni-Shia conflict comes from the belief that the sect which one professes is the only true one and that the followers of other sects should be converted to one's own sect or exterminated. The 'Other', the person who does not share your beliefs and religious observances is seen somehow as a danger to you because, being different, he cannot mean well for you.[5] Sectarianism, which was traditionally mostly confined to verbal attacks and clashes during the month of Moharram, has now degenerated into violence.[6]

More than 1000 serious incidents were recorded between 1987 and 1997, 478 persons were killed and some 2300 were injured.[7] The year 1997 was the worst so far—97 serious incidents were recorded claiming over 200 lives,[8] and 1998, which started with the Mominpura massacre, was another year of sectarian violence.[9] There has been a change in the pattern of violence: till 1995, the killings were confined to leaders and activists of both sects. Targeted attacks on religious gatherings and specific mosques followed, then it was hand-grenade attacks and time devices. In 1996, there were targeted killings of office bearers of organizations and government functionaries. The year 1997 saw a total change with indiscriminate gunfire on ordinary citizens not involved in sectarian activity, and tit-for-tat killings targeting doctors, lawyers and traders.[10]

Sectarian clashes were rare before Partition in the areas which now form Pakistan. Nobody thought in terms of Shia and Sunni at the time of the Pakistan movement.[11] Sectarian consciousness and some prejudice has always existed but has never prevented co-existence. Sectarianism does not exist at the community level even if some intolerance can now be felt: Shias and Sunnis live together in the same neighbour-hoods, they speak the same language and share the same culture. This evokes the narcissism of minor differences described by Freud: the smaller the difference between two peoples, the greater it is bound to loom in their imagination. Why is there a need for a sectarian outlook on life, why has it become much more meaningful for certain people to identify themselves as a Sunni or a Shia and why do people adhere to the principles avowed by sectarian organizations?

The roots of sectarianism

Sectarianism is often seen as the consequence of Ziaul Haq's Islamization policy which meant state monopoly on religion and dominance of a particular sect, and which brought theological differences to the fore.[12] Religion without sectarian domination has little meaning for the common man in Pakistan. The imposition of *zakat* (compulsory tax deducted by the government) in 1980 mobilized the Shia community against Ziaul Haq.[13] External factors are also enhanced: sectarianism is described as the outcome of the Iranian revolution and of the Afghan war and the ensuing influx of funds and arms, and it is often seen as a proxy war between foreign powers financing the mushroom growth of *madrasas* and using Pakistani territory to further their own interests.[14] It cannot be denied that the Iranian revolution gave a new sense of identity to the Shia community which became more assertive and entered the political arena in the 1980s. The development of sectarian Sunni organizations was partly a reaction to this new Shia militancy[15] and religion was seen, by Sunnis and Shias alike, as a means of power after the Iranian revolution. These explanations are obviously relevant but the external environment has perhaps been no more than the enabling factor which gave scale and sustenance to the sectarian phenomenon.[16] The 'foreign hand' and the intelligence agencies are inevitably blamed every time there is a crisis[17] and people are often ready to believe such stories, but this rationale too easily absolves the government and society of all responsibility.

The roots of sectarianism in Central and South Punjab go back to the political polarization of the early seventies. The rapid social and economic change leading to the emergence of new classes (without any change in the system of power which remains under the control of the elite drawn from the landed and the urban upper class) was accompanied by an extremely rapid urbanization without any industrialization. Sectarian militancy in this context can be described as a reaction to a growing sense of insecurity and hopelessness resulting from the uneven distribution of resources, and as a revolt of the uprooted and marginalized periphery deprived of access to the political arena. It is the result of extreme poverty in South Punjab[18] coupled with illiteracy and the population explosion. In a context where the traditional structures are collapsing or dysfunctional, sect has become an identity marker, a temporary refuge and a platform to articulate grievances and get access to power.[19] Sectarianism can thus be described as a phenomenon of collective anger, an emotional outburst against structures of power which must be pressurized or done away with.

The social cost of mechanization and the Green Revolution

South Punjab has been neglected since Partition. This economically deprived region had the lowest education rate according to the 1981 census. Large landholders in Central and South Punjab have managed to retain their power.[20] To escape land reforms, they converted their estates into orchards which were exempted from the limits on holdings. This was accompanied by a marked increase in mechanization which created unemployment and semi-employment, while there was already surplus labour in the Punjab. Mechanization was a substitute for labour and it displaced landless labour: a study based on sixty mechanized farms in the Punjab and Bahawalpur found that permanent labour declined from 2000 to 340 out of which 100 were employed on tractors. Another study revealed that the labour force per acre had been reduced about 50 per cent from the pre-mechanization period.[21] The big landlords have sold vast tracts of land and a new class of middle capitalist landlords has appeared. They did not hesitate to eliminate those who could not compete with them and a large number of smaller landholders were displaced.[22] Land previously cultivated by tenants was resumed, many were transformed into wages' labourers on the feudals' or new middle capitalist landlords' farms, working as tractor drivers or seasonal workers as mechanization had increased the need for casual workers. Many more were forced to migrate to the cities and this traumatic experience changed the social and political outlook of people who had been traditionally tied to the land. While in the *barani* (rain-fed) regions of north-west Punjab, there was a tradition of emigration to towns or employment in the army, such a relation with outside employment does not exist on a significant scale in the Canal Colonies of Sargodha, Multan and Bahawalpur. Allotment of land to military and civil officers at the expense of the locals has also produced a strong feeling of being neglected. Small farmers, owning between 12.5 and 25 acres, could not keep up with the increased competition. They sold their lands and moved to the towns and cities or became small shopkeepers. A comparison of the 1960 and 1972 census figures for the Punjab shows that the category of farmers owning between 7.5 to 25 acres has decreased both in area and numbers.[23] Although the Green Revolution has increased the prosperity of some, it has impoverished many in the rural areas.[24] Due to landlessness and unemployment the peasantry has been proletarianized:[25] 30 per cent of the population is now considered as living under the poverty level compared to 20 per cent ten years back.[26] Most of the people of South Punjab could not afford to pay recruitment agencies to get a job in the Middle East—anyway this safety valve does not exist anymore[27]—and Karachi has become more and more problematic because of the law and order situation. In traditional rural society, everybody was employed and had a place in village society, everyone had something to do and had some social utility. Traditional functions have been eliminated, auxiliary professions (blacksmith, carpenter, etc) are not needed anymore. Farmers have opted for cash crops— mostly cotton in South Punjab—they hardly grow vegetables anymore, and food has to be bought from specialized shops. There has been a realignment of the class structure: due to the traditional sense of superiority among the farming classes, they are reluctant to enter other professions. However, manual labourers have entered different professions and have made profit as entrepreneurs, merchants and intermediaries. Many *kammi*[28] families are now more prosperous than small farmers and their income is more stable. If there had been industrialization, many people would have left the villages to

work in factories thus reversing the trend of land fragmentation.[29]

The market towns are in the hands of Punjabi
immigrants,[30] especially the *mohajirs* from Rohtak, Hisar and
Karnal districts who control most of the trade.[31] For the locals
displaced from their lands, no jobs are available which gives
rise to much bitterness. The region has not been indus-
trialized, as the Seraiki belt concentrates on agriculture. The
South (Rahim Yar Khan) has witnessed the development of
agro-based industries; the traders have invested but certain
landlords have resisted the growth of industry which they
see as a threat to their vested interests.[32] The Pakistan
Peoples Party (PPP) was the main beneficiary of the
discontent,[33] but its image of defender of the downtrodden
suffered a lot after it allied itself with the feudals of the
Multan area. The sense of hopelessness was channelized for
some time into nationalist sentiment (Seraiki identity) which
traditionally appeared every time the locals felt that they
were left out of the power structure. People felt that they
had been colonized economically and also psychologically
which resulted in a deep sense of alienation.

The mushroom growth of *madrasas* in South Punjab

Educational facilities were absent because the landlords did
not allow the establishment of schools[34] and also because it
carried the threat of alienation: educated sons were likely to
leave the village, attracted by a job in town.[35] According to
the survey of 'ghost schools' conducted in 1998 by the army,
there are over 5000 such schools in Multan division and 800
in Sargodha division, the buildings being used by feudals as
dera[36] or cowsheds. This explains why *madrasas* proliferated
in South Punjab. According to an official report published in
1995, out of a total of 2512 registered *madrasas* in Punjab,[37]
1619 were located in South Punjab. Bahawalpur, a very poor
area, had the highest number in the province (883), Dera
Ghazi Khan came next (411) and Multan had 325. It should be
recalled that West Pakistan had only 137 *madrasas* in 1947.

The total number of students at any time is about 214,000 with Bahawalpur division on top. About 100,000 students graduate every year. The number of unregistered *madrasas* is thought to be much higher, according to some sources, Jhang district has over 500 *madrasas*.[38] Not all *madrasas* are sectarian but the sectarian ones have multiplied.[39] In a feudal environment where violence is part of the socio-political culture and is even valued,[40] the sectarian *madrasas* identify with the parties which protect them, preach violence for enforcement of their kind of Islam and the elimination of other sects.[41] The students are taught a wrong concept of *jihad* (holy war): if they kill a member of the other sect, called a *kafir* (infidel), God will reward them because they have protected the true faith.

The sons of these uprooted peasants did not go willingly to the *madrasas*, they were forced by poverty. Parents send their children to the *madrasas* because they have no other alternative to ease their financial burden. Students come from the poorest and far away places. They are lodged, get two meals a day and receive an average of 100 rupees a month. This means less mouths to feed for their parents. *Madrasas* are also the only means of social advancement for these children and the only hope for a career in the future. The parents gain the respect of the local *mullah* for sending their children to these schools, a *hadith*[42] says that the parents of a *hafiz-e Quran*[43] will be blessed with a luminous crown on the Day of Judgement. *Madrasa* students are taught in a language they do not understand—all the books studied in Sunni *madrasas* are in Arabic, a language which many of the *mullahs* hardly know. Physical abuse is the norm, it is considered a good method of ensuring discipline and attaining excellence and the parents agree to it most of the time. Children are chained 'to put the fear of God in their minds' according to a *mullah*. More than 80 per cent of the students in the *madrasas* of Lahore[44] studying the *hifz*[45] and *dars-e nizami*[46] courses do not belong to the city. The *mullahs* say that those with families in the city would find it easier to escape from the *madrasa* so children from Lahore study in other cities. The young students are completely cut off from the outside world; they cannot watch television and newspapers and magazines are prohibited.[47] Their attitude towards secular education is one of contempt. However, they are often conscious of their low status in society so they seek to compensate by serving the cause of religion.[48] According to Eqbal Ahmed: 'The madrasas have provided the religious parties with a potential constituency and a pool of cadres, workers and martyrs.'[49]

For *madrasa* graduates, the surest way of earning a livelihood is to become the *imam* of a *masjid*.[50] The mosques have become business entreprises with adjoining shops which can be rented out. The proliferation of mosques is due to urbanization and to the high number of *madrasa* graduates: Okara had one Sunni mosque in the early fifties, in 1994 there were over 160 Sunni Barelvi[51] mosques and dozens of other Sunni mosques and Shia *imambargahs*.[52] Investing in a mosque is a tremendous source of social prestige, more than half of them are built on public or disputed land. Mosques are no more open houses where everyone can come and pray, there is a system of sectarian apartheid and the names of the mosques often indicate their affiliation clearly. Sectarian interpretations of Islam have replaced traditional perceptions and the mosques have been taken over by extremists who are outsiders, the local community being marginalized.

Some *madrasa* graduates become teachers of Arabic and Islamic Studies. Ziaul Haq had compelled the University Grants Commission in 1980 to recognize the *Wifaqs*[53] and treat their degrees as equivalent to M.A Arabic/Islamiyat. Only Peshawar University accorded recognition to these degrees and the practice virtually stopped after Zia's death. But most of the graduates remain unemployed and feel bitter. Held in contempt by the westernized elite, they burn with rage against it. Without any connections and no links to their own village, they feel a deep sense of alienation in a society where they have lost their way.

Sectarianism as the outcome of poverty and unemployment

Not all sectarian extremists have a *madrasa* background, many are drop-outs of the Urdu medium system of education, half educated, and with no qualifications and no connections to get a government job.[54] Full of anger and frustration with the corrupt system, they are ready to join a sectarian organization which will give them a sense of belonging and power.[55] They will have access to arms in a society where the display of arms and their utilization to intimidate one's rival is a widely accepted practice.

They are misfits in society because they have no skills and no relevance to the job market. They cannot go back to their families who are too poor to support them so they find themselves rootless, with no place in traditional society. Frustrated and bitter, they do not believe in politics and elections, they cannot identify with the corrupt elite which has failed to deliver, and place no trust in the traditional religious parties, too ready to compromise. They are looking for a messiah, a charismatic leader who blames everything on another group and exhorts them to exterminate it.[56]

In South Punjab, where the Sunni-Shia divide was previously blurred by the *pir*[57] factor and where 80 per cent of the population was Barelvi, the puritanical brand of Islam was not favoured before the proliferation of *madrasas* and the proselytism of the Tablighi Jamaat which promotes a certain kind of sectarianism. The young *madrasa* graduates and those who had been 'converted' by the Tablighis became staunch Deobandis and harboured strong anti-Shia feelings. It is then not surprising that the Sipah-e Sahaba (SSP, Army of the companions of the Prophet), a sectarian party which appeared as an offshoot of the Jamiat-i-Ulema-i-Islam (JUI) and defined itself as the defender of the downtrodden—and later the terrorist movement Lashkar-e Jhangvi—were born in Jhang where Shia landowners have traditionally held power.[58] Religion has become a tool and a social demarcation rather than a faith, the members of the other sect are viewed as rivals and as a threat to the material status of one's community.[59] Sectarianism has been used as an umbrella for the struggle of the emerging classes against more entrenched interests and the beginning of a challenge to feudalism.[60] The new middle class—Sunni immigrants from East Punjab with a strong sectarian tradition[61] controlling 80 per cent of the trade and business of the cities—,[62] who were in competition with the traditional elite,[63] were compelled in the ideological environment of the 1980s to use anti-Shia rhetoric and they found allies in the ideologically motivated *madrasa* graduates. Most people joined the SSP for political interests because it was the only party which provided a political platform against the powerful feudal families and which could give them access to the political arena. Sectarian politics thus became a surrogate for political empowerment and material gains.[64]

Religious violence as a means of empowerment

Jhang was the first city to fall prey to sectarian violence in the mid-eighties,[65] it then spread to the poor parts of the region, notably Leiah and Muzaffargarh[66] then to Bahawalpur and Bahawalnagar where the percentage of Shias is minimal and where there was no separate *imambargah* till 1970.[67] It all started when Maulana Haq Nawaz Jhangvi, the provincial *amir* of the Jamiat-i-Ulema-i-Islam (JUI)—who founded the SSP in 1985—hailing from a poor rural background and being an ordinary *maulvi* of a local mosque,[68] gained prominence when he persuaded poor Sunnis to send their young sons to his *madrasa* to be educated free of cost.

The presence of a large number of *mohajirs** in the small towns became a catalyst for violence. This new under-class of small traders finances the SSP while physically staying out of the conflict.[69] While Shia militants belonging to the Imamia Students' Organization (ISO) or to Sipah-e Mohammad (SMP) are locals, mostly middle class, and financed by the landlords,[70] Sunni militants belong to the lower and lower

---

* Although most East Punjabi immigrants do not call themselves Muhajirs, the 'locals' refer to them as such. There is a very strong divide in South Punjab between the Seraiki-speaking locals and the Muhajirs—both Urdu and Punjabi-speaking. This divide together with the caste factor plays a central part in the sectarian conflict, and should not be underestimated.

middle classes. Many of them, Sunnis and Shias, are unemployed or do not have a steady job. But Sunnis are convinced that they are discriminated against and that the government supports the Shias.[71] Maulana Ziaul Qasmi, Chairman of the Supreme Council of SSP, said recently: 'The government gives too much importance to the Shias. They are everywhere, on television, on radio, in newspapers and in senior positions. This causes heart-burn. The jobless Sunni youths find all doors closed, they have no option but to join extremist groups.'[72]

The traditional religious parties have no control over the sectarian organizations and anarchy prevails. The rivalry has degenerated into a chain reaction of vengeance and tit-for-tat killings in a society where revenge is viewed by most as a natural sentiment linked to ones identity and ones honour.[73] Determined gunmen, who are trained in the same camps as the Harkat ul Ansar[74] militants who fought in Kashmir or in Afghanistan and have firearms at their disposal, have taken the lead. They are often recruited as bodyguards for the leaders or 'muscle men' for political rallies.[75] A gun gives them a sense of power, violence is a thrill and when they have tasted blood, they are transformed overnight. They resort to robberies to finance their activities[76] and rely on the network of *madrasas* to hide. Highly motivated and committed to a cause, most of them do not kill for money although they need it when they are on the run. They feel that the religious parties have failed to defend their faith and they are disillusioned. Bitter and indignant at the hypocrisy and injustice found in society, they have become desperate. They have seen that the religious parties are corrupt, that they compromise and think only of making money. They are willing to kill and to die. They believe that they are waging a *jihad* to cleanse the *ummah* (Muslim community) of impurities from within, certain that they will go straight to Paradise, that martyrdom is at their doorstep, and that they do not have to travel far to fight an alien enemy.[77] *Jihad* has come to be identified with the cult of violence. They are persuaded that they have a religious mission and that violence is legitimate to accomplish that mission. They are sure that they are defending their faith in

a war which has been imposed on them and that it is
permitted by the *Sharia*. They want to take the message of
Islam all over the world. When asked why his group targeted
specifically doctors, lawyers and traders, a militant said: 'It
is useless to kill the *malangs*.[78] We kill people who pollute
their minds.'[79] They want to spread terror and for that
purpose killing community leaders is very effective. They
have no material or social stakes, no hope. They are
ideologically opposed to the state. Unable to fit into society,
they try to create a society where they will be useful. They
have in some cases succeeded in creating territories
independant of state control, 'no-go areas' such as Niaz Beg
in Lahore.[80] They want to avenge alleged wrongs and settle a
succession controversy which took place 1400 years ago.

The culture of sectarian violence

Maulana Ajmal Qadri from the Jamiat-i-Ulema-i-Islam (JUI)
said recently: 'Sectarian violence has become a culture and it
is here to stay'.[81] Students and staff of educational
institutions supported by religious leaders have started
exploiting sectarian differences to extort concessions from
teachers and the administration. Blackmailing by students'
organizations who exploit sectarian differences to get their
own ends is becoming commonplace, as illustrated by a recent
case in Multan.[82] The government is backing off; it fears the
street power of the religious organizations and does not want
to disavow those who fight in Kashmir. More than 120
sectarian cases are pending in the courts and very few have
been adjudicated, while judges and policemen are under
threat.[83] Society seems to have learned to cope with the
sectarian violence, it does not resist either physically or
intellectually, there is no rational interpretation of Islam as
a counterweight. Political parties believing in secularism are
on the defensive and have sometimes entered into alliances
with the sectarian organizations.[84]

Conclusion

There are still some reasons to be optimistic: society does not approve, sectarian organizations have only a marginal appeal and no roots in the population. They have not succeeded in radicalizing the population on sectarian lines. The Sunni-Shia conflict has never assumed the proportion of Hindu-Muslim riots in India, and sectarian hatred has not penetrated to the grassroots level of Pakistani society.[85] People do not blame the other sect when sectarian motivated killings are perpetrated, they turn their anger towards the state: no Sunni home or shop was attacked after the Mominpura massacre in Lahore but the crowds burned the district commissioners office and the district court. The limits of sectarian movements might have been reached as they have no permanent source of financial support and they cannot last without foreign funding as the decline of SMP shows. The idea of Islam as a religion which will provide social justice and punish criminals is what appeals to the population. The solution lies in creating a new culture through an education which emphasizes nationhood, teaches tolerance and restores Islam to what it truly is and what it was when it first came to the subcontinent: a message of love and peace as propagated by the sufis.

NOTES

1. Shehzad Amjad. 'Nation, State and Terrorism. Sectarian War vs Operation Cleanup.' *The News* on Sunday. May 11, 1997. Most of the references in this paper are taken from the press as few scholars have so far done academic research in the field of sectarianism in Pakistan.
2. Patrilineal descent group which is also, at least ideally, the main unit of endogamy. This notion, which has a 'sliding semantic structure' is sometimes used to denote caste (*zat* or *qaum*) (see Hamza Alavi. 'Kinship in West Punjab Villages' in *Contributions to Indian Sociology*, New Series, 6 (1972), pp. 1-27).
3. Mumtaz Ahmad. 'Revivalism, Islamization, Sectarianism, and Violence in Pakistan.' in Craig Baxter and Charles Kennedy

(eds) *Pakistan 1997*. Westview Press, Boulder, 1997. pp. 101-123.

4. Till 1998, the conflict was between Deobandis and Twelver Shias (no Bohra or Ismaili was ever targeted), and it was often analysed as a proxy war between Saudi Arabia and Iran on Pakistani soil. An Ismaili scholar was assassinated in Karachi in September 1998 and the Urdu daily *Khabrain* published in December 1998 a statement attributed to the Sipah-e Sahaba Karachi which claimed that an Aga Khani state was being created in Gilgit and that Muslims would not tolerate it.

5. *Dawn*, January 23, 1998.

6. Khaled Ahmed. 'The Sunni-Shia conflict in Pakistan.' *The Friday Times*, January 30-February 5, 1997.

7. *The Nation*, May 26, 1997.

8. Azmat Abbas. 'Punjab's worst year of sectarian violence.' *Dawn*, January 1, 1998. *The News*, January 3, 1998. Gul Rukh Rahman. 'Sectarian violence: where will it all end?' *The News*, January 19, 1998.

9. Zaigham Khan. 'The tragedy of Mominpura.' *The Herald*, February 1998. According to *Dawn* (December 26, 1998) 78 people were killed and over 80 injured in 36 incidents of sectarian violence in 1998 in the Punjab province alone.

10. Awais Ibrahim. 'Hostage to terrorism.' *The Nation*. January 18, 1998.

11. *S. H. Rahman*. 'Sectarianism must be fought.' *The Frontier Post*. January 23, 1998.

12. Mumtaz Ahmad. 'Sectarianism and Zia.' *The News*. April 15, 1998. 'Revivalism, Islamization,' op.cit. (3).

13. Afak Haydar, 'The Politicization of the Shias and the Development of the Tehrik-e-Nifaz-e-Fiqh-e-Jafaria in Pakistan.' in Charles H. Kennedy (ed) *Pakistan 1992*. Westview Press, Boulder, 1993. Saleem Qureshi, 'The Politics of the Shia Minority in Pakistan: Context and Developments.' in D. Vajpeyi and Y. K. Malik (eds) *Religious and Ethnic Minority Politics in South Asia*. Manohar, Delhi, 1989. Munir Ahmed, 'The Shi'is of Pakistan.' in M. Kramer (ed) *Shi'ism, Resistance and Revolution*. Westview Press, Boulder. 1987.

14. Mohamed Hanif. 'The Anatomy of Sects Appeal.' *Newsline*. August 1990.

15. Sunni militant organizations received huge funding from Saudi Arabia and Iraq in the early 1980s to counter Shia militancy.

16. I am thankful to Nasim Zehra for this suggestion.

17. The Sunni-Shia conflict is sometimes depicted as 'the fourth India-Pakistan war'.

18. Mohammad Rauf Klasra. 'Poverty fanning sectarian tensions in S. Punjab.' *Dawn*, September 26, 1996.

19. Sharif al Mujahid. 'Sectarian strife. The economic dimension.' *The News*, June 5, 1997.

20. From 1880, through an extensive irrigation programme, the British government converted vast tracts of wasteland in the Punjab and Sindh into rich agricultural land known as 'canal colonies'. The large landholders of Central and South Punjab were the main recipients of land in recognition of their services to the British Raj. See Imran Ali. *The Punjab under Imperialism 1885-1947*. Princeton, 1988 and Imran Ali. 'The Punjab and the Retardation of Nationalism' in D. A. Low (ed) *The Political Inheritance of Pakistan,* Macmillan, 1991, pp. 29-52.

21. Swadesh R. Bose and Edwin H. Clark II. 'Some Basic Considerations on Agricultural Mechanization in West Pakistan.' *The Pakistan Development Review,* 1969.

22. Shahid Javed Burki. 'The Development of Pakistan's Agriculture: An Interdisciplinary Explanation.' in R. D. Stevens, H. Alavi and P. J. Bertocci (eds) *Rural Development in Bangladesh and Pakistan.* University of Hawaii, Honolulu, 1976. pp. 290-315. Shahid Javed Burki. 'Development of towns: The Pakistan experience.' *Asian Survey*, vol 14 n¡ 8, 1974.

23. Moazam Mahmood. 'Change in Land Distribution in the Punjab.' *The Pakistan Development Review*, 28: 4 Part II 1989.

24. Hamza Alavi. 'The Rural Elite and Agricultural Development in Pakistan.' in *Rural Development*, op. cit. pp. 317-387.

25. *Poverty fanning*, op. cit (18).

26. Mahbub ul Haq and Khadija Haq. *Human Development in South Asia, 1998*. Oxford University Press, 1998.

27. The Gulf States expelled thousands of illegal South Asian workers in 1996 and 1997 and Saudi Arabia, faced with a financial crisis and rising unemployment among its nationals, has embarked on a 'saudization' policy both in the public and private sectors.

28. Members of the lowest castes assigned menial works in rural Punjab where the main divide is between *zamindar* (landowning castes) and *kammi*.

29. Kaiser Bengali. *Why unemployment ?* Pakistan Publishing House, 1991. Syed Javed Burki. *Migration, Urbanization and Politics in Pakistan*. in W. Howard Wriggings and James F. Guyot (eds) *Population, Politics and the Future of Southern Asia*. Columbia University Press, 1973.

30. The Punjab accommodated 5.3 million refugees which accounted for 25.6 per cent of its population in 1951. They influenced the

local population and enhanced consciousness about Islam. See Mohammad Waseem. 'Partition, Migration and Assimilation: A Comparative Study of Pakistani Punjab.' *International Journal of Punjab Studies 4*, 1 (1997) Sage Publications.

31. At the time of Partition, the areas which form Pakistan had a low level of urbanization and middle class occupations were largely dominated by Hindus and Sikhs (about 75 per cent of urban immovable property in the Pakistan areas belonged to Hindus before Partition). Immigrants from East Punjab constituted more that half the population of major cities in 1951. Sargodha had 67.9 per cent refugees, Jhang 37.9 per cent, Sahiwal 40 per cent, Lyalpur (Faisalabad) 70.4 per cent, Multan 43.7 per cent. Asad Sayeed. 'Growth and Mobilisation of the Middle Classes in West Punjab: 1960-1970.' in P. Singh and S. S. Thandi (eds) *Globalisation and the Region*: *Explorations in Punjabi Identity*. The Association for Punjab Studies, Coventry, 1996. pp. 259-286.

32. Ameneh Azam Ali, Zahid Hussain and Talat Aslam. 'Punjab: The Silent Majority?' *The Herald*, May 1987.

33. The land reforms and their consequences for the rural population explain partly why the PPP had such a large vote bank in rural Punjab in 1970.

34. *Dawn*, September 26, 1996.

35. *The Rural Elite*, op. cit. (24).

36. Extended residential site of a landlord.

37. *The Frontier Post*, August 3, 1997. Ahmad Bashir. 'Sectarian violence will grow.' *The Frontier Post*, January 15, 1998.

38. Jhang city, which had 3 madrasas in 1947, had 47 in 1998.

39. Nasir Jamal. 'Religious schools: who controls what they teach.' *Dawn*, October 28, 1996. '746 Punjab madrasas involved in sectarian activities.' *The News*, March 7, 1995.

40. Iqbal Ahmed. 'Roots of violence in Pakistan.' II. 'Feudal culture and violence.' *Dawn*, February 2, 1998.

41. Shahid Ibrahim. 'Pakistan's Achille's heel—sectarian terrorism.' *The Pakistan Times*, April 8, 1998.

42. A saying of the Prophet Muhammad (PBUH).

43. Someone who has learnt the Quran by heart and is thus entitled to add Hafiz to his name.

44. 649 *madrasas* were functioning in Lahore in 1998. *Pakistan's Achille's Heel*, op. cit. (41).

45. Memorization of the Quran by heart. It is the first level of *madrasa* education and usually lasts three to four years.

46. Traditional curriculum of religious schools introduced in the middle 18th century in India by Maulana Nizamuddin.

47. Imrana Khawaja. 'The making of an Islamic militant.' *The Friday Times*, January 12-18, 1995. See also the annual reports of the Human Rights Commission of Pakistan (HRCP).

48. See Mark Juergensmeyer. 'The logic of religious violence: The case of the Punjab.' *Contributions to Indian sociology* 22, 1 (1988) on the empowering of marginal groups through the use of violence.

49. Talat Aslam. 'The Madrasah Factor.' *The Herald*, September 1992.

50. Ahson Saeed Hasan. 'Sectarianism: roots and possible solutions.' *The News*, February 11, 1998.

51. Barelvis are the followers of Ahmad Raza Khan (d. 1921) a native of Bareilly who led a reaction against the import of Wahabism into Indian Islam. Barelvis believe in the special powers of *pirs* (spiritual guides) and they worship the graves of saints. They believe that the Prophet Muhammad (PBUH) has unique knowlege of the unknown and is composed of God's light and they hold major celebrations for his birthday (*Milad un Nabi*).

52. Mohamed Hanif. 'In the Name of Religion.' *Newsline*, September 1994.

53. Umbrella organization of religious schools.

54. 'A white collar job at a desk in an important office with some elements of power and patronage is the only goal of the majority of young [urban] persons.' Government of Pakistan. Report of the National Manpower Commission, 1989. Islamabad, Ministry of Labour and Manpower and Overseas Pakistanis. p. 82.

55. Aamer Ahmed Khan. 'Blind Faith.' *The Herald*, June 1994.

56. Tariq Rahman. 'The making of a Mominpura.' *The News*, February 18, 1998.

57. Spiritual guide.

58. Hasan Mujtaba and Mazhar Zaidi. 'A Tale of Two Cities.' *Newsline*, September 1994.

59. Ayesha Jalal (talking about Partition). *The News*, May 25, 1998.

60. Talat Aslam. 'The New Sectarianism.' *The Herald*, August 1991. 'The Lady and the Maulana.' *The Herald*. Election Special 88. 'The Jang in Jhang.' *The Herald*. Election Special 90.

61. For example, a poster widely circulated in Karnal District during the campaign for the 1937 election quoted *fatwas* from leading *ulema* suggesting that a vote for a Shia candidate was a vote for a *kafir* and that Sunnis should not sit with Shias or assist them, they should not follow their funerals nor bury them

in their graveyards. (See David Gilmartin. 'Divine Displeasure' and Muslim Elections: The Shaping of Community in Twentieth-Century Punjab.' in *The Political Inheritance of Pakistan*. op. cit. (20). pp. 106-130.) Such *fatwas* are often quoted in SSP literature.

62. The lower class in the urban areas is also mainly Sunni.

63. About 65 per cent of the land in Jhang belongs to the Shias (*Newsline*. September 1994).

64. *Revivalism, Islamization*, op. cit. (3).

65. Abdus Sattar Qamar. 'Jhang: High Tension?' *The Herald*, August 1990. Abdus Sattar Qamar. 'Sects and Violence.' *The Herald*, August 1990. Sohail Akbar Warraich. 'Jhang: A City Divided.' *The Herald*, February 1991.

66. Khalid Hussain. 'The Jehad Within.' *Newsline*, August 1990. Sharif al Mujahid. 'The rise of sectarianism.' *Dawn*, May 3, 1997.

67. Adnan Adil. 'Sectarian violence threatens Bahawalnagar and Bahawalpur.' *The Friday Times*, November 21-27, 1996.

68. Muhammad Qasim Zaman. 'Sectarianism in Pakistan: The Radicalization of Shi'i and Sunni Identities.' *Modern Asian Studies* 32, 3 (1998) pp. 689-716.

69. Ibid.

70. Adnan Adil. 'Who will untie the sectarian knot?' *The Friday Times*, July 28-August 3, 1994. Adnan Adil. 'Among the believers.' *The Friday Times*, March 2-8, 1995.

71. Monthly *Al Haq*. vol. 14, n¡3. December 1978, pp. 26-27. 'The Shias are also controlling the key positions in the (civil and military) services and are in majority (in these services). This is despite the fact that they are hardly two percent of the total population of Pakistan [...] We must also remember that the Shias consider it their religious duty to harm and eliminate the Ahl-e Sunna.' (Quoted in *Sectarianism in Pakistan* [op. cit. 68]). Such statements are commonplace in the publications of sectarian Sunni parties.

72. *The News*, January 14, 1998.

73. *Roots of violence*, op. cit (27).

74. An extremist anti-Shia movement created in the early 1990s in Central Punjab for the accession of Kashmir to Pakistan.

75. *Revivalism, Islamization*, op. cit (3).

76. Aamer Ahmed Khan. 'The Rise of Sectarian mafias.' *The Herald*, June 1994.

77. 'Unemployed youths are recruited by the sectarian parties in the far flung villages in the name of jihad and with the promise

of lucrative financial reward.' Asma Jahangir. *The News*, February 8, 1998.

78. Meaning here the ordinary people.
79. Personal communication, Lahore, May 1998.
80. Adnan Adil. 'Siege of Niaz Beg.' *The Friday Times*, July 21-27, 1994. Adnan Adil. 'Intra-SMP battle leads to peace at Niaz Beg.' *The Friday Times*, November 28-December 4, 1996.
81. Azmat Abbas. 'Who controls terrorist organizations?' *Dawn*, February 3, 1998.
82. Rauf Klasra. 'Exploiting sectarian differences to get concessions.' *Dawn*, January 27, 1998.
83. Rauf Klasra. 'Reasons for court's failure to decide sectarian cases.' *Dawn*, January 19, 1998. Judge Nayyar Iqbal Ghauri who awarded death sentences to 14 culprits—Sunnis—involved in the Iranian Cultural Centre case and to 8 culprits—Shias—involved in the Masjid ul Khair (Multan) case has reportedly decided to stay permanently in the USA as he was terrified for his life since he declared the judgment on December 16, 1998 (*Dawn*, January 15, 1999).
84. The PPP entered into an alliance with the SSP in 1995. Two SSP leaders became provincial ministers in the Punjab government and since Maulana Azam Tariq, leader of the SSP and member of the National Assembly from Jhang, was an enemy of Syeda Abida Hussain, a Shia leader despised by Benazir Bhutto, he enjoyed complete immunity during the Bhutto government (*Revivalism, Islamization*, op. cit. (3)).
85. *Revivalism, Islamization*, op. cit. (3).

Nationalism, Ethnicity, and the Mohajir Political Movement in Sindh[1]

The deduction that the transformation from anti-ethnic to pro-ethnic thinking among the Urdu-speaking migrant population of Sindh, who call themselves *mohajirs*,[2] signifies the ill success of the original aim of Pakistan to be a separate 'homeland for the subcontinent's Muslims',[3] and merits a reference to the contexts within which the logic of the two processes is situated. It also merits a reference to the multiple dimensions of the *mohajir* identity, and to the circumstances of its emergence and sustenance for the past fifteen years.

Fifty years after the creation of Pakistan, an analysis of the *mohajir* political movement in urban Sindh permits a recollection of the social dynamics of the indices that impelled Partition; the nature of the state structure that came to power, given the socio-economic character of the areas inherited by Pakistan, and the strategies pursued by the state in keeping with defined priorities; and the half-a-century history of centre-province relations. The *mohajir* case is examined both for its specific features, i.e., the particularities of the *mohajir* identity and those of the political party that represents them, as well as for the analogy that can be drawn between the case and the conditions that have favoured the activation of boundaries, relative to present needs, that have been reinforced around the historically based identity criteria of the populations of the other provinces of Pakistan as well.

This draws attention to the circumstances that countenanced the legitimization of the claim of the Muslims of India to be a separate 'nation' as opposed to the Hindus. Whereas the changing pre-Partition political context highlighted only the cutting edge of differences that subsumed all others, the national context redirects attention, as in the case of India, to the distinctions that have defined the historical pattern of social existence in the sub-continent. The emergence of the *mohajir* identity as a separate category in Sindh, therefore, throws into relief the conditions that have favoured a polarization of class and inter-provincial relations in Pakistan on the one hand; and the state and society on the other. The *mohajir* ethnic identity as such, is juxtaposed against the maladies of that horizontal and vertical polarization, and the rationale of its sustenance is related, in large part, to the escalating process of diverse centrifugal forces.

The Population Composition of Sindh

The *mohajir* political movement surfaced in 1984. Urban Sindh, particularly Karachi, the largest metropolitan city of Pakistan,[4] has since been ravaged by street violence and bloodshed. The intensity of the conflict manifested in Sindh, and the perpetuated jeopardy of public peace has commonly been defined in terms of the confrontation between the rural and urban populations of the province, particularly the Sindhis (concentrated in the interior), and the *mohajirs* who came primarily from the United and Central Provinces of India during the decade following Independence and Partition of the subcontinent in 1947, and the bulk of whom settled in the port city of Karachi, and the towns of Hyderabad, Sukkur, and Nawabshah.

Urban Sindh, however, is not inhabited by the *mohajirs* alone. Also the Urdu-speaking *mohajirs* were not the only ones to migrate to Sindh after Partition. Although the *mohajirs* constituted the large majority (20 per cent) of the migrants from India after partition,[5] members of primarily the Gujrati-speaking business community from Western

India, albeit relatively much less in number, also migrated to Sindh in search of opportunities. As of the 1960s, in-migrants from the Frontier and Punjab provinces, and to a lesser degree Balochistan and Kashmir were also drawn to Karachi, which developed as the industrial capital. Illegal immigrants (mainly from Bangladesh, Burma, Sri Lanka, and to a lesser degree Thailand and the Philippines) arrived in Karachi in the 1970s, in search of employment. Refugees from Afghanistan were added to Karachi's population in the 1980s in the wake of the Afghan war with the former Soviet Union.[6] The population of the city is said to continue increasing by an average of 250,000 persons annually.[7]

The population, collectively known as 'Sindhi' to outsiders, is also not ethnically homogeneous. On the eve of partition, moreover, native Sindhis were in bare majority in the province. About 25 per cent of the population that had 'migrated from the Punjab',[8] and that emigrated to India after partition, was Hindu. Thirty per cent of the Muslim population of Sindh had also originated outside its borders.[9] The main groups among the latter were the *Syeds* and the Baloch. The *Syeds*, and the powerful *Pir*[10] families among them, notes Talbot, had settled in Sindh in the twelfth and thirteenth centuries after fleeing their homes in Central Asia in the wake of the Mongol invasions. The Baloch totaled 23 per cent of the Muslim population of the province. Among them were not only the pastoral nomads who had historically frequented the fertile Indus Valley with their livestock, but also the Baloch who had been encouraged to settle in Sindh towards the close of the Mughal period in appreciation of their martial qualities. The chief of the Talpur tribe had seized power from the Sindhi Kalhora rulers at the end of the eighteenth century. Hence, it was the *Mirs* of the Baloch tribes who ruled Sindh before it was annexed by the British in 1843.[11]

Among the non-Sindhi origin of the Muslim populations of the province represented in smaller numbers were: the Memons, Khojas, and Bohras on the one hand; and the Punjabis on the other. The Punjabis had settled in Sindh after the completion of the British irrigation projects and the construction of the Jamrao Canals in 1900 and the Sukkur

Barrage Canals in 1932.[12] Despite native Sindhis having a thin majority in Sindh before Partition, the fact that more than half the total population of the province reported Sindhi as their native tongue[13] reveals the degree to which the populations of external origin had associated with the region. At the time of partition, however, of the 70 per cent of the migrants to the Punjab and the Bahawalpur state,[14] Sindh was asked to accommodate a large number with a rural background of immigrants. This entailed a secondary southward descent from the Punjab, twice as many as Sindh had been willing to accept.[15]

In so far as ethnicity, in the modern context, constitutes a 'reactive political activity' promoted by competition over access to limited resources,[16] the Sindhis and the *mohajirs* who are identified as the main contenders, are not in as dramatic a conflict with each other as can be explained by the scale of the violence that has been unleashed, particularly in Karachi. The economic niches exploited by the two continue, by and large, to be as various as they were at the time of Partition. The absence of any marked pre-Partition urban-rural divide, and the independent post-Partition development of urban Sindh, moreover, has left largely unaltered the primarily agricultural and feudal character of what in contrast became rural Sindh, where the Sindhis are concentrated. The *mohajirs*, who for the most part came from the cities of Northern India, continue to be urban-based.

In order to understand the nature of the conflict, and the anatomy of violence rampant in urban Sindh, we may draw a comparison of the population ecology of present Sindh with the socio-economic conditions of the province before Partition, and attempt to interpret the transformations since, within the regional and national contexts.

Transformations in the Wake of Partition

Pre-Partition Sindh was sparsely populated, and communication between the distant villages was poor.[17] With the exception of the small business community that dominated trade and commerce,[18] and the middle-class professionals,[19] the bulk of the population was horizontally divided into the *waderos* (the large landowners); the *zamindars* (the mid-level landowners); and the cultivators, collectively known as the *haris*. The *waderos* and *zamindars* belonged not only to indigenous stock, but also included the historically dominant *Syeds* and Baloch. The *haris*, mostly from the Rajput, Jat, Sammat, and Soomro tribes, were almost exclusively comprised of the original population of the province.[20]

Since the western border of the province (the Kirthar Range) was bound by hills, and its eastern belt constituted part of the Thar Desert, cultivation was largely limited to the banks of the Indus. Although wheat and cotton had been introduced, notes Talbot,[21] productivity suffered on account of the unfavourable ecological, and inadequate technological conditions, and also because of the absence of motivation among the *haris* to increase production due to the despotic hold of the landholders (particularly the *waderos)* over them. The ruthless and exploitative behaviour of the former was emulated by the *zamindars* who depended on the *waderos* for local social support. In contrast, the Punjabis (invariably army personnel) had been granted land in the alluvial tracts of Sindh (in keeping with the British practice of cultivating the goodwill of the army by granting them revenue-free land). As compared to the Sindhis, the Punjabi cultivators were prosperous, and also independent of the influence of the local landholders. As such they invoked the jealousy of the socially subordinate native *hari* population.[22]

The two-way movement of populations across the border of the new states of Pakistan and India dramatically altered the ethnic landscape and character of the province. According to the figures compiled by the Pakistan-Sindh Joint Refugee Council,[23] 'more than 700,000 Muslim refugees had entered Sindh by the end of May [1948] with nearly three-quarters of the newcomers settling in Karachi, the majority of the rest in the larger cities, and only about 60,000 on land'. Although the migrants to Sindh constituted only 20 per cent of the refugees from India, 'in 1947', note Rashid and Shaheed, '95 per cent of the population was Sindhi. By 1951, according to the population census, 50 per cent of the urban population in Sindh was made up of those whose mother tongue was Urdu.

This proportion reached 80 per cent in Karachi, and 66 per cent in Hyderabad'.[24] Unlike refugees to the Punjab, who had migrated almost simultaneously with Partition, refugees from Northern India, moreover, continued to pour into urban Sindh, particularly Karachi, for eight years after Partition.[25] Individual migrations (to join relatives settled on this side of the border) furthermore, continued beyond the second decade despite border restrictions.

The arrival of the refugees in Sindh (the absence of relative violence in the province notwithstanding)[26] entailed the departure of the 25 per cent Hindu community from the province.[27] Among the latter, as noted by Khuhro, the *Banias* (who had moved to Karachi after the decline of Shikarpur as a trading and financial centre following the British conquest) had managed the commercial enterprises of the province. The *Amils* (or agents of first the Kalhora and Talpur rulers, and then as 'native officers' at the British commissioners' office) were concentrated around the capital Hyderabad. They also owned the press[28] and were constituted of middle-class professionals for whom acquisition of English had been essential to serve as 'go-betweens' of the British and the local authorities. Hence, they had contributed in the field of education as well.[29] The replacement of the Hindu community by the Urdu-speaking migrants from Northern India (whose migration obtained foremost from their role in the creation of Pakistan); and (primarily) the Gujrati-speaking entrepreneurs from Western India, two-thirds of whom settled in the urban areas[30] was inherently different in nature and context to the pre-Partition migrations to Sindh.

This was the first time that migrants to Sindh settled in the province within the context of a nation state. For the first time also, the political outlook and self-image of the new settlers differed dramatically from that of the indigenous population. For the Urdu-speaking refugees from Northern India, Pakistan represented the 'Promised Land'. Since the Muslims of the minority provinces had played the pioneering role in the Pakistan Movement, the migrants from these provinces also expected to play a prominent role in the politics and economy of the country they saw themselves as having struggled to create. The entrepreneur class of refugees from

Western India sought to explore the business potential of their new homeland, particularly the port town of Karachi which also boasted land and air channel facilities.

In contrast to the rural populations of Sindh, the migrants from India, moreover, represented 'an advanced urban capitalist culture'.[31] The social and cultural distinction of the new arrivals from the not-so-productive rural feudal order in Sindh differentiated the latter notably from the existing population of the province. In the early years after Partition, however, Sindh circumscribed groups distinguished by virtue of indigenous or migrant status. Both categories were cut across by smaller identities defined by language, area of origin, and period of settlement on the one hand; and yet smaller identities of tribe and lineage on the other. These categories were a means of social identification in a transformed context. Despite nascent tensions with the populations of rural Sindh, or inevitable complaints against the rehabilitation measures of the central government, during the decade following Independence, the distinctions between the rural and urban populations of the province had no political role.[32]

The repercussions of the indices that increasingly privileged the Punjab over the other provinces in the decades to come, however, began to bear on the relations between the centre and the provinces in Pakistan. Guerrilla warfare began in Balochistan soon after Independence. The year 1971 saw an armed conflict between Baloch tribal groups and the army. The most decisive outcome of hostilities becoming overtly manifest led first to the nationalist movement in East Pakistan, and (following India's military offensive) the eventual creation of Bangladesh in 1971. Fifteen years down the road, the somewhat complex nature of the violence in Sindh is interpreted primarily in terms of the confrontation between the Sindhis and the *mohajirs*.

A reference to policies that fostered a distortion of the relationship between the centre and the provinces may enable the conflict in Sindh to be partially understood within the context of inter-provincial disparities, and the tensions generated by the non-representation of the provinces in the authority structure of the state.

Centre-Province Relations

Pakistan, notes Jalal (in her exploration of the international dimension), began its independent existence without a 'central state apparatus' (the British unitary central apparatus being inherited by India).[33] In constructing a state structure in the newly independent state, she postulates, the early leadership of the country was guided by two principal concerns: conditions that could guarantee the sovereignty of the state (given its strategic location,[34] and the priority of defence against India); and their perceived role of Pakistan in the international political system. Both these considerations were seen to favour the creation of a strong centre, and rationalized the pursuit of a political economy of defence.[35]

Since Muslim League officials, in their bid to obtain quick results,[36] had relied on 'the ready-made networks of the elite representatives of the majority provinces, rather than going through the slow and painful process of building up party support', unlike the minority provinces, the organization of the Muslim League in the majority provinces was weak.[37] Given, moreover, the restriction of the support base of the elite representatives to the confines of their provinces, the accession of the civil and military bureaucracies to a position of dominance in the state structure was favoured by 'their relative autonomy from the internal class structure'.[38] Both Jinnah and Liaquat Ali Khan, furthermore, relied on the bureaucracies for the formulation and execution of state policy.[39] The latter were consequently propelled to a position of prominence and authority in the central government.

The question of ethnicity in multinational ex-colonial 'state nations', particularly those that evolved rapidly, note Rashid and Shaheed, is linked to the legitimacy of those who dominate the structures of state power.[40] Effective state building involves enabling achievement of parity in access to state resources among the participants in competition. The role of the state in reducing competition by subjecting diverse and disconnected small-scale ethnic groups to the same laws and regulations, observes Hannan, causes local political boundaries to dissolve in favour of a uniform set of relations which henceforth become consequential in interactions between the various peripheries and the centre. Sub-national economic and political differences thereby tend to become irrelevant.[41]

In Pakistan however, the administrative mode of governance engineered at the outset became a lasting feature. The attention of the establishment has remained focused on policies that could cater to its defence priorities. The importance and authority of the army within the state structure, as a consequence, came to be enhanced. The military bureaucracy also gained access to the 'Western dominated centres of power', and eventually a growing interest in maintaining that dominance in order to perpetuate the gains that could be made thereof.[42] Since state resources were meagre,[43] and the defence budget exceedingly large, inadequate provincial budgetary endowments led to 'class based demands for distributional justice'.[44]

Representation from the regions within the civil and military bureaucracies that dominated the state structure, moreover, was dramatically uneven. With the exception of Bengal and Punjab, Pakistan inherited provinces where the traditional pattern of subsistence economies predominated. The bulk of the Urdu-speaking migrants, in contrast, had come primarily from the United Province (the seat of the Mughal, and colonial governments), which was also the home of Aligarh University. The largest number of Muslim civil servants in the British Indian Civil Services had been schooled at Aligarh. Those who were already in service were assigned counterpart positions in Pakistan. Others were able to fill the vacuum for absorption in services (to which they came to have relatively easy access in a supportive political environment). The civil bureaucracy thus initially came to be dominated by the migrants from Northern India. Since the British followed a policy of recruiting the bulk of the British Indian army from the 'martial races' of particular districts of the Punjab alone,[45] the military bureaucracy in turn was, by default, dominated by the Punjabis. The other largest group represented in the army were the Pathans.[46]

In the decades to follow, rather than the initiation of measures that could enable the populations of the provinces to attain parity in representation within the state structure, and a more equitable access to state resources, the disparity in the political and economic growth of the regional populations continued to increase. The incidental shifts that occurred merely served to reduce the capacity of the environment to support the competitors in equilibrium. The participation of the Pathans for instance, progressively expanded in industrial and commercial enterprises.[47] This, however, happened to the detriment of the migrants from Western India. The crucial shift in the inter-provincial political and economic balance of power occurred when the benefits of the Green Revolution in the 1960s accrued to the Punjab. The accompanying prosperity in the Punjab, notes Zaidi, became manifest in the expansion of education and diversification of economic activity.[48] Punjabi representation in the civil bureaucracy thus gradually increased. This resulted in an inverse decrease in the strength of the Urdu-speaking migrants who had hitherto dominated the civil bureaucracy. The Bengalis, despite their numerical superiority and eligibility, were deliberately ignored. Although the Bhuttos later came to power, and Pakistan has seen two Baloch Presidents (one of them a caretaker President), the Sindhis and the Baloch have remained marginal to the power exercised at the centre. No substantive transformation in the traditional power structure, moreover, has come about in the latter provinces.

During the different regimes the state has varied in its efforts to strengthen and/or curtail the power of the social and economic interest groups of the country: the landlords; the industrialists and traders; and civil bureaucracy.[49] However, vested interests, the pursuit of development strategies in keeping with defence priorities, and politically motivated concessions and exemptions, (whether the head of state was democratically elected, or a martial law administrator) have continued to obstruct the expansion and strengthening of the state. Increasing regional disparities thus came to accentuate tensions between the Punjabi dominated centre and the provinces. The ineffectiveness of measures to control the authority, or increasing prosperity of the diverse interest groups, moreover, has promoted an escalation of social and class polarization.

The perpetuation of a non-representative, administrative mode of governance thus eroded the development of political processes and created a distance between the state and society. In order to maintain its control over the discontent developing within the provinces, notes Jalal, in addition to preoccupation with defence to counter external threats to the sovereignty of the state (whereby centralized state authority has continued to be justified), the state also became guilty of resorting to the use of force to counter internal political threats to its power from within the provinces as well.[50] These measures included curbs placed on the freedom of expression.[51]

Against this background, we may take a closer look at the developments in Sindh since Independence.

Post-Partition Population Ecology of Sindh

The support for the Pakistan Movement in Sindh, notes Talbot, had been vociferous primarily among the prosperous Punjabis landowners settled in the alluvial tracts of the province (particularly after Punjab joined the Movement) and the Khojas, Bohras, and Memons, whose business interests conflicted with those of the Hindu *Banias*. Given the feudal character of the province, and the divisive areas of influence of its elite, the pre-Partition politics of the representatives of Sindh had been riddled with feud and factionalism, and accompanying changing alliances. The manoeuvring of the Muslim representatives of Sindh was guided more by motives of securing personal political office and expanding their local power base than by strengthening the cause of Pakistan. Hence, the Muslim League alliance that had been cobbled together before the 1946 elections whereby Sindh acceded to Pakistan, reverted just as quickly to traditional rivalries. Whether they belonged to the Muslim League, or were among those who had favoured a sovereign and autonomous status for their province (as defined in the Pakistan Resolution), the general mood of the powerful elite of Sindh continued, after Independence, to subscribe to a 'hands off Sindh' policy by the central government for their province.[52]

The elite of Sindh, however, were able to benefit in some measure from the departure of the Hindus from the province (in that they came to have access to the land mortgaged to the *Banias* by extravagant landowners against loans).[53] The Muslim tenants of those lands, the *haris*, in contrast, had to share tenancy privileges with the (Punjabi) refugees who were settled on land.[54] Given their essentially provincial outlook, and the common bind of the autocratic feudal structure, the *Syeds*, Baloch, and Sindhis henceforth assumed a common collective 'Sindhi' identity as distinct from the other earlier and incoming migrants to the province. The replacement of the Hindu community (that had contributed to the reproduction of the traditional social system of the province) by twice as many refugees with 'less proven attachment to the region' hence, was regarded by this new 'Sindhi' grouping with general scepticism.[55]

The Khojas, Bohras and Memons (concentrated in Karachi) constituted the remaining petty bourgeois class of Sindh. Given the large potential for advancing business interests in the newly independent state, the arrival of immigrant Khojas, Bohras, and Memons from Western India, rather than creating competition for the earlier settlers, encouraged affiliation with the former on cultural and linguistic grounds. The context of the nation state, moreover, enabled a collective distancing of the latter groups from the rural feudal order of the province, with which the earlier settlers had been associated. The distinct identity of the Punjabis of Sindh also received a boost following the pivotal role of the Punjab in the creation of Pakistan during the final stages of the Movement, and the predominant representation of the Punjabis in the military and bureaucracy. Despite a modification of the boundaries that defined the identities of the rural and urban populations of Sindh after Partition, the absence of any direct threat either to the local power of the elite of Sindh, or economic advancement opportunities for the *haris* that could challenge the structure from within, stayed these boundaries from becoming politically charged. The confirmation of Karachi as the capital of the new state in 1948, however, was received with reservation by the new 'Sindhi' grouping (henceforth collectively referred to as

Sindhis). Karachi's conversion to federal territory meant its separation from the province. For the provincially inclined Sindhis, therefore, this was not a readily acceptable option.[56] After the departure of the Hindu business community, not only was the pre-Partition entrepreneurial or petty bourgeois class of Sindh all but eliminated, but the Punjabis also owned the very little industry in the province. In the absence of a readily available labour force in Sindh, the labour for these industries was recruited from the Punjab. Although the (urban-based) migrants from India had 'a relatively large entrepreneurial class along with an administrative and educated petty bourgeois service class' [and] 'a large and well trained working class',[57] they did not seek a niche in the provincial context. Given an urban educated background, and a 'national' outlook, the migrants to urban Sindh sought to assume jobs for which they were most eligible, and for which there was a large potential in the newly independent state.

During the initial years of Independence hence, the Urdu-speaking migrants came to figure significantly in jobs in both the public as well as the private sectors. Although they constituted only 3 per cent of the population of East and West Pakistan, notes Waseem, the migrants from Northern India held 21 per cent of the jobs. Out of the twelve biggest business houses of Pakistan, moreover, the Gujrati-speaking migrants from Bombay controlled seven of these in Karachi.[58]

The challenge to the migrant political and bureaucratic dominance, as well as their business leadership, however, began to emerge not long after the first decade following Independence. The assassination of Liaquat Ali Khan in 1951 was the beginning of the process that brought the army into a position of political power at the centre.[59] The boost received by the business community in the wake of opportunities provided by the Korean War in the 1950s came up against competition from the Punjab as of the next decade. As capitalism made inroads into the Punjabi economy in the wake of the Green Revolution, notes Zaidi, 'the new dynamic [Punjabi] entrepreneur [was] born'.[60] With mechanization of agriculture, moreover, the displaced Punjabi peasant was also able to travel to the cities and provide competition for jobs. The increase in educational opportunities in the Punjab furthermore, enabled more Punjabis to become eligible for desk jobs, causing jobs in both the public as well as the private sectors to become more competitive and scarce.[61]

The challenge to the Urdu-speaking migrants' domination in the civil bureaucracy thus emerged primarily from the Punjab. The screening of civil servants on corruption charges, and lateral entry of 'technical specialists' and army personnel in the Civil Services in the following decades, though free of ethnic considerations, was significantly detrimental to the migrants from Northern India who were represented in the civil bureaucracy in large numbers.[62] Migrant business leadership also received a setback with their loss of control in the 1960s of the two key trade bodies of the country, namely: the Federation of Pakistan Chambers of Commerce and Industry, and the All Pakistan Textile Mills Association.[63]

Despite the land reforms of 1959 and 1972, the power structure in rural Sindh did not undergo substantive change. Since urban Sindh developed independently, the disparity between the prosperity of the urban and rural areas widened. Furthermore, the British practice of allocating land to army personnel (to retain their goodwill) was continued during the Ghulam Mohammad and Ayub Khan eras. Since the army personnel were invariably Punjabi, the practice saw a further allocation of the most choice lands in Sindh to the Punjabis. Given their accompanying affluence, further industries in Sindh were also set up by the Punjabis. The bulk of the labour for these industries, as earlier, continued to be imported from the Punjab. The Sindhis thus remained insulated from the developments in the province, and the emergence of a Sindhi middle class was hindered.[64]

Other strains were simultaneously compounding. As Karachi developed into the industrial capital, strains were placed on opportunities for smaller businessmen and on skilled and unskilled wage labourers, with the arrival of competitors from the Frontier and Punjab provinces as of the 1960s. The Pathans came not only as labourers, but also gradually took over, almost entirely, the public transport system of the city.[65] Migrants from the Punjab were more diversified in the choice of economy niches they exploited. Not only were they in the civil bureaucracies (postings in

Sindh being possible even after the capital moved to Islamabad in 1959 because the One Unit form of government remained intact until 1969), but also in services in the private sector, as well as businesses, public transport (a niche they shared to a lesser degree with the Pathans), and skilled and unskilled wage labour.[66]

The Sindhi presence in Karachi was nominal. The present Sindhi population of Karachi is estimated to be about 8 per cent[67] of the total population of the city.[68] For the most part, Sindhis in Karachi were incorporated as a result of the accession of their villages to the expanding circumference of the city. They were primarily fishermen and transporters (who drove camel and donkey carts), and were engaged in skilled and unskilled wage labour. Until the 1970s, the changes that were taking place at the federal and regional levels did not dramatically impact on the economic niches the Sindhis had hitherto exploited. A manifestation, in embryonic form, of the tensions between the less and the more affluent, and/or the populations perceived as being more privileged, however, became visible by the mid-1960s. The main identities along which the populations of Sindh first split, surfaced in 1964 when Ayub Khan's electoral victory over Fatima Jinnah was celebrated by the Pathans in Karachi, and was resented by the non-Pathans (i.e., the migrants, the Punjabis, and the Sindhis). A public reaction to the threat posed by the ethnic group perceived as being supported by the centre took the shape of a bipolar conflict between the 'favoured' ethnic group as distinct from all the others.

These divisions and the identities they invoked dwindled with Ayub Khan's power in 1968. The next clash took place in 1972 after the break-up of the One Unit, and the restoration of provincial governments, when the Sindh Chief Minister tabled a bill to institute Sindhi as the official language of the province. The outcome saw a public protest by the non-Sindhis, spearheaded by the Urdu-speaking migrants. The latter championed the cause of Urdu, whereas the Sindhis demonstrated in favour of the legitimacy of Sindhi. The decision to make Sindhi the official language of the province, however, was diluted by the intervention of

Zulfiqar Ali Bhutto, who allowed a twelve year period for the language to be learnt. Implementation of the decision in schools, moreover, has been weak for want of qualified teachers. The clash, however, was symptomatic of the growing Sindhi concern with losing ground to 'outsiders'.

Crystallization of Ethnicity in Sindh

Sindhis received their first effective boost in the 1970s after the coming to power of Zulfiqar Ali Bhutto. Although Bhutto, the first democratically elected head of state, did not win the elections on ethnic grounds, his Sindhi identity became important to the Sindhis as well as the non-Sindhis, in the same manner as Ayub Khan's Pathan identity had become important to the Pathans and non-Pathans, in terms of the expectations for greater representation by the population sharing the ethnic identity of the head of state. The Sindhis, who since independence had had the opportunity to become literate and thereby eligible for administrative and technical positions, began pressing for maximum representation in all sectors on the grounds that as Sindhis they deserved priority over others in their home province. By the 1970s thus, notes Zaidi, the Sindhis were beginning to have a stake in the prosperity of Karachi.[69]

Bhutto tried to redress some of the grievances of the Sindhis by enforcing rural-urban quotas for provincial services. The process that typically sought to mainstream the Sindhis became the initial cause of enhancing Sindhi ethnicity. Limiting the recruitment of non-Sindhis to civil posts in urban Sindh (i.e., Karachi, Hyderabad, Sukkur and Nawabshah) directly affected the Urdu-speaking migrants, who, in addition to competition from the Punjabis at the federal level,[70] now faced competition from the Sindhis at the provincial level as well. Given their educated middle and lower middle class background, moreover, the quota allocated to them fell far below their fundamental[71] potential for those posts. This resulted in an increase in the number of Sindhis in the provincial civil bureaucracy, and a simultaneous escalation in the number of unemployed educated Urdu-speaking migrant youth.

During the Z.A. Bhutto regime, the business community of Karachi also suffered another, and major, setback. The nationalization of the capital sector (about half of which was owned by the migrants),[72] and the intermediary goods sector (in which migrant ownership was more widespread) became the cause of substantial discontent.[73] The livelihoods of those engaged in skilled and unskilled wage labour were also threatened (in addition to earlier competition from the in-migrants) by the arrival in the 1980s of a sizeable number of illegal immigrants from Bangladesh, Burma, Sri Lanka, and to a lesser degree Thailand and the Philippines. The illegal immigrants were significant for increasing the population of the city and providing labour at cheaper rates, thereby placing a strain not only on access to fundamental civic amenities and economic opportunities, but also lowering the wages of the earlier unskilled labourers of the city. The carrying capacity of Karachi (which was near saturation) by the constant influx from within and outside the country over the past decades, saw the additional arrival of refugees from Afghanistan in the wake of the Afghan war with the former Soviet Union. The Afghans brought arms and drugs with them.

Multiple pressures and causes for discontent hence had compounded in Sindh by the 1980s. Although the *waderos* and the *zamindars* had themselves resisted change in the rural power structure, the insulation of the Sindhis from the developments in their province, and the contrasting affluence and constant influx of non-Sindhis in the province was a growing cause of anxiety for them. The *haris* grudged these developments because their perennial lowly status in their own province remained largely unaltered. The migrant business community in turn was frustrated by the competition from the Punjabis, and the setbacks they underwent as a consequence of the nationalization of industries. De-nationalization during the following Ziaul Haq regime, moreover, they estimated, did not result in the reversion of the de-nationalized industries to their original owners, even though they fulfilled the conditions. The trauma of marginalization from state power was notably dramatic for the 'national' oriented Urdu-speaking migrants, who looked upon Pakistan as the haven for the Muslims of India, and for the creation of which they saw themselves as having struggled and sacrificed. The arrival of the in-migrants, the illegal immigrants, and the Afghan refugees not only increased work competition, but also placed a further strain on the already saturated carrying capacity of the industrial capital. The import of automatic weapons and drugs, furthermore, provided the potential for accumulated tensions to assume a violent form.

The challenges faced by the different sections of the populations in Sindh, and the tensions these invoked, however, do not isolate the Sindhis and the Urdu-speaking migrants as the sole aggrieved parties. The competition between these two groups, moreover, is restricted to jobs in the provincial civil bureaucracy. The small percentage of Sindhis eligible for government jobs on the one hand, and the possibility of the private sector to accommodate the Urdu-speaking migrants on the other, tends to release some of the pressure. The results of a household sample survey conducted in 1986 (which is commonly assessed, also by the authors of that survey report, to be currently valid), furthermore revealed the migrants to be better placed than all the other ethnic groups living in Karachi, in terms of housing facilities, access to utilities, literacy[74] and income. Their employment rate was about the same as the Pathans and the Punjabis.[75] If the grievances of the populations of Sindh, both rural and urban, in terms of the challenges to their economic advancement, and their non-representation in the authority structure of the state, are not substantively different from the plaint of the populations of Balochistan, and to a lesser degree, the NWFP, how then must we understand the emergence of the *mohajir* political movement in Sindh in 1984, and the violent clashes that have taken place between the Sindhis and the Urdu-speaking migrants since the formation of the *Mohajir* (later *Muttahida*) *Qaumi Movement* (MQM) as a political party?

Let us see how we can answer this question.

Sindhi-Mohajir Conflict: An Artificial Creation?

More than any other section of the population, the Urdu-speaking migrants subscribed to a 'national' self-image. Accordingly, they forwarded the concept of homogeneous Pakistani nationalism based on common religious faith, and in 1955 had favoured the One Unit form of government. The Sindh Legislative Assembly (at the behest of Khuhro, who was disgruntled by Sindh's faction-ridden elite) had also supported One Unit.[76] Any desperate response to the challenges that were emerging (although resented by the provinces of West Pakistan other than the most represented Punjab province at the centre) tended, as far as the Urdu-speaking migrants were concerned, to be contained within the framework of the One Unit. It was after the One Unit dissolved in 1969, and the migrants were brought within the fold of the politics in Sindh, that their economic and political alienation from the centre and the provinces was brought home to them. Their faith in the centre to guarantee their welfare, or even survival was also shaken after witnessing the fate of the Biharis who became stranded in former East Pakistan with the creation of Bangladesh.[77]

The economic disparity between the regions, and the absence of measures to strengthen civil institutions or foster national cohesion, by the creation of an enabling democratic environment for equitable representation from the provinces in the authority structure, was less than inspiring. In so far as a distinct identity would enable the Urdu-speaking migrants to articulate their disenchantment with the 'Promised Land', and the criteria for identity formation would highlight their distinctive role as pioneers of the Pakistan Movement, and thereby serve the implicit purpose of reiterating the legitimacy of their civic rights over their competitors, a transition from a 'national' to an 'ethnic' identity, as a political strategy for self-assertion in an increasingly polarized scenario, was likely to find fertile ground. The origins and activities of the political party that represents them, however, are less coherent. The relative economic well-being of the *mohajirs*, and their discerning support for the MQM, moreover, does not testify to the inevitability of a *mohajir* political movement without external impetus, particularly after the easing of tensions with the removal of Z.A. Bhutto, nor to the designation of Sindhis as their main competitors. The nature of the violence that ravages urban Sindh, particularly Karachi, also cannot be explained solely in terms of 'the *mohajir* mode of protest'. How then do we explain the Sindhi/*mohajir* conflict?

The credit for authoring the MQM and instigating the current conflict in Sindh, is laid at the threshold of Ziaul Haq as part of his efforts to eliminate internal political threats to his authority. Having come to power after deposing and eventually seeking the physical elimination of a popular, democratically elected leader through a military coup,[78] and under the pledge to hold elections within three months of assuming office, Ziaul Haq tried variously to gain legitimacy, not least by launching his brand of an 'Islamization' process, expected to appeal to the masses, and hold the elite in check, but also by cultivating specific economic and social interest groups of the country.[79] Not assured of having successfully eliminated the threat of mass support for the PPP, nor, therefore, of having pre-empted the possibility of its return to power, under the leadership of Benazir Bhutto, Ziaul Haq attempted to fuel tensions between the Sindhis and Urdu-speaking migrants by extending his patronage to Altaf Hussain.

As a student, Altaf Hussain had become vocal by 1979, about the perceived discrimination of the state against the Urdu-speaking migrants, in the aftermath of the language bill and the rural/urban quotas. Although Ziaul Haq had earlier had him jailed 'on charges of stoning, arson, illegal assembly, and taking down the Pakistan flag and replacing it with a black flag',[80] the All Pakistan Mohajir Students Organization, led by Altaf Hussain, was transformed into a political party in 1984.[81] With the formation of the MQM, the Urdu-speaking migrants were designated as Mohajirs, and transformed into a well-defined 'ethnic' group. A militant cadre of the MQM formed almost simultaneously with the party. This was facilitated by the availability of automatic weapons brought in by the Afghan refugees.

The use of the word 'Mohajir' to describe the identity of the Urdu-speaking migrants thus entailed exclusive appropriation, thirty-five years later, of the term that had designated all the refugees from India at the time of Partition, regardless of the language they spoke: Punjabi, Urdu, Gujrati, or other. The term also has a religious connotation. The word *'hijrat'* (to migrate) recalls the migration undertaken by the Prophet of Islam from Mecca to Medina, following his persecution in Mecca. It, therefore, inspires the welcome and hospitality that a *mohajir* expects in the land chosen for his/her refuge. The political use of the word *'mohajir'* thus plays on the dual inference of the term: on the one hand it draws attention to the circumstances of the arrival of the Urdu-speaking migrants as a consequence of *'hijrat'*, following Partition; and on the other, it lays emphasis on the distinctiveness of their identity *vis-à-vis* the other populations of Pakistan. Whereas the religious connotation of the term may be the insinuated message for the general body of MQM supporters, the MQM leadership, despite its vigorous and long standing affiliation with the *Jamaat-i-Islami* during university days, has publicly distanced itself from the Islamist lobby[82] (and therefore the identity invoked during the Pakistan Movement, and subsequently as the criteria for homogeneous nationalism), and as a mark of protest, has emphasized its 'secular' standing. In keeping with these orientations, the *mohajirs* manifest a degree of disdain towards the mystical version of Islam followed in rural Sindh.[83]

The violence that has become endemic to urban Sindh sparked soon after the formation of the MQM. The first clashes, however, took place between the Mohajirs and the Pathans, when a Pathan bus driver in Karachi ran down a migrant girl in 1985. Subsequently, an alliance of the Sindhis and the Mohajirs collided with the Punjabis, and then the Pathans and the Punjabis were pitched against the Mohajirs. Despite the divisiveness of the Sindhi leadership,[84] and the absence of sufficient compelling economic grounds to incite the Mohajirs, the conflict between the Sindhis and the Mohajirs eventually took centre-stage. As distinct from the other groups, the confrontation between the Sindhis and the

Mohajirs pivoted around the 'mutually exclusive' incentive of establishing the supremacy of their civic rights, and of reinstating their self-images.

The Mohajirs describe themselves as the custodians of 'Mughal culture'. A sense of ethno-linguistic arrogance pervades the Mohajir psyche. They believe themselves to be inherently more 'cultivated' than the original populations of what became Pakistan, and in keeping with their role in the creation of the country, 'naturally' endowed to assume a privileged position in society. The cultural arrogance of the Mohajirs not only renders a reiteration of their ethno-linguistic distinctiveness inevitable, but their perception of Pakistan as a legacy for the Muslims of India,[85] lends credence to their belief in their inherent right to dominate the power structure, failing which, their right to adopt a confrontationalist attitude towards their competitors.

For the Sindhis, unlike any other identity group, Sindh constitutes their home, and Karachi an integral part of the province. Any presumed challenge to that right legitimizes a liability to their wrath. The 'self-righteous' attitude of the Mohajirs, therefore, is resented by the Sindhis. Proud of their ancient Mehran culture, the Sindhis are impatient with the cultural arrogance, and 'persistent dominant presence' of the Mohajirs in their midst. Immediately after Partition, the Sindhis profess to have supported not only the Mohajirs, but also the central government '...who had not legs (sic) to stand on, no chair to sit and no papers to write'.[86] Despite their initial hospitality towards the Mohajirs, the latter, the Sindhis observe, have never tried to assimilate with them, as did the *Syeds* who settled in Sindh in the twelfth and thirteenth centuries, and the Baloch who settled in the province around the seventeenth century. The Punjabis moreover, they point out, have been settling in interior Sindh since the construction of the Sukkur barrage, as early as 1932, and subsequently the Guddu and Ghulam Mohammad barrages. Unlike the Mohajirs, the Punjabis, or the in-migrants, the Sindhis remark, have never tried to dominate them in their own province. Even after fifty years of co-existence, furthermore, the Sindhis scoff at the Mohajirs wanting to retain a 'migrant' identity.

The manner in which the Mohajirs perceive themselves, and their expectations of the 'Promised Land' thus juxtapose the views of the provincially-oriented Sindhis. The perceptions of the Sindhis and Mohajirs of each other contrast with the attitude of the in-migrants. Although permanent settlers, the identity of the in-migrants remains associated with, and is reinforced by their home province. So long as their province of origin does not overtly protest against the centre, the in-migrants show little inclination to agitate. As compared to the Mohajirs, the differential association of the migrant business community with Pakistan; the structural disadvantage of the minorities, and the illegal immigrants; and the 'special' status of the Afghan refugees; places the latter sections of the population in a non-competitive category *vis-à-vis* the Sindhis and the Mohajirs.

The conflict between the Sindhis and the Mohajirs hence, it may be ventured, is more speculative than real. In large part, the confrontation has been artificially engineered, and its contrived nature is eclipsed by genuine discontent common to the smaller federating units *vis-à-vis* the (Punjabi dominated) centre. The substitution of democracy by military or civilian authoritarianism, and therefore, the arrested political processes, the worsening economic crunches, and the lack of faith in institutionalized authority to uphold the rule of law, or demonstrate the political will to address the multiplying civic grievances, continue to sustain the tensions. The association of the Mohajirs with Pakistan, in terms of their pioneering role in its creation, their urban background, educational advantage, greater political awareness, as well as their enhanced organizational ability, facilitated further by physical proximity, and the absence of any traditionally sanctioned strife, distinguishes the Mohajir ethnicity. The formation of the militant cadre, and the violence associated with the party, however, need to be differentially understood, as does the oscillating stance of the MQM, and the accompanying variance in the support of the Mohajirs for their party.

During the early years of its formation, the tightly knit, cult-like[87] organization of the MQM was able to command the near absolute support of the Mohajirs. The numerical superiority of the Mohajirs in urban Sindh, particularly Karachi, enabled the MQM to win the local bodies elections in 1987, and the national elections in 1988, 1990, and 1996.[88] Although initially the MQM reiterated its demands,[89] sceptical of its potential to be 'adequately' assertive,[90] the party for the most part has concentrated on emphasizing the distinct identity of the Mohajirs, and on pressing for the recognition of Karachi as the 'fifth province'. No notable interest is demonstrated in evolving a coherent agenda for power sharing, or of adopting a sustained political means of pressing for a more equitable participation of Mohajirs as members of civil society. A show of militant strength thus became the preferred means of exercising power, and asserting the party's presence. The party formed and broke alliances with both the PPP as well as the PML governments. These alliances, based more on momentary political expediency, on both sides, rather than on the will to address the problems afflicting the populations of Sindh, were destined to be short lived. As the third largest political party of the country nevertheless, the MQM capitalizes on its importance for the parties that vie for its support. Escalation in conflict thus serves the purpose of perpetuating political clout.

Failure of the party to deliver on promises, and the sustained violence and crime in the city, of which the Mohajirs have often themselves been the victims,[91] has tended to decrease Mohajir support for the MQM. The waning support, however, is periodically reinforced by sporadic provocation from the establishment. Force, as an emergency measure, has been used, with or without the semblance of constitutional sanction, through the police, the para-military forces, as well as the army, acting either at its own initiative, or being asked to do so by the government.[92] In the first instance, like the MQM, the army was also suspected by the Mohajirs of fermenting conflict in order to create an opportunity to exercise power in the civil affairs of the state. The Mohajirs, moreover, availed of these occasions to remind the establishment that the state itself was responsible for 'brutalizing' and 'weaponizing' urban Sindh. The provocation in turn heightens the belligerence of the MQM, and has generated counter violence.

In 1990, the MQM made an effort to increase its power base and assume a national face by changing its name to *Muttahida* (United) *Qaumi Movement*, thereby aspiring to become the spokespersons of all the poor and middle classes of the country.[93] The measure cost the party some loss of members, and created dissident factions, namely: the *Haqiqi*;[94] and the *Aman Pasand* (or the 'Peace Loving').[95] The party, however, did not gain any support in the rest of the country by changing its name, nor did a change of name entail any real change in the agenda, or the aspirations of the MQM to becoming a national party. In-fighting between the Altaf Hussain and the *Haqiqi* factions, however, resulted in *Haqiqi* controlled 'no go' areas in Karachi.

In the on-going strife-ridden scenario, urban crime found a favourable environment to flourish. The lucrative business of trafficking arms and drugs led to the creation of powerful *mafias* that thrive on violence.[96] Extortionists and criminals in turn, took advantage of the disturbed law and order situation. Instances of sniper shooting, and casualties resulting thereof, arson, armed robberies, and kidnapping for ransom became frequent occurrences. The break-down of civic amenities under the weight of over-population further aggravated the travails of the citizens.

Does the grave and complex nature of this conflict, the social and class polarization of which it is a part, and the accompanying transformation from anti-ethnic to pro-ethnic thinking among the Mohajirs, defy the logic of the 'two nation theory' and the creation of Pakistan as a separate homeland for the Muslims of India? Let us examine the comparative validity of this contention.

Nationalism and Ethnicity

Nationalism and ethnicity are not synonymous. The latter may also not lead to the former.[97] Ethnicity, invoked on the basis of traditionally determined criteria that are interpreted to meet the needs and ambitions of the present,[98] in fact challenges nationalism, where defence of common interest engenders the formation of a group that defines its separate identity against the state. The state, in this instance, is designated as 'a specified third player in the process of boundary construction between groups'.[99] Nationalism is the exclusive realization of that separate identity. 'The cultural and ideological dynamics that bring to life the two phenomena, in both cases, are indebted to a history that can be read and interpreted in several changing ways'.[100] The specification of the 'Other', however, is fundamental to both ethnicity and nationalism.

The marginalization of the Muslims implied by the 'nationalism', cast as Hindu revivalism, propagated vociferously by the Bharatiya Janta Party, and overtly or covertly by the Congress as well (albeit under the garb of 'secularism') during the Independence movement, obliged Jinnah to take the position that the distinctive traditions of the Muslims of India qualified the latter as a separate 'nation' as distinct from the Hindus. The movement for the creation of Pakistan sought to legitimize that claim. Although initiated in the minority provinces, Pakistan became possible after the Muslim League captured Bengal and Punjab. Hamza Alavi attributes the catalyst role of the UP in Muslim nationalism to the loss of their privileged position following a decrease in their share of government jobs since 1857 from 64 per cent, to 35 per cent in the early twentieth century.[101] According to Noman, the greater involvement of the Muslims of UP in the negotiations for the transfer of power from the British was related to their proximity to the seat of government in Delhi.[102] More fundamentally, a separate Muslim consciousness, and its salience during the independence movement, was linked to the implications of the minority/majority identity distinctions in the emerging scenario.

Muslim inceptions in the region, and the conversions to Islam that took place in their wake, countenanced a cognitive divide between the Muslims and the Hindus. The Mughal politics of 'inclusion' and 'exclusion' and the land settlement policies of the British served to reinforce identity distinctions. However, since the patterns of socio-economic survival remained largely unaltered, many social forms from the past were perpetuated, and the absence of any notion of marginalization allowed concordant social existence. From the period of the Montagu-Chelmsford constitution, and the formulation of separate electorates, political divisions along communal lines were further consolidated. The factor that gave the impetus for Partition, however, was the impending transformation of the subcontinent into a 'nation state' in the aftermath of de-colonization.

The prospect of converting the entire subcontinent into a single federation not only defied the historical logic of an autonomous, or semi autonomous mode of social existence in the subcontinent, but the only commonality on the basis of which such a move could be justified was the Hindu caste structure that fed the concept of 'Mother India'. The question of national character, as portrayed tacitly by the Congress, and more vocally by the Hindu fundamentalist parties hence, tantamount to a virtual denial of the preceding thousand years of the subcontinent's history and the developments that took place during that period. As such, it challenged the very existence of the Muslims, and by implication de-legitimized their potential claim to equal citizenship in the independent Indian 'nation state'. The anti-colonial struggle hence did not progress as the struggle of a civilization, which in no way could claim to qualify as *a single nation state*, against British rule. Rather, it became a struggle, from the Muslim perspective, for independence not only from the British, but also from the influences of the earlier Muslim period. The Congress failed to dispel the impression that the Muslims of India did not belong to the category of colonisers' as did the British, and the struggle for independence as such was not a struggle for liberating the subcontinent of all 'foreign' influences: British as well as Muslim. The failure to do so magnified the tensions emerging from equating the movement for independence with Hindu revivalism, on the one hand; and a single civilization with a single nation state, on the other.

The idea of a separate Muslim majority centre hence crystallized in response to a combination of ideological, political, and economic concerns, against a given historical background. Initially, the Muslims of the minority provinces turned to the Muslim League because the forum provided the opportunity, once the British left, to safeguard Muslim interests in at least one part of the country. In this way, they believed that Muslim interests could be guaranteed in the rest of the country. The élite of Sindh and Punjab had sought provincial autonomy in order to protect their socio-economic interests. Bengali Muslims were already disposed towards autonomy—a preference developed after the treatment meted out to them by the Bengali Hindus—prior to the partition of Bengal by the British. Because of the manner and the rapidity with which the Movement evolved, the politics of Muslim provincialism were abandoned in favour of Muslim nationalism. The elite of the majority provinces, who had campaigned from the late 1920s against the introduction of a responsible government at New Delhi thus, capped on the Pakistan Movement to create a centre of their own.[103]

The success of the Muslim League in being able to 'turn the tables on its rivals' hence, lay not in its cynical manipulation of religion, as is often conjectured, but rather in providing a solution, albeit partial, to the growing clamour of Hindu nationalism by demanding a separate Muslim state. Islam as a community symbol gained importance during the final stages of the Movement in reaction to the Hindu attacks on Muslim minorities in Bombay and Bihar in 1946. During the final negotiations, moreover, the Congress leadership itself preferred partition to sharing power with the Muslims at the Centre: convinced as it was that, given the disadvantages with which it was to begin its independent existence, Pakistan would not survive as a state. Failure to do so would stem the Muslim struggle for self-determination, and neutralize the opposition.

The Muslim identity that had been defined in opposition to the majority Hindu population of the subcontinent, and which had became highly salient and symbolic during the Pakistan Movement, lost its point of reference, and therefore its relative validity, after the creation of Pakistan. In Pakistan, the right to Muslim self-determination was no longer at risk. Within the national context hence, the resurgence of the varying scope and form of ethnic expressions relate to the inadequacy of conditions that foster national cohesion. The definition, and redefinition of ethnic boundaries has thus become the means of associating with a larger or smaller group, sharing a particular criteria, that offers a better chance of political self-assertion. Ethnicity hence, serves to claim a greater share in the power structure and economic resources of the state, and to register opposition to the highly centralized, non-representative nature of state structure, dominated by the bureaucracies.

The question whether the polarization of the polity refutes the rationale of the 'two nation' theory hence, is ill formulated. The validity of the theory drew its rationale from the relativity of the pre-Partition context. Its current applicability can similarly be verified by re-invoking the option of an undivided India, and determining whether the populations of Pakistan would accept to be part of the Indian federation. Would the Mohajirs, for instance, be willing to undo Partition after the present experience and return to India? Do the dynamics of the present Pakistan-India, Bangladesh-Pakistan, and Bangladesh-India relations falsify the arguments on which the 'two nation theory' was founded? Similarly, why does India feel compelled to stall the Kashmir issue, or fear to test her international commitment to hold a plebiscite? Again, why has the Indian establishment been devoted to undermining Pakistan ideologically, strategically, and militarily? Why even does India's *Hindutva*-subscribing leadership demand to see tears in the eyes of the Indian Muslim population when India loses a cricket match against Pakistan?

The postures that divide the political consciousness of the Muslims and Hindus of the subcontinent are based, in part, on the historical dominant-subordinate Muslim/Hindu syndrome sustained over centuries before colonization. They represent 'one of the fault lines of South Asian society',[104] along which the British empire was liable to give way in the wake of de-colonization and the emergence of a subcontinental nation state. An analogy with the grievances of the citizens of Pakistan against the structure and policies of the state, therefore, is untenable. The latter draw attention to the earlier autonomy exercised by the provinces on the one hand; and are aimed at questioning the limits to which state policies can be justified to the detriment of civil interests, on the other.

Conclusion

Despite the enthusiasm accompanying its creation, the difficulties peculiar to Pakistan *vis-à-vis* other multi-national ex-colonial states, particularly those that evolved rapidly, in seeking to reconcile diverse competing social and economic interests within the polity to a homogeneous set of relations that could become consequential in the interactions between the centre and the provinces, spring from the absence of any degree of 'stateness' prior to Independence, and the organizational weakness of the Muslim League in the Pakistan areas. Unlike India, that appropriated the name of the subcontinent, and has thereby been able to banish the last thousand years of history from its collective memory with relative ease, it has been more difficult for Pakistan to try and live with only one thousand years of history, or more precisely only fifty years. The priority attributed to defence, moreover, has rationalized the maintenance of a large defence budget, and continued to justify the centralization of state authority, and the pursuit of a political economy of defence. Concern with warding off external threats to the sovereignty of the state furthermore, translated into vigilance against internal political threats to state authority from within the provinces as well.

The permanence assumed by the distorted relationship between the centre and the provinces, inherent in the nature, and the non-representative content of the state structure, coupled with the allocation of endowments to provincial governments relative to defence, have resulted in a negligence of the service sectors and basic needs. Regional grievances and class differences have thereby been accentuated. The continued substitution of democracy by military or civil authoritarianism has thus hindered the development of political processes, or the expansion of the state. An ethnic manifestation of discontent as a means of defending common

interest, became manifest in all the provinces, other than the
most represented Punjab province at the centre, not long
after Independence.

Alienation from the authority structure of the state was
more dramatic for the Mohajirs, not only because the
Mohajirs had earlier been significantly represented in the
civil bureaucracy, but also because of their association with
the 'homeland' for which they perceived of themselves as
having struggled and sacrificed.[105] The initial impetus for the
formation of the MQM, and the designation of Sindhis as
their competitors, however, was provided by the Zia regime
to subvert a potential 'Sindhi threat' to its authority. Vested
interests of the establishment on the one hand; and greater
political awareness among the Mohajirs, combined with their
lack of faith in institutionalized authority to tackle intra and
inter-provincial grievances, on the other; has succeeded in
sustaining the status quo. The facile availability of automatic
weapons, a fall-out of the Afghan war, opened the chapter of
violence in Sindh. Selective use of force, targeting mainly
armed activists of the MQM, by an alienated, politically
expedient Establishment is equated with the authority
exercised by the colonial state that stood 'outside' or 'above'
society. Rather than restoring normalcy, such actions have
generated counter violence, heightened insecurity, and caused
tensions to escalate.

The severe nature of centre-province tensions, however,
represents a protest against the denial of participation, rather
than a refusal of the provinces to participate in the national
political process. Not only do all the provinces participate in
elections, but in case of Sindh, the rigid and hostile attitude
of the Sindhis and the Mohajirs towards each other, despite
the Sindhi 'nationalist' currents, conceal elements of a mutual
coming to terms with the inevitable realities of co-existence.
They also reveal symptoms of accommodation, and the
potential for the conditional acceptance of the 'Other'.[106] The
more educated strata of the Mohajirs, moreover, tends to feel
that the Mohajirs should press for their political and economic
share in the resources of the state *along* with the Sindhis,
rather than fighting them.[107] As compared to the relatively
provincial orientation of the Sindhis, the Mohajirs

furthermore, continue to retain a 'national' perspective in their analysis of inter-provincial disparities, and the ensuing centre-province tensions.[108] Despite the conflict ravaging Sindh, the populations, particularly of Karachi, also do not consider the situation to be a lost cause. The support of a large section of the Mohajirs is withheld conditional to the conflict being addressed and treated as a 'political' problem that would allow local representatives to be a party to the urgent demand for structural reforms.

Karachi is considered a mini-Pakistan. Its populations represent all the identity groups of the country, in addition to illegal immigrants, and Afghan refugees. Given the inclinations towards accommodation, the upper limits on ethnic boundaries can be caused to decrease, provided the centre pursues policies that cater to the interests of society. In the alternative, the perpetuation of a self-seeking non-representative authority structure, and the accompanying decay of the political, administrative, and judicial institutions will continue to multiply internal fission, and prevent intra-population strife from subsiding. Although optimism continues to be expressed regarding the return of peace to Sindh, the potential for a more representative future is held hostage to the lack of faith in the existing leadership to meet the multiple challenges.[109]

NOTES

1. ***Author's note:*** The analysis of ethnic tensions in Sindh is based on qualitative research, conducted by myself in Karachi in May 1998. The main technique was focus group discussions with Mohajirs and Sindhis in the afflicted areas of Karachi. The data was complemented by in-depth interviews of some key informants: political representatives from opposing parties; journalists; local administrators; and squatter settlement development managers. The paper updates my earlier study of 1989, also in Karachi.

   I am grateful to Akbar Zaidi for his insightful comments on an earlier draft of this paper. His observations have substantially helped enhance its quality. The usual disclaimers apply.

2. *'mohajir'* literally means migrant. The word referred to all the language groups (Punjabi, Urdu, Gujrati etc.) that migrated from India after partition. Its appropriation by the Urdu-speaking migrants alone represents the ethnic use of the word to designate a separate political identity.

3. Ansari, 1995, p. 95.

4. According to the 1981 Census, Karachi covers a total area of 3.527 sq.km. Pending the results of the recently concluded census, the city is estimated to house a population of about 14 million people (which demographers feel is under-enumerated).

5. Rashid and Shaheed 1993, p. 12.

6. Mumtaz, 1990, p. 237.

7. Karim, 1988, p. 33.

8. Khuhro, 1992, p. 22.

9. Talbot, 1990, p. 36.

10. Religious guides.

11. Ibid.

12. Khuhro, ibid., p. 19.

13. Talbot, ibid., p. 35.

14. The latter received a total of 5,281,194 migrants from East Punjab, Kashmir, and North-west India (Census of Pakistan, 1951. Vol.7. W.P. 2-1). Also see, Rashid and Shaheed, ibid., p. 12.

15. According to Ansari, Khuhro had agreed to take 100,000 migrants from the Punjab. Liaquat Ali Khan, however, coaxed the Sindh government, accepting 200,000 in 'a spirit of Islamic solidarity' (1995, p. 105).

16. Hannan, 1979, p. 265.

17. Talbot, ibid.; Khuhro, ibid.

18. Constituted of the Hindu *Banias* and the Muslim Khojas, Bohras, and Memons.

19. Constituted of the Hindu *Amils*.

20. Talbot, ibid., p. 37.

21. Ibid., p. 33.

22. Ibid.

23. Cited in Ansari, 1955, p. 104.

24. Ibid., p. 12.

25. The influx of migrants from India declined, according to Hashmi (in Mumtaz, 1990, p. 232), as of the second half of the 1950s due to a more vigorous implementation of immigration rules.

26. Partition, particularly in the divided Punjab province, was accompanied by 'wholesale butchery'.

27. The departure of the Hindus from Sindh, notes Ansari, was prompted by the fear of retaliation from Muslim refugees arriving from Northern India who had suffered loss of family members, and borne the brunt of violence at the hands of the Hindus in their districts of origin. The Sindh Maintenance of Public Safety Ordinance (which was promulgated on 21 September 1947 to pre-empt the potential for lawlessness in Sindh, and protect minority interests), had the reverse effect of heightening the insecurity of Hindus who perceived an arbitrary use of the powers of the Ordinance as potentially detrimental to their community (Ansari, 1995, p. 99).

28. The ownership of the press by the *Amils*, notes Talbot (ibid., 35), played an important role during the Pakistan Movement in moulding public opinion in favour of the Congress.

29. Ibid., p. 23.

30. Shahid Kardar, in Rashid and Shaheed, ibid., p. 12.

31. Zaidi, 1990, p. 2.

32. Mumtaz, 1990, p. 234.

33. Partition, observes Jalal, did not result in the division of India into successor states (unlike the argument on which Jinnah had based his political strategy). It was India that inherited British India's central state apparatus. Pakistan was cast in the light of a seceding state, and began its independent existence without the semblance of a central state structure (ibid., p. 264).

34. 'and the emphasis placed on warding off the potential threat of a Soviet attack on its North-western frontier' (ibid.).

35. 1990, pp. 265-267.

36. In the aftermath of the 1937 debacle.

37. Talbot, ibid., p. 112.

38. Jalal, ibid., p. 262.

39. Noman, 1988, p. 9.

40. Ibid., p. 2.

41. 1979, p. 265.

42. Jalal, ibid., p. 300.

43. Pakistan's share of the sterling balances Britain owed to undivided India (which was held in a common pool at the Reserve Bank, pending an agreement as to how it was to be released) was estimated at 17.5 per cent. Pakistan's main foreign exchange earners (raw jute and raw cotton) moreover, had hitherto been manufactured in factories located in India (Jalal, ibid., p. 265).

44. Noman, ibid., p. 33.

45. Young, 1995, p. 178.

46. Noman, ibid., p. 182.
47. Noman, ibid., p. 182; Shahid Kardar in Rashid and Shaheed, ibid., p. 11.
48. Ibid., p. 4.
49. Noman, ibid., p. 183.
50. Jalal, ibid., p. 266.
51. Noman, ibid., p. 69. Noman for instance, notes the constraints placed on the press; the judiciary; and the academia during the martial regimes (ibid.).
52. Talbot, ibid., p. 52.
53. According to Shahid Kardar (1988), it was the Mohajirs who took over 40 per cent of the two million acres of land that had been held by the *Banias* (in Rashid and Shaheed, ibid., p. 12).
54. Ansari 1995, p. 105.
55. Ansari, ibid., 1995, p. 100.
56. Ansari, ibid., p. 102.
57. Zaidi 1990, p. 2.
58. 1996, p. 621.
59. Jalal ibid., p. 300.
60. Ibid., p. 4.
61. Ibid.
62. Apart from suspensions during the Ayub Khan regime, 303 civil bureaucrats were removed from service by Yahya in 1970, and 1300 were removed by Z.A. Bhutto in 1972.
63. Bengali and Sadaqat 1997, p. 190.
64. Zaidi, ibid., p. 10.
65. The report of Enquiry into Karachi's Affairs commissioned by the Prime Minister in May 1988 showed only 557 buses in the city to be Government property. In contrast, the bulk of the 1253 private buses, and a total of 85,709 privately run taxis, *rickshaws*, trucks, and mini-buses were owned by migrants from the NWFP.
66. Mumtaz, ibid., p. 241.
67. 15 per cent according to Noman (1988, p. 183).
68. Bengali and Sadaqat 1996, p. 172.
69. Ibid., p. 7.
70. According to the figures recorded by Rashid and Shaheed 'jobs in the federal government [were] given out on the basis of the following formula: 10 per cent on pure merit; 50 per cent for the Punjab; 7.6 per cent for urban Sindh (including Karachi, Hyderabad, and Sukkur); 11.4 per cent for rural Sindh; 11.5 per cent for the North West Frontier Province; 3.5 per cent for Balochistan; 4 per cent for the Federally Administered Tribal

Areas; and 2 per cent for Azad Kashmir and Jammu' (ibid., p. 31).

71. That is the 'combination of environmental states' within which a population can survive (Hannan 1979, p. 265).

72. See Table 1 (based on Rashid Amjad's 'Industrial Concentration and Economic Power) in Noman, (1988, p. 78).

73. Rashid and Shaheed, ibid., p. 18.

74. The literacy rate of the Mohajirs was at 68 per cent; followed by the Punjabis at 58 per cent; 41 per cent among the Pathans; 35 per cent among the Baluch; and 34 per cent among the Sindhis (Bengali and Sadaqat, ibid., p. 173).

75. Bengali and Sadaqat, 1997, pp. 171-173.

76. Ansari, ibid., p. 107.

77. Rashid and Shaheed, ibid., p. 17.

78. Z.A. Bhutto's controversial policies; accusations of having rigged the 1977 elections; and a joint alliance (the Pakistan National Alliance) of opposing political parties challenging his legitimacy to state power did not dent Bhutto's popularity sufficiently to jeopardize his chances of winning the elections.

79. Rashid and Shaheed, ibid., p. 12. The powerful provincial landlords and leaders were tackled by the cancellation of the agricultural income tax proposed by Zulfiqar Ali Bhutto; and by holding non-party elections, which benefited individual rural elite (mostly dissidents and opponents of the PPP) without enabling them to pose a collective threat to Zia. The industrialists were differentially won by selective de-nationalization (banks for instance, were not de-nationalized, nor were certain industries returned to their original migrant owners, although they claimed to fulfil the required conditions). The civil servants were pacified by a formula of power sharing with the military. The Afghan war with the former Soviet Union furthermore, enabled Ziaul Haq to subdue his international isolation (in reaction to the execution of Z.A. Bhutto), and secure 3.2 billion dollars in military and economic loans for Pakistan (Noman, ibid., pp. 121-126).

80. According to Verkaaik (1994, p. 1) Altaf Hussain had burnt the Pakistan flag.

81. Rashid and Shaheed, ibid., p. 29.

82. The MQM, Rashid and Shaheed note, 'neither claims nor bears any special responsibility for Pakistan, nor the upholding of the Islamic ideal' (ibid., p. 29).

83. Rashid and Shaheed, ibid., p. 33.

84. As a national party, the Pakistan Peoples Party acted as a counter weight to the 'nationalist' currents in Sindh. The

smaller Sindhi 'nationalist' parties moreover, rivalled each other.

85. According to Azeem Tariq, 'anybody who is a Muslim has the right to Pakistani nationality' (*Herald*, 1990, in Rashid and Shaheed, ibid., p. 30).

86. In Ansari, ibid., p. 103.

87. Solemnised by blood pacts.

88. The MQM boycotted the last national elections in 1997 in protest against the Anti-Terrorism Act that was formulated without their consultation, despite the MQM being an ally of the PLM Nawaz Sharif government.

89. The grievances highlighted by the MQM have ranged from the identification of general civic problems common to all the populations of Karachi (such as the provision of adequate public transport); to 'Mohajir' specific issues, namely: the repatriation of (250,000) Biharis stranded in Bangladesh (who like the Mohajirs would have no territorial affiliation with the provinces that constitute the state of Pakistan, and are therefore expected to increase the Mohajir strength in the city); the opening of the Khokhrapar route to India (which Sindhis fear would further facilitate Indian Muslims to clandestinely migrate to Pakistan), the allocation of federal funding for educational institutions; and jobs to Mohajirs by priority on the basis of fixed quotas rather than the urban/rural classification instituted by the Bhutto regime (thereby revising their earlier position on recruitment by merit; or, as a first step, the strict implementation of existing quotas, until further revisions can be agreed upon). (In Rashid and Shaheed [ibid.] pp. 30-31). To pre-empt competition from the in-migrants, the Mohajirs also demand restriction of voting rights to residents settled in Sindh for at least twenty years, and the prevention of the more recent settlers from acquiring property in Sindh.

90. Since Karachi has 13 out of 202 seats in the National Assembly; and urban Sindh (i.e., Karachi, Hyderabad, Sukkhar, and Nawabshah) has 25 out of 99 seats in the Provincial Assembly, the MQM is unable to form a government either at the provincial, or the national levels, even if the party sweeps the elections in its constituencies.

91. The affluent population of Karachi (Mohajirs and non-Mohajirs alike) have become victims of armed robberies, kidnapping for ransom, and extortion. Some MQM militants claim to have taken up the latter activities by way of 'their profession' (because they are unemployed). These activities are

distinguished from the party's commitment to represent the grievances of the Mohajirs.

92. In 1992, the army (itself instrumental in the formation of the party) became concerned with the growing rate of crime in the city, the increasing importance of the MQM, and the offensive launched by the party militants against dissidents and opponents. As a 'corrective' measure therefore, the army cracked down on Mohajir militants, and after two-and-a-half years of intensive operation (which included 'siege and search' operations to track down suspected terrorists, and 'clean up' the streets), the army withdrew, with little success to its credit. In 1995-96, during the second Benazir government, extra-judicial killings of believed terrorists were carried out under the supervision of the Minister of Interior. Towards the end of 1997 (and the beginning of the current Nawaz Sharif tenure), an emergency law, the Anti Terrorism Act, was formulated with the express purpose of controlling the unrest in Karachi, and rendering 'speedy justice' in 'special anti-terrorist courts'. The most recent among this series of 'emergency measures' was the imposition of Governor's rule in Sindh on 30 October 1998.

93. The MQM claimed to champion the cause of the poor and middle classes of Pakistan. The party, it said, was not against the Sindhi peasant. Rather, their struggle was against the quasi-feudal system of the country that exploits all the depressed strata of society.

94. The creation of the *Haqiqi* faction is believed to be an effort of the military establishment to crack the monolithic facade of the MQM Altaf Group.

95. Under the Chairmanship of Azim Tariq.

96. The Mohajirs give the MQM militants the benefit of the doubt, considering 'other' criminal *mafias* are also operating in the city.

97. Verkaaik, 1994; Phadnis, 1989.

98. See Hobsbawn and Ranger (1983); Anderson (1983); Tonkin (1989).

99. Barth, in Verkaaik, ibid., p. 7.

100. Verkaaik, ibid., p. 3.

101. In Rashid and Shaheed ibid., p. 12.

102. Ibid., p. 4.

103. Page, 1987, p. 259.

104. See Imran Ali's article in this volume.

105. The Mohajir concern with Punjabi domination at the centre, and their sensitivity towards the consequent tensions between

the centre and the provinces thus, is relatively recent. The resentment of the provinces (other than the Punjab at the One Unit form of government) was not shared by the Mohajirs so long as they were significantly represented within the central power structure, nor until their threat of marginalization had found a forum for expression.

106. Justifications to establish civic rights in Karachi are offered by the Mohajirs as well as the Sindhis. The former (conscious of their 'migrant' status in the 'land of the Sindhis') point out that it was they who built the city from a small military port to the industrial capital of the country, which now generates 33 per cent of the GDP. However, the Mohajirs complain that Karachi gets back only 2 per cent of the contribution it makes to the national revenues. The Sindhis share the plaint of the Mohajirs regarding the inadequate budget allocated to the province. They also cannot manifestly deny the claim of the Mohajirs to having built Karachi. However, they would rather acknowledge the contribution of the in-migrants in that regard (since the latter, as the Sindhis put it, have never challenged the legitimacy of the Sindhi claim to Karachi). As a strategy to check Mohajir 'hegemonistic' designs, therefore, the Sindhis suggest distribution of political power not only among the Sindhis and Mohajirs, but the in-migrants as well.

107. Some changes in the population dynamics of Karachi during the last decades have also had a bearing on structuring strategies of self-assertion in the competitive environment. The Mohajirs for instance, are no longer estimated to constitute the majority group in the city. Until the secession of Bangladesh in 1971, urban Sindh continued to be a magnet for the Muslims of India. As of 1971, increase in Mohajir population has by and large been restricted to natural reproductive growth rates. In the recently concluded census hence, the motivation to over-report their numbers had been high among the Mohajirs. For the same reason, Mohajirs favour the formal grant of citizenship to not only the illegal immigrants in Karachi, but also demand repatriation of the stranded Biharis in Bangladesh who would expand their support base.

108. Mohajirs express concern not only for the Sindhis, but also for the other populations of Pakistan facing problems similar to their own. They also show signs of acknowledging that they alone are not experiencing economic deprivation. Resources, they accept, are scarce for all the underprivileged populations of Pakistan.

109. Which ill-conceived decisions of the establishment itself have often helped compound over the last five decades.

Bibliography

Anderson, B. 1983. *Imagined Communities*. London, New York: Verso.

Ansari, Sarah. 1995. "Partition, Migration and Refugees: Responses to the Arrival of Mohajirs in Sindh during 1947-48." *South Asia: Journal of South Asian Studies*. Special issue, vol. xviii: 95-108.

Bengali, Kaiser and Mahpara Sadaqat. 1997. "Economic and Political Dimensions of Ethnicity: The Case Study of Karachi." In *The Politics of Ethnicity and Nationalism in Europe and South Asia*. 167-181. Karachi: University of Karachi.

Census of Pakistan. 1951. Karachi: Government of Pakistan.

Habsbawn, E. and Ranger, T.R. eds. 1983. *The Invention of Tradition*, Cambridge: Cambridge University Press.

Hannan, Michael T. 1979. "The Dynamics of Ethnic Boundaries in Modern States." In *National Development and the World System: Educational, Economic and Political Change 1950-1970*, ed. J.W. Meyer and M.T. Hannan. 253-275.Chicago: University of Chicago Press.

Jalal, Ayesha. 1990. "State Building in the Post-War World: Britain's Colonial Legacy, American Futures and Pakistan." In *South Asia and World Capitalism,* ed. Sugata Bose, 262-301. Delhi: Oxford University Press.

Jalal, Ayesha. 1995. *The Sole Spokesman: Jinnah, the Muslim League and the Demand for Pakistan*. Lahore: Sang-e-Meel Publications.

Karim, Mehtab S. 1998. "Demographic Dimensions of Karachi's Problems." In *Karachi: The Urban Development Institute*. (Occasional Paper Series No.1).

Khuhro, Hamida. 1998. *Mohammed Ayub Khuhro: A Life of Courage in Politics*. Lahore, Rawalpindi and Karachi: Ferozsons (Pvt.) Ltd.

Mumtaz, Soofia. 1990. "The Dynamics of Changing Ethnic Boundaries: A Case Study of Karachi." *The Pakistan Development Review*, Vol. 29, No. 3 and 4. 223-248.

Noman, Omar. 1988. *The Political Economy of Pakistan 1947-85*. London, New York: KPI Limited.

Page, David. 1987. *Prelude to Partition*. New Delhi: Oxford University Press.

Phadnis, Urmila. 1989. *Ethnicity and Nation Building in South Asia*. New Delhi: Sage Publications.

Rashid, Abbas and Farida Shaheed. 1993. *Pakistan: Ethno-Politics and Contending Elites*. Discussion Paper 45. Geneva: United Nations Research Institute for Social Development.

Talbot, Ian. 1990. *Provincial Politics and the Pakistan Movement. The Growth of the Muslim League in North-West and North-East India 1937-47*. Karachi: Oxford University Press.

Tonkin, E. ed. 1989. *History and Ethnicity*. London: Routledge.

Verkaaik, Oskar. 1994. *A People of Migrants: Ethnicity, State and Religion in Karachi*. Amsterdam: VU University Press.

Waseem, Mohammad. 1996. "Ethnic Conflict in Pakistan: The Case of MQM." *Paper and Proceedings*, Part II. Twelfth Annual General Meeting of the Pakistan Society of Development Economists, Islamabad, Vol. 35, No. 4. 617-630.

Yong, Tan Tai. 1995. "Punjab and the Making of Pakistan." *South Asia: Journal of South Asian Studies*. Special issue, vol. xviii: 177-192.

Zaidi, S. Akbar. 1990. *Sindhi vs. Mohajir? Contradiction, Conflict, Compromise*. Paper presented at the Democracy Development in South Asia Conference, Tufts University. (Unpublished).

The New Global Order: Politics and the Women's Movement in Pakistan

I write this at a moment in history when several events of great significance have come together: Indonesians are struggling and dying for their right to live; Palestinians are struggling and dying for their right to a homeland; India is asserting itself as a super power based on its nuclear capability; Pakistan is suffering an almost full scale sectarian war and Islamic fundamentalist groups of all hues and colours work towards resurrecting a Taliban-type control over the Pakistani people; and a Bishop commits suicide in protest against the Blasphemy Law in Pakistan which has tended to target the Christian community.

Yet these events are neither isolated, nor co-incidental. Indeed, they are the necessary fall-out of President George Bush's New World Order, the so called 'failure' of socialism and the 'end of ideology and end of history'; the 'success' of the 'free' market ideology; the global village etc; all of which have given rise to articulations of identity, conflict and destruction.

This study deals generally with these issues and traverses through the labyrinth of issues of identity, Pakistani history and the implications of this on women in Pakistan, and reflections of issues for the women's movement and indeed for all progressive movements for the future.

In almost every part of the world people are asserting their identities and looking within to find the essential in themselves. At present this is most acute in the former Soviet Union, Eastern Europe, Africa and South Asia where, from the dream of an over-riding internationalism we see the people of these nations shedding skin after skin of multiple identities: national, provincial, cultural, ethnic, linguistic, religious... hoping to get at the essence of what they are. But however creative, this type of paring away is necessarily painful and almost always violent. Furthermore, this breaking into smaller and smaller communities where people can express what is really their 'own' is offset by a new 'internationalism'.

This monolithic 'New World order' and 'new economic order' is trying to subsume all diversity and the alternatives to the linear development that it upholds. In this creation of what is being termed a uni-polar world, one can only see a future controlled by a new Imperialism. But this uni-polar world rests on creating a multi-polar substratum and on pitting the world against itself: across national borders, within nation states, and within ourselves. Creating the 'Other' is essential to this formulation, and its success lies in making this 'Other' believe that the expression of its identity emerges from itself. I am not suggesting that all expressions of nationality, religion, race, identity, and culture are part of a global conspiracy. Yet Islamic fundamentalism was created and encouraged by global capitalism, particularly by the United States, for its own political and economic purposes. For the people of those countries where Islamic fundamentalist regimes were imposed and supported, this meant two things, one that a monolithic and one-dimensional Islam was forced upon them, and secondly, that this imposition of a repressive and narrowly defined Islam led to intense divisions within these countries because of the various sects, and multiple interpretations that exist within Islam. Pakistan was one of the countries where an Islamic fundamentalist regime was forced upon the people, and which was supported militarily and economically by the United States.

Pakistan was created on the basis that the Muslims of India had a different identity, yet the question of its identity has never been resolved. The seeds of this crises lies in its history and indeed in the history of the national liberation struggle of pre-Independent India. Indians are taught that the Muslims divided India by raising the hollow issue of religious separateness; Pakistanis are taught that the Muslims of India created Pakistan because the Hindus of India would not allow them a say or space in an undivided India. Pakistan was, therefore, a rejection of Hindu dominance rather than an affirmation of Islam.

After the creation of Pakistan other identities surfaced: linguistic, ethnic, sub-national, provincial, and ideological. It took nine years for the nation to come to some sort of an agreement on a Constitution, but in these years, far from anything getting resolved, the other identities became more articulate. With the Jamaat-i-Islami (an Islamic fundamentalist political party which had opposed the creation of Pakistan, but which nevertheless decided to establish itself in the country) pushing for a more religious state, the Constitution of 1956 declared Pakistan to be an Islamic Republic with 'Almighty Allah' giving temporal authority to the people as a sacred trust. Affirmative action for women was recognized in the 1956 Constitution with women getting two votes, one for the general constituency and one for the reserved women's seats.

Meanwhile, the imposition of Urdu as the national language had alienated East Pakistan; the issue of who is a Muslim had surfaced with the Islamic credentials of the Qadiani sect being brought into question; and sub-nationalities were resisting a homogenization by the Centre.

The military took over in 1958. It sought to 'modernize' and liberalize Pakistan, and opened the doors to capitalist development. General Ayub Khan made changes in the Islamic personal law by promulgating a Muslim Family Laws Ordinance which gave some rights to Muslim women, and even removed the word 'Islamic' in the Constitution of 1962, although this was amended in 1963, and Pakistan again became an Islamic Republic. While Ayub Khan suppressed fundamentalist religious forces, he also suppressed all other dissent, and all articulations of sub-national, provincial, ethnic and linguistic rights in both parts of Pakistan. After a violent war of liberation, East Pakistan declared independence in 1971. Islam had not managed to hold the country together. This called into question the very basis of Pakistan, and only intensified its lingering crises of identity. Did Pakistan now have a rationale for its existence?

Z.A. Bhutto, President and then Prime Minister, initially tried to give Pakistanis an identity as Pakistanis. He himself was a Sindhi, a sub-nationality, his Urdu was faulty, he took to wearing *shalwar-kameez*, he was liberal and progressive in terms of women's rights, and he was able to give a voice to the people. Yet he was unable to withstand the pressure of the Islamic parties, and nor was he himself willing or able to transcend his own Muslim identity. The 1973 Constitution not only reinforced Pakistan as an Islamic Republic but held that all laws would be governed by the Quran and *Sunnah*. He established the Council of Islamic Ideology; hosted an Islamic Summit of Muslim states; and, misreading the opposition to his populist but repressive regime, he tried to establish his credentials with Islamic fundamentalist forces opposing his regime. Bhutto was overthrown by the military in 1977.

In the early 1970s in Pakistan, however, and especially when President Bhutto was preaching a brand of socialism, there was some shift in development planning from the purely productive and physical infrastructure, to socially oriented programmes such as health, education, housing and population control. For many of these programmes, the mobilization of women was crucial to their success. The development of women, therefore, became synonymous with national progress. In fact, the 1973 constitution declared as much, stating not only that 'there shall be no discrimination on the basis of sex alone' but that 'steps shall be taken to ensure full participation of women in all spheres of national life'. Consequently, not only was emphasis placed on the education and training of women but many occupations and professions normally closed to women were thrown open, including the highly exclusive Foreign Service. This policy was also prompted by the fact that Bhutto had a lot of support among women because they saw him as a 'progressive' man who would support equal rights for women. Bhutto responded to this not least because women were considered his allies against the right wing obscurantist forces opposing him.

The International Women's Year in 1975 was the perfect opportunity for Bhutto to prove to the women of Pakistan that he supported them, especially since it came at a time when a general election was on the horizon, and the women's vote crucial to Bhutto's success in it. Mrs Bhutto, therefore, led the Pakistan delegation to Mexico where she pledged that the 'people's government of Pakistan was fully committed to the complete equality, emancipation and integration of women in the development process'.

On 31 January 1976, Bhutto set up a Pakistan Women's Rights Committee to 'consider and formulate proposals for law reforms, with a view to improve the social, legal and economic conditions of the women of Pakistan and to provide speedier legal remedies for obtaining relief in matters like maintenance, custody of children, etc. Further, the Committee was to make suggestions for improving their economic conditions. The Committee suggested numerous, very progressive changes in several laws, and significantly in the Family Laws Ordinance, the Divorce Act and the West Pakistan Land Revenue Act. These suggestions included not only maintenance for a woman after divorce but a divorced woman's right to a share in her husband's property. It suggested simpler ways for a woman to get a divorce when she wanted it; allowed her to claim custody of the children beyond the ages specified in Islam and allowed her to claim maintenance for children in her custody. In addition to this, the Committee recommended changes in the labour laws affecting women in social security and maternity benefits and suggested all factories should have crèches (a point made also in the 1973 Constitution). Political power was also meant to be shared with a greater representation of women in local government institutions and in the provincial and national assemblies. Apart from the reserved assembly seats, the Committee suggested that it be made mandatory that political parties put up at least ten per cent female candidates for the seats contested in a general election. The Committee placed emphasis on education and on the employment of women in all occupations, including all government services. In fact, it suggested that until such time as women themselves gained the confidence needed for certain careers, that a certain percentage of positions be reserved for qualified women. Women were to be encouraged in the fields of sport, culture and the media. There were several other progressive suggestions but the most crucial was the proposal that it be made mandatory for a woman to get her share of inheritable property including agricultural land: and that a permanent Commission on the Status of Women be established, not only as a watchdog, but as the highest policy making body for women's interests in the country. Little of this was given time to be implemented.

The year 1977 was a turning point for Pakistan. General Ziaul Haq declared Martial Law, and justified his take-over by saying that he had to Islamize Pakistan. Apart from the support of the United States, other Western countries and the military, Islamic fundamentalist parties supported him, and the Jamaat-i-Islami joined his government. At one level it meant no more than military repression using the language of religion, yet Pakistan today borders on being a theocratic state not because the clergy is supported by the people, but because the state, in giving a voice to the clergy, has created its own nemesis.

While not being able to 'convert' the nation, or to bring about any fundamental changes in its capitalist economy, Ziaul Haq concentrated on issues such as Islamic punishments; on legal changes; and on refining the definition of Islam and what it means to be a Muslim. Fasting in Ramzan, saying one's prayers, forced deductions of *zakat* (charitable donations) by the government from bank accounts and other assets, in the exact percentage determined by Islam became the parameters of being a Muslim, while the larger morality got lost in the ritual. In separating the wheat from the chaff, non-Muslims were completely marginalized and are now only nominal citizens.

However, the linchpin of this process of Islamization was women. In his first address to the nation, Ziaul Haq vowed to uphold 'the sanctity of *chaddar* and *chardivari*' (the veil and the four walls). The State moved to take over the lives of women, to control their bodies, their space, to decide what they should wear, how they should conduct themselves, the jobs they could take, the sports they could play, and took it upon itself to define and regulate women's morality. This was done through a series of legislative changes such as the Zina and Hudood Ordinances, and the Islamic Law of Evidence; through directives such as the dress code, women not being allowed to participate in spectator sports; but mainly through a persistent ideology that women were not equal to men and that they must be regulated.

While the people of Pakistan and particularly women, have resisted this kind of Islamization, the process has been very detrimental to the nation. It has given legitimacy to fundamentalism and has put the nation, especially the progressive, liberal, urban middle class on the defensive, by constantly having to prove its identity. There is always a tendency that in asking larger questions such as what is a Pakistani or a Muslim, one ends up with narrower answers and narrower identities, because the more refined the definition, the greater will be the exclusion. This constriction is continuing in Pakistan, with even Islamic sects being pushed out of the central discourse.

Also, since Islam has no ultimate authority on earth to determine what Islam is, or who a Muslim is, the attempt to impose a single interpretation of Islam has pitted Muslim against Muslim, and sect against sect, and has also led to a proliferation of sub-sects. All of this has made every one, other than those in one's own community, the 'Other' and has made for a very disintegrated and violent society.

Women, in particular, have been fighting back, especially since 1981. The Hudood Ordinance, which specifies Islamic punishments, was passed in 1979. It requires the evidence of four Muslim males of good repute for maximum punishment, and makes no distinction between rape, adultery or fornication. The enormity of its implications became evident in 1981 when a woman and a man were arrested for adultery and sentenced to a hundred lashes each and stoning to death. This galvanized women into coming together and forming the Women's Action Forum (WAF), which was then an alliance of several women's groups and individuals. Since then, women's organizations have fought every anti-women measure, and the first demonstration against Islamization and Marital Law was a women's demonstration in 1983 against the proposed Law of Evidence which stipulated that the evidence of two women would be equal to that of one man. The women's movement grew in size with several other groups and organizations being formed.

On 15 December 1984, six women's organizations in Lahore passed the following resolution:

> General Ziaul Haq has asked all the citizens of Pakistan to judge his performance on the basis of the past 7-1/2 years (in the Referendum held on the 19th of December 1984). For Women, these Years have been the most repressive since the creation of Pakistan, for we have seen not only the enactment of retrogressive laws but have suffered the encouragement of an atmosphere that is derogatory and denigrating to women. The Hudood Ordinance of 1979, the Law of Evidence, 1984, and the proposed Law of *Qisas* and *Diyat* have systematically and deliberately snatched away the rights previously granted to women. Similarly, proposed changes in the Family Laws Ordinance, the Child Marriage Act and the Dowry Bill will degrade the status and dignity of women still further.
>
> In addition to this, these past years have threatened women's participation in all spheres of national activity and in some cases have actually curtailed women's participation such as in the field of sports, culture, the media and the administration. When we add to this the atmosphere of vilification against women; the increasing crimes against women and the encouragement of viewing women only as sexual objects we can only say again that these past 7-1/2 years are years for which the nation must be ashamed. All this has been carried out under the garb of Islamization... We warn the women of Pakistan of the dangers inherent in the continued process of Islamization as it is perceived and implemented by a few self-proclaimed guardians of Islam. A mandate for the continuation of these policies, as asked for in the referendum, must be rejected by the women of Pakistan.

Women fought a continuous battle with the State from 1984, with many more groups being formed and with various tactics and strategies. There were a few moments of reprieve at least on paper and in public statements under the two governments of Benazir Bhutto but in real terms little has been implemented.

However, while women's organizations and the women's resource centres and organizations that grew out of the women's movement in Pakistan have worked with dedication, the movement itself has lost its political sharpness and its energy. What is even more unfortunate is that the women's movement has begun to be defined only by a few women-centred groups, mainly in the urban areas. This has tended to exclude and to overlook the efforts that women have been making all over Pakistan in their own areas of work or expression, and this in turn has meant that the media, the government, international agencies and even these organizations, believe that it is only they who give legitimacy to the movement. There is, however, little validity in the assumption that the interests, issues, understanding, and in some cases, sophistication of urban/professional groups are different from those women not considered part of the movement. If anything, experience shows that women from different class, ethnic, religious, and professional back-grounds are much more able and willing to understand and grapple with issues of their own subordination. For example, it is often said by urban/professional, or women's rights groups that the women's movement cannot be very political, or confrontational, or secular, or conceptual, or feminist, because the 'average' woman is not yet ready for any of these. Yet, we have often found that these women are much more willing and able to understand and identify with these notions than middle class urban women, and that these women (and some men) are more willing to travel long distances for their jobs; stay away from their families; and even take enormous personal risks; to be a part of something that they believe in. To them the issues of class contradictions in society; the patriarchy inherent in all religions; militariza-tion; poverty; unemployment; suppression of creativity etc are not only concepts or objective realities, but also what they deal with on a daily basis. They are, therefore, much more interested in why this happens and how it may be resolved.

The question then is, what is the women's movement in Pakistan? The tendency, as said above, is to see it as either the Women's Action Forum in itself, or as WAF and a few other 'known' women's rights groups. This is unfair even to these organizations since they are then put in the position of constantly explaining what they are doing and why they are not doing what other movements and groups expect them to do. There is a genuine expectation from the women's movement, or specifically from a few women's groups, that far outweighs its size or its capacity. Feminists are also criticized for not living up to their own principles of feminism. To some extent this criticism is justified since many feminists and women's groups replicate male norms and mainstream organizations. The problem, however, also lies in the fact that the women's movement has not attempted to make a distinction between the feminist movement and the movement for women's rights. There is a difference. The women's movement is a struggle for democracy and equal rights for women within the liberal feminist tradition. Feminism on the other hand, is the recognition of patriarchy as a system of male oppression and domination which has a material ie, economic base. Feminists, therefore, seek a more holistic, ideological and structural transformation of society and a transformation of all relations including the personal. The women's rights movement is a necessary stage towards this transformation, just as a democratic, liberal stage may be necessary for social and economic structural transformation in general, but as far as feminism is concerned, equal rights within the existing system is not an end in itself. If the women's movement were to make this distinction, it could be much more inclusive since it could include and mobilize all those women struggling for women's rights. This would, in itself, make the movement larger and stronger. Feminists who struggle for a more profound transformation would also be a part of this movement. In this sense the movement would not only include all those struggling for equality in the public and private sphere, but also those struggling in their individual capacities such as writers, poets, artists etc, quite apart from women's and human rights groups, development NGOs, etc.

This would not only give strength to the movement but it would limit the criticism that the women's movement is simply the aspiration and articulation of a small group.

Recently, there have been attempts at redefining the movement by including development activities and projects. In many cases, however, projects, programmes, and action plans have subsumed and/or negated the very activism and the commitment that the movement is premised on. These initiatives have, in a concrete sense, depleted much of the dynamism, energy, and flexibility of the movement. For instance, in most cases these activities require and obtain financial support which invariably brings with it the constraints of paper work, proposals, reports, accounts etc, quite apart from the fact that often activities also get defined by the agendas and the constraints of funding agencies. This also leads to professionalism since management and efficiency become important, and to a competition for resources and financial support.

Paid political and social activism, whether it is in NGOs, or the press, or other institutions that supposedly work in the public interest, also gives a false sense of commitment and fulfilment. If, for example, one is spending several hours a day doing 'good works' there is a tendency to switch off when one is 'free'. Activism in this sense has increasingly become a job or a task, and the issues and actions not necessarily internalized. This not only leads to a further fragmentation of the self and to a false consciousness, but, by reinforcing the separation of the public and the private, it negates what the women's movement is trying to struggle for.

Further, given that all political and progressive movements are increasingly being subsumed by funded/professional activity, and since the 'business' side of development has got confused with development activism, there is a need to identify and accept the development professional as a new professional category. This category should then be subject to the same ethics, rules and norms as other professional groups. In other words, development professionals, especially those in consultancy work, should not be confused with development/social/political activists. A distinction should also be made between activism and action plans. Action plans do not necessarily lead to activism and do not necessarily produce social and political activists. Much of the confusion on these issues in development initiatives and processes has also played a role in diffusing the politics and energy of the women's movement.

The area that has, however, diffused the political edge of the movement the most is the issue of 'gender', especially the positing of 'gender' as opposed to 'feminism'. Gender is a complex, and even profound, concept which came out of the socialist feminist tradition. Unfortunately, it has been trivialised to the point of losing not only its original meaning, but also its history. It is increasingly promoted by the World Bank, the United Nations, bilateral aid agencies, by governments, and by NGOs, all of whom link this concept to development assistance. It has become an integral part of many activities in the women's movement. In many instances, it has simply replaced the word 'women' by the work gender (or is understood as meaning only women) because the use of the word women is much more politically charged, and the divisions much more clear. The women's movement has, therefore, lost its political edge, its sharpness and its tension, and is increasingly also losing its autonomy.

The women's movement has moved from being a movement, to becoming institutionalized, and a part of the establishment. The antithesis has, therefore, been through the synthesis and is increasingly becoming the thesis. Women's groups are now institutions, feminists are members of the establishment, women's studies is rapidly being incorporated in many universities, women's list are carried by mainstream publishers, women's issues are being addressed by governments, and key women are being included in decision making in state structures. If one has a dialectical understanding of history, this thesis or establishment, will produce a new antithesis to challenge it. This is a global as well as a national phenomenon, and the movement everywhere is not necessarily responding to the challenge within it with an openness and a flexibility that would allow it to move to a higher stage of development and a higher stage of politics. The question is, how do we get out of this stagnation and out of the apathy that funding and post-modernist ideology inculcates, or, where does one go from here?

There is still space within the women's movement to respond to this challenge, but the tendency has been to move away from the principles of feminism such as 'consciousness raising', 'speaking out', 'the personal is political', 'holistic' 'non-hierarchical', etc. Challenge and reflection are often dismissed as divisive or a 'waste of time, and in any case, too painful'. Yet there is a need to re-examine and redefine these principles rather than to dismiss them out of hand. This is its greatest challenge. If this challenge is not addressed, or confronted, or resolved, there is a danger that the trappings of the movements' issues and struggles will be co-opted by patriarchy and capitalism, while the substantial changes that it seeks get lost in the process.

Another challenge is the fact that economic and social development has been impeded by geo-political considerations as well as by structural adjustment policies in which development is determined by global market forces and by the privatization of various sectors including the social sector. With price increases of all goods and services, poverty levels and unemployment have increased. The privatization of the social sector has limited the access to quality health, education, and facilities to those who can afford them, thus reinforcing the existing class divisions.

All of this has had an impact on women who tend to get even more marginalized in crises situations: within the family, in the community, and in all aspects of society. In addition to this, the militarization of society, the increase in internal conflicts and crime, and the fact that the retrogressive ideology and legislation promoted and promulgated by General Ziaul Haq has not been reversed, have left women particularly vulnerable physically, politically, economically and socially.

All this has been done in the name of development, but what is 'development' anyway? The word 'develop' itself has a wondrous meaning, and is poetic in its implications. It means: 'to unfold; to unfurl; to unveil; disclose; reveal; discover; to lay open; to remove that which enfolds; to bring out all that is potentially contained therein; to bring forth from the latent or elementary condition; to make manifest what already existed under some other form or condition; to progress; to grow. Likewise, development is the process and the fact of this, that is, the concrete result of this process. In other words, development is unfolding...a bringing together into fuller view that which is latent. It is the 'production of an actual force, energy or a new form of matter from an existing state of being to one of a more vigorous, dynamic and creative condition'

The present model of development is not only class dominated, but is uni-linear and quantitative. Furthermore, it is economistic and materialistic and subsumes the more profound aspects of humanity. It has also never been culturally neutral and never gender-free. On the contrary, it is decidedly class dominated, Eurocentric and androcentric with patriarchy permeating all aspects of it. The history of this model is a history without women, and women continue to be invisible even when the parameters of this model are enriched by the social sciences and the humanities. Thus, when we talk about development, even when we talk about the development of the poor, the rural poor, women, human development, sensitization, etc, the development of women is still the underside of it; the periphery; the afterthought...

Although the concept of women and development has done much to focus attention on the formerly 'invisible' woman, it still treats woman one-dimensionally. Those of us women involved with this issue are as much to blame, for we too have accepted the worldview that separates poetry from science, and the personal from the political; and we too have struggled to integrate women and ourselves into this worldview. We have fought many a struggle to bring women into the mainstream; we have challenged the invisibility of women's contribution to society. We have fought for women's rights to wages and to work; for access to education, health, the law, and decision making. We have made endless programmes, run countless projects, written numerous reports, and books, and papers, and participated in many meetings, and all to one end: to acknowledge; to reinforce; to give a value to women's work and thereby to give women a place in society; as if this were an end in itself.

But if we understand that the development of a people is much more than this, we must challenge the very premises on which these concepts are based and we must be prepared to reconstruct our own knowledge and our own lives, and indeed our own ideology. As women we must start looking for a new vision, an alternative way of developing. Feminism and especially socialist feminism can show us some of the possibilities of finding a new space, or searching for a new understanding, since feminism is a distinct shift from what has been a universal construct. It seeks to question and redefine progress and development. It impacts on all aspects of our lives. Unfortunately, too much has gone wrong in Pakistan for too long, and we are tired from struggling against the forces that confront us. Yet the future looks even more bleak if we withdraw now. Neo-imperialism is much more insidious and we are all liable to get entrapped in it, since it does not clearly identify itself as imperialism. This neo-imperialism is deciding our options for the future and if we want any degree of independence, we have to fight for it... both within and outside the country.

We must take on the challenge that the future poses. How do states address their human, social, and moral responsibilities towards all their citizens without subsuming their individuality? How can individual creativity be encouraged while fulfilling the common good, and ensuring a just, equitable and classless society. How can identities be expressed without them becoming divisive? This challenge is not just strategic, it needs, dare I use the term, an ideology. Indeed, an ideology of the left that can address these complexities before they are consumed by ideologies of the right. The ideologies of the right ride over all of us, be they of religious fundamentalism; fascism or capitalism; and none of them address complexity. Right-wing ideologies ask simple questions and get simple answers. For a just future we need an ideology that recognizes that the answers are not simple, and this is a challenge that we must address globally.

PART FOUR

THE POLITICAL
ECONOMY OF
PAKISTAN

Economic Strategies and Policies in Pakistan, 1947-1997

On 14 August 1997, Pakistan celebrated its fiftieth anniversary as an independent nation—and over twenty-six years of existence within its present geographical boundaries. With a 1997 GNP per capita of US$470,[1] and a population of over 135 million, Pakistan is the seventh most populous country in the world, just ahead of Japan. Some 90 million persons are of working age, 38 million are in the labour force, and 36 million are employed. Until recently, Pakistan had been one of the fastest growing economies in the world. Naturally, this growth has been accompanied by considerable structural diversification.

Yet, a persistent criticism of Pakistan's economic performance has been the failure of this growth and structural change to improve the lives of the bulk of the population by the degree of improvement experienced by a small exclusive élite—euphemistically referred to as inattention to 'social' sectors. A second criticism is the government's inability to establish a sustainable pattern of public finance, relying first on foreign grants, then loans, supplemented by domestic non-bank borrowing, and of late, even by borrowing from short-term private sources. As a result, Pakistan faces a profile of future debt service payments which can not be met without resort to extremely repressive social measures.

Basic data on Pakistan's economic performance are presented in Table I. The first two periods in Table I correspond to 'United Pakistan' (1947-71), while the last three (1971-97) correspond to the present boundaries of Pakistan.

Under united Pakistan, four phases can be identified: 1947-53, occupied by reconstruction and self-reliant development; 1953-58, occupied by the preparation of the First Five-Year Plan (1955-60), with US intellectual and financial assistance; 1958-65, the 'miracle' years of aid-financed crony capitalism; and the consequent 1965-71 period of disintegration, leading to the secession of East Pakistan.

Table I
Growth and Structural Change, 1950-97

	1950-58[a]	1958-71[a]	1971-77	1977-88	1988-97
Growth Rates (% p.a.)					
Population	2.5	2.8	3.2	3.1	3.0
Real GNP(mp) per capita	0.9	4.2	3.3	3.0	1.1
Consumer Prices	2.3	3.2	17.4[b]	7.5	10.4
Real GDP (fc)	3.3	6.2	4.8	6.6	4.9
Value Added in Agriculture	1.8	4.3	2.2	3.9	3.9
Value Added in LS Manufacturing	19.8	12.1	2.3	9.4	4.0
Employment	..	1.6	3.0	2.4	2.1
In Agriculture	..	0.8	1.8	2.0	-1.0
In Large-Scale Manufacturing	..	3.6	3.0	1.7	-0.9
Structure (% GDP, end period)					
Agriculture	51.8	41.2	36.6	22.9	22.4
Large-Scale Manufacturing	6.1	11.9	10.3	11.6	11.1
Overall Budget Deficit (-)	..	..	- 8.6	- 8.5	- 6.3
Trade Deficit (-)	- 4.9	- 3.2	- 7.8	- 5.0	- 4.8
Current Account Deficit on the BOP (-)..		..	- 7.0	- 4.4	- 7.1
M&LT External Debt (DOD US$ billion)					
(as % of GNP)	..	..	8.3	20.0	30.0
Liquid External Reserves (US$ billion)..		0.1	0.4	0.5	2.5
(as months of merchandise imports)	..	(2.3)	(1.9)	(0.9)	(2.5)

Note: All growth rates have been calculated by fitting an ordinary least squares (OLS) trend.
.. not available.
[a] (West) Pakistan only.
[b] Only 11.1% (OLS, or 9.5% simple average), if 1971-72 and 1973-74 (when imported inflation was extraordinarily high) are excluded.
Source: *Economic Surveys*, Annual, and Federal Bureau of Statistics.

In the contemporary period (1971-97), three phases can be identified quite naturally: the first, 1971-77, sought to correct the excesses of the crony capitalism of the 'miracle' years by resort to the Islamic Socialism of Bhutto; the second, 1977-88, undid the nationalization of the first period, but continued to buttress their power by appeal to Islamic values and symbols under what might be called the Islamic Capitalism of Ziaul Haq; and the final present phase, 1988- , in which crony capitalism is once again being promoted (like 1958-65), albeit in very different political and economic circumstances. Given the role of the International Monetary Fund (IMF) and the World Bank (WB) in this period, this can also be identified as the 'stabilization and adjustment' or 'reform' phase in Pakistan's economic history.[2]

The Roots of Macro-economic Disequilibrium

The budget is the root of all economic problems in Pakistan. It is important, therefore, to understand the evolution of the crisis of public finance in its structural and historical context. Although the state of Pakistan was created in 1947 and its present boundaries date from 1971, the *economy* of Pakistan—a system of resource allocation for the production and distribution of goods and services—is the third oldest in the world (pre-dated only by Iraq and Egypt).

Since the earliest times local communities had been able to provide for their needs, even after paying the king's demand (in kind). This demand was usually moderate, especially during famines, but it did become onerous during times of war. In either case, however, revenues from agricultural produce or land (the principal form of wealth) were adequate to finance the king's court and his wars. Colonial government continued with this pattern of public finance. Until the end of the nineteenth century, government revenues are thought to have been around 5-7 per cent of GDP, public expenditures were well under 10 per cent of GDP, and the fiscal deficit was usually under 2 per cent of GDP.

Two historical developments served to alter this pattern of public finance:
- First, with the weakening of central authority during the 'twilight' of Mughal rule (1707-1857), the balance of power shifted away from the kings to the local landlords— *zamindars*, who as agents of the king collected land

revenue from tenant farmers, and *jagirdars*, who were allowed to collect revenues on their own account in return for loyalty or special services. Although motivated by entirely different concerns, Cornwallis' permanent settlement of Bengal in 1793 formalized this situation, by recognizing the *zamindars* as permanent owners of the land, subject to their payment of a fixed annual revenue to the government.[3]

- Second, with the assumption of direct control by the British in the wake of the revolt of 1857, efforts were initiated to appease local influentials through schemes of community development. Early in this century, when requirements of political expediency were joined by the demand for democratic reforms by liberal opinion in England, the idea that the budget should provide for expenditures to sustain government—especially, governments that sought to implement (real or illusory) democratization of society—acquired legitimacy.

These developments had a number of important consequences:[4]

- the tax system was deprived of buoyancy (by fixing the settlement for long periods, with payment in cash rather than in kind), and became subject to exemptions (for preferred *jagirdars* and by size of holding, among others);
- the full burden of military expenditures was transferred to the state, while relieving wealthy landowners of any specific responsibility for the provision of supplies or finance for war;
- an additional burden of schemes for local improvement—development projects, in modern parlance—designed to mobilize political support for the government, was assumed by the budget; and
- the delicate balance of customary rights and responsibilities was upset in the rural areas, with ruinous results for agriculture and the condition of the rural poor.[5]

Development Strategies and Policies

In the initial years after Independence (1947) the government addressed itself to meeting these problems, along with the demands of reconstruction, by ensuring austerity and developing the tax base. With the start of the Cold War (1949-89), however, Pakistan entered into its fateful alliance with the United States of America. As a result, a growing inflow of military and economic assistance—initially (1955-60) mainly as grants, but after 1960 increasingly as loans—served both to mask these structural weaknesses, and to add a new burden on the budget: that of debt service payments. In addition, an aid-dependent pattern of development in which fundamental structural reforms were perennially postponed and policy-making became a marketing activity in pursuit of aid flows, was firmly established.

This has provided an essential underlying continuity to the apparent turbulence which has characterized the first fifty years of Pakistan. Throughout this period, the performance of agriculture and the volume of military and economic assistance received have been the proximate determinants of economic performance. This leads to a peculiar difficulty in attempting any serious analysis of development strategies and policies on economic outcome—pronouncements of strategy and policy have been motivated almost exclusively by a concern for maximizing foreign assistance;[6] any serious plan for action by the government has been implemented by *ad hoc* executive decisions which have seldom been announced. Any linkage between strategy and outcome, therefore, has been strictly fortuitous, even though plan and programme reviews submitted by the government to donors have sought to establish such linkages whenever favourable to their case.

In any periodization of the economic history of Pakistan, therefore, relations with sources of foreign assistance—mainly the United States of America—must constitute an important criterion of demarcation. The periodization given below distinguishes first between 'united Pakistan' (1947-71) and the subsequent phase (1971-97) which corresponds to contemporary Pakistan. Within each period, the three constitutions (1956, 1962, and 1973) and the two martial law periods (1958-73 and 1977-85) which intervened are also distinctive.[7] Far more important from an economic perspective, a distinction can be made between periods of especially close relations with the United States of America (1951-62 and 1981-90).[8] An added criterion, although of much lesser consequence in the more recent period (due to a shift in development fashions), have been the eight Five-Year Plans—especially the Second Plan (1965-70) and to a much lesser extent the Sixth Plan (1982-87)—which purport to lay out strategies and policy frameworks, in quest of aid.

'United' Pakistan 1947-71

Within the scope of this study, it is not possible to do justice to the lessons yielded by a close examination of this first period of Pakistan, even if confined to development strategy and policies. Nevertheless, as a prelude to a discussion of the more recent period (1971-97), a summary overview is presented below.

Sovereign Development (1947-53)

At its birth on 14 August 1947, amidst dire predictions of imminent collapse, Pakistan had few foreign friends. The paramount concerns of public policy were non-economic—defence, rehabilitation of refugees, and the development of institutions and infrastructure essential to a sovereign state. In the economic realm, the principal concerns, apart from institutional development, were the maintenance of external and domestic solvency amidst the many crises which attended its early years.[9] Although the ideas of development strategy or policy, as we know them, were yet to be born, there was a sense of development activities as schemes for local improvement and the idea that investment decisions needed co-ordination by government.[10] In response, the government sought to organize itself, but despite some talk of investment co-ordination and plan formulation, there is little evidence of any concrete movement toward these ends.

The First Plan Period (1953-58)

While the government struggled with ensuring military security while managing the many crises which beset the polity, economy and society, a new global order—in short, the Cold War order—had begun to take shape. In the wake of events succeeding the end of the Second World War, the idea of military containment of the Soviet Union had been buttressed by the ideology of development—motivated largely by the fear of a communist revolution, especially in South and South-East Asia, like the 1949 revolution in China. US assistance started in 1951 and was sealed by the 19 May 1954 Mutual Defense Agreement, under which a 'special relationship' was established between Pakistan and the United States of America. In 1953, the Harvard Advisory Group (1953-70) was established, to 'assist' the Planning Commission in preparing the First Five-Year Plan.[11] The First Plan is certainly a good essay on the economic development problems of Pakistan. Lacking political 'ownership' however, it proved to be an entirely unfeasible plan.

The 'Miracle' of Pakistan (1958-65)

Completed in late 1957, the First Plan was overtaken by the imposition of martial law in October 1958. It was the Second Five-Year Plan (1960-65), however, which was the *pièce de résistance* of economic plans in Pakistan, not least because it covered a period regarded (by some) as the 'golden age' of economic development in Pakistan. Critics, however, question how much of it was fortuitous, what was the share of 'hype' in favour of a strong US ally—not unlike that for the East Asian 'Tigers' these days—and whether the social costs of the hard-headed growthmanship which characterized this period was sensible.[12] On the evaluation of this experience rest many contemporary positions on strategy and policy: the advisability or otherwise of closer ties with the United States, plan vs. market, industry vs. agriculture, the desirability of inequality, or of a direct attack on poverty or benign neglect (under the so-called 'trickle-down' strategy), among others.

Disintegration (1965-71)

There was always a feeling that a 'miracle' based on continued provision of military and economic assistance from the United States, not a natural ally of Pakistan,[13] may not prove durable. The beginning of the end came with the 1962 Sino-Indian hostilities, in the wake of which India finally turned to the United States for military assistance. With the September 1965 Indo-Pakistan war, the US suspended military assistance to Pakistan (and India), bringing to an end the US-Pakistan aid relationship (1951-62), and the accompanying miracle.[14] As a result, the Third Plan (1965-70), with its assumptions of large and increasing aid flows, was still-born.[15] With it perished the platitudes about tempering modernization with religious, moral and cultural values and preventing 'excessive concentration of income and wealth in the hands of a few' (Government of Pakistan, 1964). By the time the Fourth Plan (1970-75) was being formulated, the prospects for foreign assistance had become even more bleak. In the face of resource scarcity, the East and West wings of the country failed to reach agreement on the Plan. By late 1968, civil disturbances had started which culminated in the secession of East Pakistan in December 1971.

Contemporary Pakistan 1971-

Following the secession of East Pakistan, both elections and the military lay completely discredited within Pakistan and Pakistan itself became a pariah in the international community. Once again, from an economic perspective, the 1981 agreement on a 'new relationship' with the United States provides a more meaningful breaking point than the conventional division by civil and military regimes. In deference to tradition, however, we can consider this modern period according to the persons in whom the popular imagination has seen power as being vested: the Islamic Socialism of Bhutto (1971-77), the Islamic Capitalism of Ziaul Haq (1977-88), and the Chaotic Liberalism of Pakistan's second democratic experiment (1988-1999).

Islamic Socialism, 1971-77[16]

Once again, the early years (1971-73) were spent in dealing with security concerns and the recovery of prisoners-of-war. Responding to heightened criticism of social inequalities, the regime nationalized major industries and financial institutions within the first six months of assuming office. With the suspension of US aid (and associated bilateral assistance from US allies, and multilateral assistance from international financial institutions), the nature of plans and planning in Pakistan stood exposed. At the same time, developments in the international economy in the early 1970s both imposed additional strains on economic management, and provided a release by large-scale emigration of labour (mainly to neighbouring Muslim countries). Since the main balance of payments surpluses were with Arab countries, there was a powerful impetus to combine popular values and the necessity of securing Arab financial aid by invoking Arab-Islamic symbols and rhetoric. Although the Fourth Plan (1970-75) was finalized and a semblance of planning was maintained, the 'Islamic Socialism' period is also referred to as the non-plan period.

Islamic Capitalism, 1977-88

The imposition of martial law in 1977, in the wake of widespread disturbances following the first elections held by the previous government, did not really mark any essential discontinuity in the aid mobilization strategy. Abandoned by America, both regimes continued to invoke Islam in an effort to base power in popular values. The new government did, however, undo the nationalization measures of the previous regime to a certain extent, and turned to the private sector for spearheading economic activities once again. There was no real change in the status of planning activities, even though a Fifth Plan (1978-83) was drawn up. The economy, however, was in serious straits:

'By the time martial law was imposed in July 1977, the economy had been bankrupt for some time. At the end of

June 1977, for the first time in the history of Pakistan, net foreign assets of the banking system were negative by Rs 566 million (or US$57 million). In 1976-77, although the investment rate had risen to 19.3 per cent of GDP and the surplus on the consolidated revenue budget to Rs 1.7 billion, the deficit on the current account of the balance of payments was above US$1 billion (or 6.7 per cent of GNP); the rate of growth of GDP had fallen to 2.8 per cent, so that per capita GDP growth had been negative; while consumer prices had risen by 11.8 per cent.'[17]

The return, once again, to the present era of aid-dependent development, came from two fortuitous events in 1979: the revolution in Iran and the Soviet invasion of Afghanistan. Although all US aid was cut off to Pakistan in 1979, both events led to a fundamental re-assessment of Pakistan's strategic importance to the United States, and a fresh search to resuscitate the old patterns of dependence. With these US overtures to Pakistan, the prospects for formulating plans, strategies and policy statements once again became bright. In 1980, the US agreed to reschedule some US$160 million in debt service payments due from January 1981 to July 1982, subject to the negotiation of a suitable agreement with the IMF. In November 1980, the government promptly entered into a three-year Extended Fund Facility (EFF) agreement with the IMF.[18] Shortly thereafter, US assistance was once again resumed in October 1981 under a fresh, long-term agreement to provide military and economic assistance, as the basis of a 'new relationship' between the US and Pakistan. On this basis, the Sixth Plan (1983-88) was drawn up. With its judicious combination of Quranic verses and Jeffersonian idealism, it provided a clear pronouncement on Pakistan's commitment to economic liberalism, appropriate to the international climate of opinion.

Chaotic Liberalization (Since 1988)

Reverting to old patterns, in the Sixth Plan period the commitment to liberalism was largely a posture, whose adverse effects were contained by the selective interventions of a bureaucracy in control. The unexpected death of Ziaul Haq in August 1988 and the decision of the army to stay out of politics were critical turning points. As an emergency measure, the army handed power to an interim government consisting of a group of senior civil servants and influential expatriates. The army also conducted elections that attracted high participation rates and were widely reported to be fair by domestic and international observers.

The interim government rushed into medium-term agreements with the IMF in the interregnum between elections and the formal swearing-in of the new government. As a result, when Benazir Bhutto took office as Prime Minister (in November 1988, and again in December 1990) she had no choice but to approve these agreements which were then approved by the IMF Board on 28 December 1988 and on 22 February 1994.[19]

There were several problems, however, with these agreements:

- First, they created opportunities for corruption but were not designed to forestall corrupt behavior by politicians.[20]
- Second, domestic institutions of governance were undermined as economic decision-making shifted to a small coterie in the Ministry of Finance, and processes of inter-ministerial review, consultation and examination atrophied.
- Third, even as they signed the agreements, the IMF staff knew that those signing on behalf of the government were in no position to deliver on long-term promises, especially as they related to the budget.

Fourth, because action on the budget was difficult, the IMF proceeded to exact concessions on the balance of payments (devaluation, import liberalization, and tariff reductions, all of which exacerbated budgetary problems), in the financial sector (de-regulating interest rates, also leading to wider budget deficits, and to enormous profits for foreign banks, whose entry was encouraged), and privatization (which in the absence of regulatory reforms in banking led to massive plunder of national assets, as erstwhile profitable public sector units were closed down after having been stripped of assets by private sector buyers, who used fraudulent or unenforceable bank guarantees to acquire these firms).

Just as research at the IMF/WB would have us expect, because of improper sequencing of adjustment efforts, the liberalization that took place was chaotic and damaging. Not surprisingly, it did not achieve any of the three goals of structural adjustment programmes: balance of payments viability, price stability and sustainable growth. As a result, Pakistan finds itself in the midst of a full-blown debt crisis, and is presently seeking IMF funds under an extended structural adjustment facility (ESAF).[21]

In 1989-90, following the disintegration of the Soviet Union, the *raison d'etre* of US-Pakistan military and economic alliance—as well as the larger global context of the Cold War which sustained the world of foreign aid, including the structure of theories about, and practice of, economic development—ceased to exist. The new realities revealed themselves in 1990 when all US military and economic assistance, provided under the 'special relationship' established in 1981, was cut off following the US President's sudden failure to provide a certification that Pakistan's nuclear programme was peaceful in nature.[22] A failure both of an appreciation of the new realities and of imagination, however, has led successive governments in Pakistan to search for a solution to their economic problems in the restoration of close military-economic ties with the US, trying this time to transform Pakistan from a military-client-state to an economic-client-state.

Misguided policies and failure to achieve necessary structural adjustments to changing environments have proven expensive. In comparison to less than US$30 billion of medium and long-term borrowing by the public sector over the last fifty years, short-term foreign exchange liabilities of Pakistan today are around US$16 billion—some US$6 billion in short-term borrowing (reportedly, at rates as high as 4 per cent above LIBOR) and some US$10 billion in foreign currency accounts. The bulk of this indebtedness represents the cost of misplaced adjustment policies in the last 3-5 years.

Adjustment Policies and Economic Growth, 1971-98

What has been the contribution of policy interventions to economic growth in Pakistan? In particular, what has been the contribution of 'adjustment' policies (or of economic 'reform'), initiated in the 1980s, to economic growth? As is now well-recognized, there are insurmountable methodological problems which inhibit a valid response to this question. The usual 'before-and-after' analyses suffer from the *post hoc ergo propter hoc* fallacy, in that it is impossible to establish a causal linkage between policies and outcomes. The alternative, 'counterfactual' analyses—which explore, within the framework of a formal model, what would have happened had policies not been implemented, and are, therefore, irrefutable by any set of data—are crucially dependent on model specification and estimation. The only option is to present heuristic analyses of suggested links between policies and outcomes.

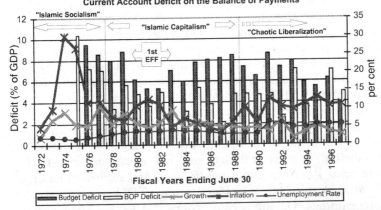

Figure 1 Growth, Inflation, Unemployment Rate, Budget Deficit & the Current Account Deficit on the Balance of Payments

Figure 1 presents trends in major macroeconomic variables since 1971, along with a demarcation of the three periods identified (for data on period averages, see Table I). It also marks the period of the first extended fund facility (EFF, 1980-83) obtained, as a pre-condition to debt rescheduling, from the IMF by Pakistan. In 1982, the World Bank (WB) also extended a structural adjustment loan (SAL) to complement the IMF's EFF.[23] The present, third period is characterized throughout by intermittent long-term arrangements with the IMF. The most recent is a US$935 million extended structural adjustment facility (ESAF) and US$623 million extended fund facility (EFF), approved on 20 October 1997, under which a first tranche of US$209 million was drawn in October and November 1997; and a second tranche of US$177 million, in April 1998.

The data presented in Figure 1 suggest that there has been a clear secular downward drift in the rate of economic growth, at least since the early 1980s (if not the late 1970s)—even though, on average, the growth rate rose during the second period, and fell in the third (Table I). Second, there has been a secular upward drift in the rate of inflation, which fell below 5 per cent in 1987, but has been rising sharply since then. Third, the rate of unemployment rose after 1975, stabilized (at around 5 per cent) from 1979 to 1990, but has been rising since then. These three trends appear to be independent of the size of the budget or the balance of payments deficits—although, naturally, the counterfactualists would argue that higher deficits would have led to higher inflation and lower growth. On balance, however, it seems that the period of adjustment has been characterized by falling growth and rising inflation and unemployment.

In the face of this evidence, it is clear that adjustment programmes have failed to achieve any of the three goals that these programmes are aimed at: (i) balance of payments viability—in the sense that at the end of the programme there would be no need for further extraordinary external financing; (ii) price stability; and (iii) sustainable growth. On the first, Pakistan continues to seek extraordinary external finance despite ten years and more of IMF/WB adjustment programmes. On the second, there has been a clear secular rise in the rate of inflation over the last decade. Finally, there has been a clear secular downward trend in the growth rate, and the sustainability of these lower rates of growth is questionable, given the explosive path of past and future debt service payments.

Why has this been the case? In a word, because of improper *sequencing* of reforms. There is ample evidence from both IMF/WB studies and from independent research that macroeconomic stability—which in Pakistan means budgetary stability—is an essential pre-condition for the success of economic liberalization. Unfortunately, in the face of binding political constraints to budget reform, international financial agencies, facing their own operational exigencies, went ahead with such 'reforms' as the government could agree to, even though the prior conditions for the success of these reforms were not met.

Fiscal Policy

The impact of fiscal policy on economic growth is difficult to quantify without the aid of a formal model. Conceptually, however, the key static first round effects may be assessed in the following terms:

- government revenues have reduced disposable income and hence private savings, private investment and growth;
- government expenditures have led to transfers abroad, domestic income redistribution, incremental demand for goods and services, and capital formation, all of which should have had a net positive impact on investment and growth, depending on the level and composition of government expenditure; and
- deficit financing, which has absorbed a large share of private savings and raised interest rates, has reduced investment and growth (among other effects).

Table II
Indicators of Fiscal Policy, 1980-97

	1979-80	1987-88	1994-95	1995-96[a]	1996-97[b]
STRUCTURE (AS % OF GDP)					
Revenues	16.4	17.3	16.9	17.5	18.7
Expenditures	23.3	26.7	22.8	23.9	22.7
Debt Service	4.6	6.8	8.7	8.7	9.3
Foreign	*3.4*	*3.2*	*4.4*	*4.1*	*4.5*
Domestic	*1.2*	*3.6*	*4.3*	*4.6*	*4.8*
Defense	5.4	7.0	5.6	5.5	5.2
Development	9.3	6.9	4.4	4.3	4.2
Administration, &c.	4.0	6.0	4.1	5.4	4.0
Overall Deficit	**6.3**	**8.5**	**5.6**	**6.3**	**4.0**
Domestic Financing (Net)	3.3	6.6	4.0	5.1	3.3
Non-Bank	*0.6*	*4.5*	*2.6*	*2.7*	*2.5*
Banking System	*2.7*	*2.1*	*1.4*	*2.4*	*0.8*
External Financing (Net)	3.0	1.9	1.6	1.2	0.7
MEMORANDUM (AS % OF GNP)					
Public Debt[c]	..	73.9	79.0	79.3	..
External Debt[c]	..	33.0	36.5	37.3	..
Domestic Debt	..	40.9	42.5	41.9	..
External Liquidity (as % of imports)	17.5	7.7	29.4	21.9	..

Note: Consolidated federal and provincial government budget figures, as presented by the Ministry of Finance in their *Economic Survey*. In the last few years, these figures have differed from those presented by the State Bank of Pakistan (SBP) in its *Annual Report*. The overall deficit is the difference between revenues and expenditures plus the surplus of autonomous bodies (not shown).

.. not available.
[a] Provisional actuals.
[b] Budget estimates.
[c] Outstanding and disbursed.
Source: *Economic Survey 1996-97*, *Statistical Supplements*, and State Bank *Annual Reports*. See Annex 4, Tables 2.3 and 2.4.

Government revenues have remained at around 17 per cent of GDP for a very long time—the higher budget target for 1996-97 is unlikely to be attained. Consequently, their direct impact on disposable incomes and saving has not been onerous. The bulk of tax revenues, however, arise from indirect taxes: mainly import duties—whose effects on industrial incentives will be examined under trade policy. Over the last decade, sales tax (mainly as a surcharge on import duties) and excise duties (collected mainly from a few items) have grown over the last decade. On balance, however, the average burden of taxation has been moderate, but the incidence on salaried tax-payers already in the tax net had become quite high. This has been corrected in the 1997-98 budget.

The major impact of the budget on investment and growth, however, has come from expenditures and their financing. First, the accumulated burden of inadequate taxation has led to an unsustainable rise in the debt burden, so that debt service payments are now growing at an unsustainably high rate: 20 per cent per year over the last ten years. As a result of the rising burden of debt service payments, government expenditure on defence, development and civil administration has all been squeezed. The decline in public investment has had both a direct impact on capital formation and an indirect one through inadequate provision of public goods (especially physical and social infrastructure). Also, as government has sought to mobilize increasingly higher amounts from capital markets, interest rates have risen and investment incentives have deteriorated. The net impact of the government's fiscal operations, therefore, have been to contribute to macroeconomic instability, and lower the rate of investment and growth.

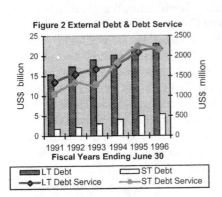

Figure 2 External Debt & Debt Service

Fiscal Years Ending June 30

LT Debt   ST Debt
LT Debt Service   ST Debt Service

Monetary Policy

Monetary policy affects investment and growth through its impact on incentives to save, invest, and produce, mainly by ensuring that credit is available, at as low interest rates as possible, in a stable macroeconomic environment. Until February 1994, when the State Bank of Pakistan Act, 1956 was amended to give the State Bank greater autonomy, monetary policy in Pakistan was conducted largely to accommodate the financial requirements of government.[24] It is too early to tell what impact this new autonomy will have on its conduct in the future.[25] In the past, however, the role of monetary policy *per se* has been minor, as the State Bank's intervention in financial markets has consisted mainly of the direct regulation of credit, in support of the government's economic objectives.

There have been three major landmarks in the history of credit regulation. First, the Credit Inquiry Commission of 1959 and the Credit Inquiry Committee of 1962 provided the State Bank of Pakistan (SBP) with clear directions to micro-manage the process of credit distribution—to primary producing sectors, and small and medium-scale enterprises—including through the establishment of new institutions. Second, under the banking reforms introduced in May 1972, elaborate institutions—consisting of the National Credit Consultative Committee (NCCC) and its sub-committees—were set up to ensure that the credit needs of specific sub-sectors was met. Finally, in 1990-91, under a Financial Sector Adjustment Loan (FSAL) from the World Bank and technical assistance from the IMF, a transition from instruments of direct control over credit to indirect influence of monetary aggregates (mainly through open market operations) was effected.[26]

Whether it had other costs or not, there should be little controversy in assuming that the direction of credit flows to priority sectors led to better fulfillment of the government's priorities: promoting investment and growth, and meeting its distributional objectives. At the same time, there is considerable evidence that without prior budget reform, financial sector liberalization was premature. Whatever impact it had on efficiency of the banking sector[27] the rise in interest rates that followed had disastrous consequences for the budget, as had been seen clearly by those who proposed it.[28]

The idea that by confronting government with higher interest rates, the government's recourse to non-bank domestic borrowing would be curtailed was flawed to begin with. In the event, after the switchover to market-based instruments, recourse to domestic non-bank borrowing—after turning negative in the year of the switchover, 1991-92— rose rapidly, and at higher rates of interest (Figure 3).

Why then were these 'reforms' implemented? With budget reforms politically impossible, lessons of theory and experience were put aside and in return for balance of payments support from IMF/WB, such 'reforms' as could be carried out were carried out. In the first instance (EFF 1980-83), the major movement was on exchange rates and import liberalization (see figure 3), along with disinvestment, de-regulation, and privatization. Subsequently, with the start of full-scale adjustment after 1988, tariff reforms and financial sector liberalization bore the brunt of policy change in return for balance of payments support from the IMF/WB. In the absence of prior budget reforms both were premature, but it was financial sector reforms which contributed most to the onset of the present debt crisis.

The common sense view was that without putting in place effective constraints on budgetary indiscipline, financial sector liberalization would lead to higher interest rates and hence a rise in the government deficit. In its eventful report, the World Bank (1987, vol. 2, pp. 6-7) also stressed the need for 'careful sequencing' of reforms—identifying price stability and the maintenance of external balance, through deficit reduction, exchange rate action, and conservative monetary policies, as prerequisites for the success of trade reform, financial sector reform and de-regulation—and warned that 'financial sector reform will not be successful unless accompanied by reduction in the budget deficit.'

The financial needs of the government and the operational exigencies of the World Bank, however, combined to ensure that change took precedence over direction. On the basis presumably of a judgement that budget deficits could be controlled, the World Bank went ahead with supporting financial sector liberalization through substantial loans. Surprisingly, on the basis of *a priori* reasoning, the World Bank (1987, vol. 1, p. 27) held that the higher interest cost on market-based government borrowing (estimated at Rs 3.2 billion over the nine-year period 1985-86 to 1996-97) would be offset by lower short-term rates on national saving schemes and greater dividends and taxes from increased earnings of the banking sector (estimated at Rs 14.5 billion):

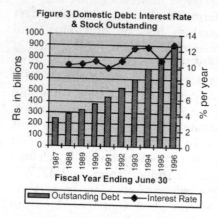

Figure 3 Domestic Debt: Interest Rate & Stock Outstanding

Fiscal Year Ending June 30

Outstanding Debt — Interest Rate

Overall, the government would gain Rs 17 billion, over a nine year period, (US$100 million equivalent per year) if it pursued the proposed strategy as against following the existing financing pattern. (Underlining in original).

In the event, these expectations did not materialize. First, budget deficits did not decline progressively from 8.7 per cent of GDP in 1986-87 to 4.2 per cent in 1996-97, leading to much larger borrowing requirements than had been anticipated. Second, the rise in interest rates on domestic public debt envisaged—from 11.2 per cent in the base case to 11.67 per cent in the recommended (staged introduction of market-based borrowing) case—proved unrealistic as both the interest cost and the stock of government domestic debt rose much faster (Figure 3).[29] Finally, the assumption that government would be able to 'earn an additional Rs 14.5 billion through higher earnings of SBP/NCB' proved entirely Utopian, not least because of the early disinvestment of some of the banks and the losses absorbed by the State Bank on the provision of forward exchange cover.

Exchange & Trade Liberalization

The second area where the government was persuaded to undertake reforms, pending meaningful action on the budget, was that of external finances. These involved exchange rate depreciation, trade liberalization (i.e. reduction of non-tariff barriers), and tariff reforms (i.e. reduction—and the lowering of dispersion—of import duties).

Exchange Rate Reforms (1982-)

The exchange control system inherited at Independence in 1947 was modified by two major external developments in the initial years (1947-55): the devaluation of the British pound, and consequently of a number of sterling area currencies, in 1949; and the Korean War boom and following slump of the early 1950s. Pakistan first devalued the rupee in 1955, and following setbacks in exchange and trade liberalization (pursued during 1959-65) once again in 1972. In February 1982, as part of the first EFF, Pakistan de-linked the rupee from the US dollar, and initiated the current regime of the managed float.

The immediate motivation for devaluation or depreciation of the rupee has always been to shore up foreign exchange reserves, even though of late the action is routinely justified as having beneficial long-term impact on resource allocation. There is, however, some controversy around the efficacy of exchange rate action, in Pakistan's circumstances.

First, it is felt that unless there is prior action to curtail excess demand arising from the budget—demand for debt service or military expenditures which are insensitive to the exchange rate—a lowering of the exchange rate merely exacerbates budgetary pressures without alleviating the root cause of macro-economic instability. Second, it is felt that the demand for Pakistan's major exports (cotton and cotton-based textiles and garments) is relatively price-inelastic, with the result that a depreciation of the rupee does not lead to a rise in export receipts. Finally, structural rigidities in factor markets inhibit a re-allocation of resources (from non-tradables to tradables), which are necessary to realize the efficiency gains from currency depreciation.

Figure 4 presents the basic data on nominal and real (consumer price index deflated) exchange rates and the trade and current account deficits on the balance of payments (as ratios of GDP). Despite the heavy nominal depreciation of the rupee, in real terms the rate of exchange has remained fairly constant. On the 'before-and-after' method, it would seem on balance that exchange rate depreciation has not had any appreciable impact on external deficits. On the 'counterfactual' method, however, it can be maintained that had the nominal value of the rupee been maintained at a higher level, the deficits would have been larger. A more definitive resolution of the question would require more in-depth analysis.

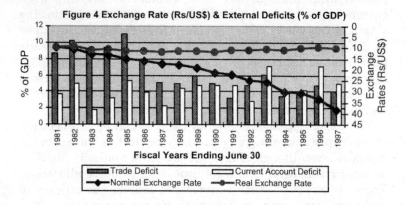

Figure 4 Exchange Rate (Rs/US$) & External Deficits (% of GDP)

Fiscal Years Ending June 30

Trade Deficit · Current Account Deficit · Nominal Exchange Rate · Real Exchange Rate

Trade Liberalization (1983-)

Traditionally, non-tariff barriers (NTBs) were used in Pakistan to curb imports in the face of acute shortages of foreign exchange. In time, they were justified on grounds of industrial promotion, even though their adverse impact on government revenues (and efficiency of resource use) was recognized. Until 1982-83, only those goods could be imported which were on the 'free' list (for which imports were allowed, subject to quantitative restrictions (QRs), after obtaining an import license) or the 'tied' list (which regulated mainly public sector imports from specified sources).

Under the first EFF, the government agreed to a radical change in its import policy. In 1980, 406 of 435 products on the free list were subject to QRs. As part of its agreement with the IMF, by 1983 the government had reduced these QRs to 5, and by 1985 no product was subject to QRs. Even more significantly, the 1983 import policy replaced the free and tied lists with a 'negative' list (and a transitional, 'restricted' or 'conditional' list[30]), leaving all items not on the two lists to be freely importable. Initially, the negative (and the conditional) list was quite large. Over the years, however, and especially since 1988, these lists have been narrowed under the pressure of successive IMF agreements.[31] In recent years, the import licensing requirement has also been removed so that an importer can open a letter of credit with a bank and import any of the importable goods.

What has been the impact of the removal of NTBs? While increased efficiency of resource use is hard to document, trade liberalization has led certainly to an increase in government revenues from import duties on previously banned imports. This gain, however, has been at the expense of increased imports, and the loss of an instrument of strategic intervention in trade matters.

Tariff Reforms (1990-)

The second major thrust of the IMF/WB adjustment programmes was the reduction of import tariffs and elimination of export duties. The manifest objective put forward by the WB/IMF was a reduction in effective protection rates (EPRs), and in the dispersion of EPRs.

Figure 5 presents a visual representation of the share of customs tariff line items in the (most favoured nation, MFN) statutory tariff rates in (fiscal years ending 30 June) 1982, 1990, 1993, 1996 and 1998.[32] In addition to the tariff slabs represented in Figure 5, the coverage of specific tariffs fell from 4.1 per cent in 1982, to 2.3 per cent in 1990, but rose to 2.6 per cent in 1993, before falling again to 1.3 per cent in 1996 and 1.2 per cent in 1998. As a result of these changes, in the same four years, the average rate of import tariffs fell from 79.2 per cent, to 59.8 per cent, to 58.2 per cent, to 44.3 per cent, while the dispersion in these rates was reduced from 49.8 per cent, to 33.9 per cent, to 24.6 per cent, to 23.1 per cent (and the coefficient of variation from 62.9 per cent in 1982 to 51.3 per cent in 1996).

In addition to tariff reductions, adjustment programmes have sought to reduce (and eliminate) the numerous exemptions and concessions provided to specific commodities, plants, industries, and even importers.

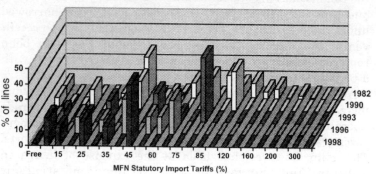

Figure 5 Tariff Reform, 1982-98

What has been the impact of trade liberalization and tariff reforms on growth and employment? First, there has been a drastic fall in government revenues—even though it has been compensated by a diversification of the structure of government revenues. Second, there has been a rise in import payments due to cheaper imports. Third, reduction in protection to industry has affected industrial output and employment. Fourth, there have been social costs, though these would be hard to quantify.

Finally, unlike reduction of import tariffs, there is unanimity of views among economists that there is often a good case for imposing export duties where the exporting country enjoys a significant degree of monopoly power in the export market. Even when this is not so, there is a case for collective action by developing countries:

> Every economist knows that for a country with monopoly power in world trade, equalization of domestic resource costs would require an 'optimum tariff,' but the relevance of this principle for developing countries is denied on the grounds that they do not possess any significant monopoly power. Although that is true for individual countries, it is not true for developing countries collectively (most notably beverages). A common export tax on those commodities, by enabling low-income countries to redistribute income toward themselves at the expense of the rich, seems to me worthy of encouragement rather than the reverse.[33]

Yet, in response to demands by its external financiers the government has been forced virtually to eliminate all export duties. This despite the fact that Pakistan enjoys considerable monopoly power in 8 export items (at the SITC 3-digit level) which account for 52.6 per cent of her 1990-91 merchandise exports (Table III). Clearly, there is a case on both revenue and trade policy grounds for reconsidering the government's policy of eliminating export taxes on these items.

Table III

Pakistan's major exports, among 70 leading commodity exports of developing Countries at the SITC Revision 2, group (3-digit) level

SITC (Revision 2) Code Commodity Group	1990-91 World Rank	Value (US$ '000)	As percentage of		
			Country Total	Developing Countries	World Total
263 Cotton	1	560,626	8.17	13.25	6.58
611 Leather	6	244,339	3.56	7.30	2.71
651 Textile Yarn	2	1,222,853	17.81	13.57	4.99
653 Woven Man-Made FIB Fabric	7	429,189	6.25	3.93	1.75
655 Knitted or Crochetted Fabric	9	50,357	0.73	1.39	0.69
658 Textile Articles NES	2	632,691	9.22	12.96	6.83
848 Headgear Non-Textile Clothing	8	340,379	4.96	5.07	3.40
894 Toys, Sporting Goods &c.	10	132,111	1.92	1.27	0.58

Source: United Nations, *Handbook of International Trade Statistics, 1994*, New York.

Conclusion

The last fifty years have been an eventful period for the Muslim community during the last one thousand years of existence in the Indus valley. Until the death of Aurangzeb Alamgir in 1707, the Indus Muslims enjoyed a degree of cultural and political autonomy which was based on strong, self-sufficient local communities. In the interregnum between 1707 and 1857, as kings grew weaker, local communities gained in strength and self-confidence. The weakness of central authority, however, prepared the way for British colonial rule (1857-1947). Economic policy during the colonial period was dictated by the requirements of the metropolitan economy. This process was aided by the development of structures of thought (through the introduction of English education), and patterns of political, economic and social organization (through the introduction of English laws).

With 'Independence' in 1947, Pakistan inherited the superstructure and the structure of the colonial state. The belligerent attitude of India at the time led to the attachment of an over-riding priority to defence by the new state. Indian expansionism in the early years of Pakistan (in Kashmir, Junagadh and Hyderabad Deccan) did not lessen these concerns. As a result, by 1954, Pakistan was forced to seek US military and economic assistance, despite the cost it entailed in terms of cultural alienation of the state from the people, and the consequent constraints to the development of democratic institutions. Even so, Pakistan's security arrangements remained highly unstable because of a deep-rooted natural inclination of the United States of America toward India. At the same time, India's consistently hostile posture toward Pakistan has not served to raise confidence either in India's intentions or the reliability of the international community in ensuring peace. With defence considerations paramount, economic policy has continued to take the back seat for most of the last fifty years.

Not unlike the East India Company in the eighteenth century, during the last decade the IMF and the World Bank have moved in to fill the vacuum created by a culturally-alienated militarily-dependent state. In the last decade then the government has dutifully followed the prescriptions of the IMF/WB to mixed results. In the process not only have public finances continued to deteriorate, but investment and production capacity have suffered. At the same time, structures and processes of economic decision-making have suffered. As a result, the economy is in the midst of a severe debt crisis, and is unable to chart an independent course for itself. To compound matters, the security environment has deteriorated further with the detonation of several nuclear devices by India in May 1998.

Where do we go from here? On past patterns, it would seem that Pakistan's military allies, its expatriates resident abroad (an increasingly powerful class), and domestic elites would like to see the past pattern of post-colonial development continue. The people of Pakistan, on the other hand, are ready for an indigenous leader who would cut the Gordian knot of external military and economic dependence. No such leader, however, appears to be on the horizon.

NOTES

1. For fiscal year ending 30 June 1997, as reported in *Economic Survey 1996-97* (Government of Pakistan, 1997, Statistical Appendix, p. 37); down from US$490 in 1995-96. According to World Bank methodology (essentially, three-year average of income, prices and exchange rates), mid-1995 GNP per capita was US$460, while on a purchasing power parity basis, it was US$2,230 (World Bank 1997, p. 214).

2. Although earlier in 1980-83 Pakistan had also concluded an extended arrangement with the IMF.

3. Actually, it was the settlement of land revenue for ten years, announced on 10 February 1790, which, with the approval of the Court of Directors of the East India Company, was declared as the permanent settlement on 22 March 1793. With the annexation of Sindh (1843) and the Punjab (1849), *zamindars* and *jagirdars* acquired ownership rights in land.

4. This discussion abstracts from a number of important historical and institutional details, as they do not affect the basic implications drawn here. The Bengal system gave rise to three or four different settlement systems—the *zamindari* system, the (Madras) *ryotwari* system (applied in Sindh), and the *mahalwari* system (adapted to the Punjab). With the imposition of 'One Unit', the Punjab system was applied to Sindh also. Also, the special status of the Punjab as a non-Regulation province enhanced the force of these observations.

5. In particular, while ownership rights were created, tenancy rights were left unattended. Moreover, when settlement rates fell below the rental value of land, there was a tendency to rent rather than farm the land, and in time, a market in land emerged. Also, when settlement was fixed in cash (rather than in kind), as was done in the Sindh and the Punjab, after independence, small farmers fell in debt and often lost their land.

6. This is especially true of employment and social sector objectives which have never been a high priority on the latent policy agenda of government, although the Fourth and Fifth Plans are

notable in their declarations of intent, in what can be seen as an ineffective lament over this state of affairs.

7. After the secession of East Pakistan, Mr Bhutto took office as President and Chief Martial Law Administrator; after the promulgation of the 1973 Constitution, he took office as Prime Minister (on the basis of the results of the elections held in united Pakistan, under the abrogated Constitution of 1962). With regard to the second period, the 1985-88 period saw a cohabitation of democracy with martial law, during the tenure of Prime Minister Junejo.

8. While it is too early to tell, beginning mid-1997 there are signs of the dawn of a new period of closer US-Pakistan relations.

9. Within days of Pakistan's creation some seven million refugees arrived from India, while the bulk of trade, banking and industry was paralysed by the mass exodus of Hindus and Sikhs—within four months, 418 of 631 bank branches had closed down, and in another six months, only 195 branches remained. The government started with no cash balances, as transfer of Pakistan's share of British Indian cash balances (Rs 2.2 million) was delayed and then received only in part. The problem was compounded by the fact that in the absence of developed ports, the bulk of Pakistan's imports arrived through Indian ports, and customs and excise duties collected at these ports accrued to India. In April 1948, India cut off water supplies in canals which flowed to Pakistan, threatening food production. In September 1949, Pakistan's decision not to devalue as India had done, led to a trade and payments deadlock (until February 1950). India also refused to transfer Pakistan's share of sterling balances with the Reserve Bank of India and of defence stores. On 11 September 1948, the founder of Pakistan M.A. Jinnah passed away, and in October 1951, the Prime Minister, Liaquat Ali Khan was assassinated.

10. Shortly before partition, provincial governments had submitted a list of development projects, to the colonial department of Planning and Development, which had solicited such a list in the closing years of the Second World War, for execution after the end of the war with grants or loans from the central government. In early 1948, the government of Pakistan established a Development Board to co-ordinate development activities, and a Planning Advisory Board, consisting of officials and private sector representatives, to advise government on development activities. In March 1948, the two Boards, until then under the Cabinet Secretariat, were transferred to the newly created Ministry of Economic Affairs. Following a decision

in May 1950, as a member of the newly formed Colombo Plan for Co-operative Economic development in South and South-east Asia, Pakistan submitted its Six-Year Development Plan (1951-57) for incorporation into the Colombo Plan. There is little evidence of any redeeming feature of the quality of Pakistan's submission, or of the activities of the Planning Board in general. In January 1951, the Advisory Board was abolished, and the Planning Board was converted into the Planning Commission. See Waterston (1963).

11. With the conclusion of reconstruction in Europe, the World Bank was looking for a new role, which was fulfilled by its turn to financing development projects. The Bank's Articles of Agreement required that project financing take place in the context of national plans.

12. Certainly, the *New York Times* of 18 January 1965 succumbed to the well-known American penchant for hyperbole: 'Pakistan may be on its way toward an economic milestone that so far has been reached by only one other populous country, the United States.' A year later, *The Times* of London of 26 February 1966 was no less exuberant: 'The survival and development of Pakistan is one of the most remarkable examples of state and nation building in the post-war world.' Quoted in Papanek (1967, p. 1)

13. It was always clear that the US would much prefer closer relations with India rather than Pakistan. However, faced with India's early proclivity toward the Soviet Union, security concerns of the US and Pakistan dictated an alliance of convenience—for the US against the Soviet Union, but not India; for Pakistan, strictly against the Indian threat. As Bhutto (1969, p. 105) put it: 'Assistance was provided to Pakistan for one set of reasons and received for another.'

14. Earlier, the Aid-to-Pakistan Consortium meeting scheduled for July 1965 was postponed.

15. An added factor was the diversion of greater resources to defence, in order to replenish defence supplies.

16. The phrase 'Islamic Socialism' is from the Third Plan, where the idea that Islamic socialism 'is nothing more' than the relocation of the idea of a welfare state (so prominent in all constitutions of Pakistan) to the moral and cultural context of Islam.

17. Government of Pakistan (1988a, p. 1).

18. One of the few relatively successful EFFs—judged, among other factors, by the length of the period for which the agreement remained in effect—to any country on record. The intrusiveness

of the IMF's demands, however, were unpalatable to an older generation of bureaucrat-politicians, who successfully resisted diligent efforts by the IMF staff after 1983 to put in place further upper tranche agreements.

19. On 28 December 1988, the Board of Directors of the IMF approved a Standby of SDR 273.15 million (cancelled on 1 December 1981, prior to expiration date, with an undrawn balance of SDR 78.67 million) and a SAF of SDR 382.41 million (which expired on 27 December 1991, with an undrawn balance of SDR 109.26 million); on 22 February 1994, an EFF of SDR 379.1 million and an ESAF of SDR 606.6 million (both of which expired on 21 February 1997).

20. Nor, in fact, by IMF/WB staff members. In his statement filed in the Supreme Court, in connection with the writ petition against her dismissal filed by Prime Minister Benazir Bhutto, the President states: 'One of the key persons invloved in this [Liberty Power] project is Ibrahim Elwan, who has the dubious honour of being the first person in the history of the World Bank who was asked to leave that institution after a full fledged corruption investigation.' (Reported in *Business Recorder*, Karachi, 16 December 1996.)

21. According to press reports, on 24 July 1997 agreement was reached between the IMF staff and the government on a Policy Framework Paper and a Letter of Intent for a US$1.6 billion or more ESAF/EFF, subject to approval by the IMF Board of Directors (expected on 8 October 1997). Earlier, on 16 July 1997 the US Senate adopted the Harkin-Warner amendment as part of the Senate Foreign Operations Appropriations Bill which would serve to overcome the obstacles to closer US-Pakistan military and economic relations placed by the Symington amendment. Earlier, the Brown amendment had alleviated some of the restrictions imposed by the Symington amendment.

22. This requirement arose from the so-called Pressler Amendment, which required a special certification from Pakistan, over and above the normal provisions of nuclear non-proliferation laid down by the Symington Amendment of 1986 (which had not affected Pakistan, because the US President had provided the required certification every year).

23. The SAL broke down over what was seen as the intrusiveness of the WB in the policy-making process. Accordingly, it was followed by sector adjustment loans (SECALs) in energy (1985) and export development (1986). The latter was a compromise operation, as the government was not prepared to accept the

trade liberalisation measures being proposed by the WB for a trade sector loan.

24. The State Bank of Pakistan Order 1948 was succeeded by the State Bank of Pakistan Ordinance of 6 July 1955 (converted to an Act of 18 April 1956).

25. According to Hasan (1997, p. 10): '...reliance on credit controls has not disappeared completely although formal credit controls no longer exist. In practice, formal controls have been replaced by equally effective jawboning when a bank's credit expansion gets out of line in the opinion of the authorities.'

26. As distinct from monetary policy, the financial sector in Pakistan was affected by three major developments in the banking sector. First, the establishment of United Bank Limited (UBL) in 1959 introduced the culture of aggressive deposit mobilization in commercial banking in Pakistan. Second, the nationalisation of banks on 1 January 1974 inaugurated an eventful era of government control over banks. This era came to a close in 1991 when the government partially disinvested two nationalised banks, and granted licenses to ten new private banks, while six investment banks (licensed earlier in 1989) started operations.

27. Serious questions can be raised about the contribution of inadequacies in banking supervision and regulation and the lack of competition in the banking sector to the high rates of profits exhibited by banks after liberalization of the banking sector.

28. High interest rates have also inhibited private investment, although there have been other non-economic reasons as well.

29. Figure 3 is based on data provided by the State Bank of Pakistan (1996, p. 91). The interest rate is estimated as the ratio of interest payments to the stock of debt outstanding at the end of the previous year.

30. The restricted list was a revised version of the tied list and sought to protect Pakistan's trade commitments under a variety of bilateral agreements.

31. The bulk of the reduction took place in 1987-88 and the next three years, respectively: 136, 169, 70 and 97 items were removed from the negative list, and 10, 51, 20 and 43 items, from the restricted list.

32. Data up to 1996 are from Arshad Zaman Associates (Pvt.) Ltd. (1997a, p. 63). Data for 1998 are from the 1997 Import Policy.

33. John Williamson (1991, p. 74). (In June 1998, when this was written, Williamson was the Chief Economist, South Asia Region, World Bank.)

Bibliography

Arshad Zaman Associates (Pvt.) Ltd. 1997a. *Pakistan: Industry and Trade Sector Study*. Prepared for the Asian Development Bank, Manila. Karachi: Arshad Zaman Associates (Pvt.) Ltd., 30 March 1997. Processed.

Bhutto, Z.A. 1969, *The Myth of Independence*. London: Oxford University Press.

Government of Pakistan. 1988a. *Seventh Five-Year Plan (1988-93) & Perspective Plan (1988-2003)*. Islamabad: Planning Commission.

Government of Pakistan. 1997. *Economic Survey 1996-97*. Islamabad: Ministry of Finance.

Hasan, Zamir. 1997. *Pakistan: Financial Sector: Perspective, Issues, Reforms*. A report prepared for the Asian Development Bank, January, Processed.

Papanek, Gustav F. 1967, *Pakistan's Development: Social Goals and Private Incentives*. Cambridge, Massachusetts: Harvard University Press.

State Bank of Pakistan. 1996. *Annual Report 1995-96*, Karachi: State Bank of Pakistan.

Waterston, Albert. 1963. *Planning in Pakistan*. Baltimore, Maryland: Published for The Economic Development Institute, International Bank for Reconstruction and Development by the Johns Hopkins Press.

Williamson, John. 1991, "Comments." In Vinod Thomas, Ajay Chhibber, Mansoor Dailami, and Jaime de Melo, *Restructuring Economies in Distress: Policy Reforms and the World Bank*. New York: Oxford University Press for the World Bank.

World Bank. 1997. *World Development Report 1997: The State in a Changing World*, Baltimore, Maryland: Published for the World Bank by Oxford University Press.

World Bank. 1987. *Pakistan Financial Sector Review* (in 2 volumes), Report No. 7049-PAK-Washington, DC: The World Bank, 11 December, Processed.

The Economy of Pakistan, the Present and the Future: the Most Dangerous Years

Following Dr Arshad Zaman's analysis of the past, let us focus on the present and on the possible future.[1] Although one could debate Dr Zaman's interpretation of the present difficulties, one cannot deny their magnitude. In fact, it would not be wrong to use the work 'crisis'. Long-standing problems have become much worse, being closely connected with political factors, both internal and external. Never before has Pakistan faced such an accumulation of interlinked obstacles to development. Foreign policy issues play a role; from Kashmir to the Taliban, tensions with Iran, a former close friend, mixed feelings prevailing in Beijing with regard to Pakistan's Afghan Policy, unstable relations with the United States... Then comes the internal situation: the succession of four governments since 1988 and their inability to promote a more appropriate development, the worsening law and order situation, including political criminality, the resurgence of very violent disturbances in Karachi, the financial and commercial heart of the country, the dubious role of the police, bloody sectarian clashes between Sunnis and Shias, erosion of the administrative framework, corruption and other difficulties.

All these factors put together cannot but seriously hinder the economy, and yet, no drastic improvement seems likely in the near future. Sultan Ahmed wrote about his country as 'an over diagnosed patient who remains largely untreated or mistreated'.[2] The [former] Prime Minister, Nawaz Sharif, while referring to corruption, is reported to have 'expressed his complete dissatisfaction with the ongoing accountability process'.[3] M.P. Bhandara reflected an opinion widespread within the country, when stating: 'Apart from foreign capital we desperately need leadership which can set out priorities for the nation'.[4]

While the immediate future looks uncertain, to say the least, one should not overlook the assets of Pakistan and of its society. Over the past fifty years, the economy has shown, on a number of occasions, much resilience. Persons of competence and integrity are not lacking either and they could contribute to a new awakening in the country.

The breaking point

In 1996 and 1997, Pakistan faced the risk of being unable to service its external debt, made worse by a severe internal indebtedness and by an inflation of 12 per cent, along with a sluggish economy. After some temporary improvement in 1997/98, economic growth slowed down again, while the external and internal financial situation became critical. It was aggravated by the consequences of the nuclear tests: Japan, the major public aid-donor, suspended its assistance, United States sanctions also had some impact. Foreign indebtedness reached $32 billion, while foreign exchange reserves fell from $1300 million in May 1998 to 400 million in November. After growing until 1997, foreign private direct investments are declining, as well as remittances of Pakistani workers abroad. Exports and imports are falling, adding to the overall sluggishness of the economy.

The agreement signed with the IMF in November 1998, providing a loan of $5 billion and rescheduling of $3 billion by bilateral donor countries, to be followed possibly with a loan of $800 million from the World Bank, and the reduction of United States sanctions gave some breathing space to the government. However, this kind of first-aid should be complemented by drastic changes in the financial and fiscal systems, which have been plagued by major defects over several decades, and this is where real reforms do not seem to be forthcoming. Even the introduction of an agricultural income tax has not been successful.

Although there is no lack of money in the country—see below—neither authoritarian regimes nor democratic governments have managed to implement a real reform of taxation. Landlords pay a very low agricultural tax. Business lobbies in towns agitate whenever new taxes are proposed. Tax evasion is flourishing. Electricity, irrigation are subsidized so that proper maintenance expenditures cannot be secured.

Other factors enter the picture, what I call the economy of leakage. According to *Transparency International* Reports, Pakistan stands among the most corrupt countries, so that, according to local guesses, black money could amount to 50 per cent of GDP. Such defects, widespread in Asia, are made worse in Pakistan by heroin and arms traffic, both consequences of the endless Afghan war. Other leakages appear in the banks. Default loans have increased from Rs 140 billion in 1997, to Rs 210 billion in August 1998.[5] Among the defaulters are prominent leaders of all the political parties.

According to various estimates, several coming from the late Mahabub ul Haq, former Finance Minister, the following data are given:

smuggling	$3 billion
tax evasion	$3 billion
losses due to corruption	$2.5 to 5 billion
default loans	$3 billion

(Source: *Dawn*, 29 August 1996; 10 October 1996)

Although Pakistan had to spend more for its oil imports after 1973, the economy benefited much from the boom in the Middle East: a large number of workers, unskilled and skilled, found work there, exports such as rice, textiles, fruit, vegetables increased. Arab countries also granted financial aid to Pakistan. The Gulf war and the slowing down of the Middle East economies have reduced their requirements of outside labour. Total workers' remittances have gone down from 9.3 per cent of GNP per year for 1980-85 to 3 per cent for 1990-96 thus, the balance of payments and the numerous families depending on that money are affected.

On top of all these difficulties comes defence expenditure, a consequence of the tensions between India and Pakistan, regarding Kashmir. The defence budget amounts to 6 per cent of GNP, i.e., around $3.6 billion per year.

The population explosion

While in many Asian countries population increase has fallen below 2 per cent per year due to family planning policies, according to the 1998 Census, the population is still growing by 2.6 per cent in Pakistan. Over the years, neither democratic nor military leaders have been concerned with family planning, except General Ayub Khan during his early years in power (1958-60). Even now, most villagers believe that family planning is against Islam, a belief also quite common in the cities. Such a belief is baseless since, as early as the eleventh century, a great theologian like Imam al Ghazali was in favour of contraception. Later scholars held similar views. There are differences of opinion on abortion.[6] In the past few years, however, more efforts in favour of family planning can be noticed, though this is not a top priority.

Decades of such a fast growth in population until recently (around 3 per cent per year) have contributed to worsening socio-economic issues: too many children, too few schools, growth of slums, poor health systems. The situation is made still worse by the limited government expenditure in these fields. As a result, Pakistan lies quite low in terms of human development compared to many Asian countries, including India: a literacy rate of 39 per cent in 1996, a life expectancy of 60-62, an infantile mortality rate of 95 per cent.

The increasing burden of population is occuring at the very time when job outlets abroad are shrinking and the economy is slowing down. Therefore, unemployment is rising which has an impact on political tensions and sectarianism.

One must add that the Census data of 1998 has raised some doubts. Is it plausible that the growth rate has fallen from 3.1 per cent in 1981 to 2.6 per cent in 1998, considering the poor record of family planning? Some Pakistanis wonder whether the urban population has not been undercounted, perhaps for political reasons, in order to prevent an increase of elected representatives from certain towns and cities.

Hydraulic works and agriculture

While finance and population are widely discussed topics in Pakistan, the same cannot be said about agriculture and irrigation where not many people, outside the circle of experts, are aware of how serious the situation has become, directly affecting 52 per cent of the active population who depend on agriculture, while agriculture still contributes 25 per cent of GNP.

The main problem is water. The Indus basin lies in an arid or semi-arid area, except its Northern part. Furthermore, the irrigation system goes back thousands of years. The huge canal systems built by the British about a hundred years ago, and the works achieved after 1947 have been a major engine of growth and relative prosperity. However, today, the canals represent the major stumbling block for further progress.

Under the pressure of population, farmers tend to spread irrigation too thinly on larger areas, but more serious is the lack of adequate maintenance of the canals for several decades. As a result, only 35 to 40 per cent of the water entering the canal heads reaches the irrigated area. Especially in Punjab, these shortcomings have been partly overcome by tubewells (more that 300,000 for the whole country). But in many districts, especially in Sindh, the groundwater is brackish so that it cannot be used for irrigation.

The total irrigated area amounts to around 18 million ha out of a total cropped area of 23 million ha, gross, i.e., including multicropping in the same year. The net cultivated area (topographical) is 17 million ha.

In addition to these defects are waterlogging and salinity. The former affects 0.5 million ha before the monsoon and

2 million at the end of it. Four million ha suffer at varying degrees from salinity. A number of reclamation projects have taken place through drainage, but much remains to be done.

The renovation of the irrigation system would involve huge expenditure and investment in view of the size of the work: 61,000 km of canals, 88,000 outlets for plots of 100-120 ha, 1.6 million km of watercourses within each plot (canal command area 14 million ha).

Such measures to recover part of the lost water would not be enough. Additional sources of water supply are needed through surface water since the untapped potential of ground water is declining. Another dam on the Indus, downstream the one of Tarbela, at Kalabagh, could store plenty of water. The project has not been approved for about three decades because of conflicts between the North West Frontier Province and Sindh which are opposed to the project on the one hand, and Punjab on the other. The issue does not look like being resolved in the near future.

In the period 1965-70 began the Green Revolution, which led to doubling rice (clean) and wheat yields so that both reached 2000-2500 kg/ha. Such progress was possible in spite of shortcomings in irrigation and in the supply of other inputs. Now, to proceed further in order to reach 3500-4000 kg/ha per crop is perfectly feasible, but it requires a much better supply of inputs. The new seeds should be replaced every four to five years, which is not done, fertilizer applications need to be more balanced between nitrogen and phosphate products. The new seeds also require more water than traditional varieties: for wheat 5-6 waterings versus 3-4. Finally, pest control should be improved, particularly for cotton.

The impact of these shortcomings has been aggravated by exceptional natural calamities. Between 1992 and 1997, very heavy rains damaged the monsoon crops, particularly cotton. The latter was, in addition, attacked by the new curl leaf virus. The small winter rains, so crucial for rainfed wheat, and helpful for badly irrigated wheat, failed in 1996/97, leading to a poor crop. On the other hand, generous rains in 1997/98 led to a bumper harvest.

The broad trends have been as follows: cotton, so important for the whole economy never reverted to its peak year 1991/92 (2.2 million t, lint). It varied around 1.6-1.8 million t. It may reach 1.7 million t in 1998/99. Wheat, by far the major cereal, showed a slow growth. After more than doubling its output between 1969/70 and 1989/90, it grew only by around 30 per cent until 1997/98, out of which 600,000 t or more went to Afghanistan. For 1998/99, imports should fall to 2 million t. Production of rice, after a breakthrough similar to the one of wheat, has not shown a sharp increase (around 4.3 million t per year for 1996-1998). It could reach 5 million t in 1998/99, enabling exports above the usual 1 to 1.5 million t. Sugarcane has shown a more dynamic trend in the 1990s, reaching a bumper harvest of 53 million t in 1997/98.

What is a matter of concern are the vagaries of weather, boosting the crops or bringing them down, although government support to agriculture did help in 1997/98.

The slowdown of major crops growth is not particular to Pakistan. It is noticeable in other countries like China and India for the same reasons, i.e., the fall in public recurrent expenditure and investment, and lack of attention granted to agriculture.

In Pakistan, as in other countries, one should not overlook more dynamic sectors. There is a process of growing diversification, away from the main crops, in favour of animal husbandry, meat, milk, fish ponds, even flowers. In Pakistan, the production of milk rose from 9 million t in 1980/81 to 22 million t in 1997/98, meat (mutton and beef) from 0.8 million t to 2.15 million t, poultry meat from 0.05 to 0.43 million t.

Improvement in fruit cultivation, citrus, mangoes, apples, apricots, are no less striking. A part of these items are exported, particularly to the Middle East, while a large part meets the rising local demand. Production could improve further with better transport, more rural roads, better marketing and packaging.

This diversification process has economic and social value: growth in output, exports and job creation. Besides, these sectors are less dependent on public investment. For instance, new water saving devices like the drip system can spread under private ownership for orchards, vegetables, and flowers. However, even when contributing to the acceleration of these activities, they cannot fully compensate for the slowdown in the growth of major crops.

The immediate future of agriculture

The next five to ten years are bound to remain very difficult. First the government cannot mobilize enough public money to wipe out the basic defects mentioned above. Second, even if money was available, it would take time to overcome the present shortcomings, particularly in the key field which is water management. As Dr Manzur Ejaz wrote: 'The irrigation system has deteriorated to the point that it is impossible to rehabilitate it in a few months. And hence the expectation of quick turnaround of agricultural sector does not appear realistic.'[7]

Various forecasts have been made, especially for wheat. According to a study of the Washington based International Food Policy Research Institute by 2010,[8] wheat imports could reach 15 million t, which seems unrealistic. Other studies mention a deficit of 6.4 million t 'by the end of the century', which again looks on the high side, and a deficit of 12 million t by 2012.[9]

While Pakistan should keep a surplus of rice available for exports, it is urgent to overcome the difficulties met with wheat and cotton. More research, better pest control and water management are badly needed. Cotton remains a crucial factor for the whole economy: for the farmers, textile mills and exports, since cotton based exports amount to nearly 60 per cent of total exports.

Industries and Services

Unlike China or India, Pakistan had practically no industry in 1947. Thanks, to a large extent, in the first phase, to big merchants who had migrated from Western India (Bohras, Khojas, Memons) a number of industries were created, mostly in Karachi and Hyderabad. Later, Punjabis and Pathans entered the field in Lahore, Faisalabad, Sialkot, Peshawar etc.

The textile industry played the major role and remains even today the most important industry. Cement, chemical fertilizers, pharmaceuticals, machinery have appeared. In the 1970s a steel mill (public sector, 1 million t) was set up in Karachi with the co-operation of the Soviets. It relies on imported iron ore and coal. Later, came semi-durable goods, refrigerators, air conditioners, the assembly and gradual production of vehicles.

In spite of this growth and the diversification of production, Pakistan remains more dependent than China or India, on imports of production goods.

After growing fast in the 1960s, industry suffered from the nationalizations under Zulfikar Ali Bhutto. Many industries, but not textiles, came under the public sector. Production was upset, while private enterprises remained fearful of expanding. A number of Pakistani trade companies and banks were also nationalized.

With the advent of General Zia to power in 1977, the economy picked up thanks to a more flexible policy. After winning the 1990 elections, Nawaz Sharif introduced drastic reforms: liberalization and deregulation of the private sector, opening towards the outside world in external trade with the reduction of trade barriers, incentives granted to foreign private investments etc. A number of public sector enterprises in industry, trade agencies, and banking were privatized.

While all these measures went in the right direction, the results, so far, have not been spectacular. The financial problems mentioned above, including high interest rates, the crisis of cotton, the slow growth of wheat etc played a negative role, but this is not all. Karachi and Hyderabad, where 35 to 40 per cent of the modern industries are located, have suffered from years of turmoil, and bloody fights between Sindhis and Mohajirs (former refugees from India). Although violence had receded in 1997, it picked up again in 1998. Such turmoil does not contribute to a climate favourable to investments. In Punjab, the deterioration of law and order in the past few years (bloody feuds between Shias and Sunnis, banditry, etc) also affected development.

On top of all these disturbances comes political instability: since 1988 there have been four general elections, with frequent changes of government.

Finally smuggling, mostly from Afghanistan, has become more serious than ever. For instance, the Pakistani market for television sets is estimated at 700,000 units per year. Now, how can local factories work when 600,000 television sets come from Afghanistan?[10] Plenty of other semi-durable goods reach Kabul from the Gulf or elsewhere and cross the border.

Infrastructure

In several Asian countries, particularly China and India, there is a growing gap between growth of GNP and of infrastructure, electricity, transport, which leads to yearly losses running into many billions of dollars, and considerably hinders efficient business.

The situation in Pakistan is less tight. In 1994, the government started a 'fast track' policy to reduce the shortage of electricity, offering very liberal conditions for the construction of power stations along the BOT formula (build, operate, transfer). Three years later, Pakistan enjoyed an extra 3000 MW as expected. This increase, but also the slowing down of industry contributed to practically wiping out load-shedding. Pakistan has a surplus of electricity, which may be sold to India. Foreign companies reacted more favourably than to the Indian or Chinese offers, because of the clear-cut policy presented by Pakistan and a high purchasing price for electricity, i.e., 6.5 US cents per unit.

But the coin has its reverse. The public corporation WADPA (Water & Power Development Authority) and KESC (Karachi Electricity Supply Corporation) are on the verge of bankruptcy due to various problems, such as poor management, and enormous losses in transmission and distribution, including plenty of thefts. Such losses for WAPDA have been estimated at 37 per cent of the output, a staggering figure, since losses in China or India are already considered to be very high with 20-23 per cent. As a result, WAPDA has no money to purchase the current supplied by the IPPs (Independent Power Projects). Moreover, the new powerhouses still under construction may not work because of delays by WAPDA in the construction of transmission lines.

Additional troubles started in 1998. The Accountability Cell in the Prime Minister's Office (responsible for fighting corruption) has charged several IPPs with resorting to kickbacks and corruption, which are supposed to have benefited Benazir Bhutto and her husband (she was the Prime Minister when the fast track policy was initiated). Foreign companies and personnel and their Pakistani partners faced various police raids, temporary arrests etc. At the same time, the government asked for a reduction of tariffs. Some of the disputes about tariffs have been reolved, others are still pending. Even if these issues are not too clear, taking into account political factors, they have a negative impact on future foreign investments.

As far as transport is concerned, the situation looks better than in China and India. No doubt the railways work poorly as a consequence of decades of neglect, but roads are improving. On the main highway Karachi-Lahore-Peshawar (1743 km), 740 km enjoy four lanes. A new road, the expressway with toll, is being opened connecting Lahore to Rawalpindi via Sargodha.

Secondary roads are also progressing, a key factor to boost production of perishable goods like milk, fruit, and vegetables.

Energy

Pakistan has only a few small coalmines. Its hydro-electrical potential is quite high thanks to the Indus and the other rivers. Out of the total installed capacity of 13,446 MW, as much as 6,241 MW are from hydel power. Natural gas supplied from Balochistan plays an important role. New discoveries of natural gas have been made in 1996 but their precise importance is not yet known. Some experts believe that Pakistan should enjoy a large surplus of gas after 2000; others say there could be a deficit.

As to oil, Pakistan relies on its own fields for only 20 per cent of its requirements. Oil exploration continues, but prospects look uncertain.

Foreign Direct Investments (FDIs) and foreign trade

On the whole, Pakistan has been more open to FDIs than India. However, there are still complaints from foreigners about bureaucratic red tape and heavy regulations in spite of progress since the reforms. Tariff and non-tariff barriers have been lowered. Various incentives have been introduced in order to attract FDIs. From 1980 to 1996, total disbursed FDIs amount to $4.1 billion versus $7.6 billion for India which is a much larger country.

Foreign corporations can find—as in India—a number of professionals for senior jobs and medium cadres without difficulty, so they do not need so many expatriates which reduces their costs. For instance, while Unilever needs eighty expatriates in China, they have only a few in their companies in India and Pakistan. Even compared to Indonesia, Pakistan is better off in this regard.

Substantial FDIs have come in during the past few years in power stations, in agro-business, pharmaceuticals, pesticides, and the automobile industry. The turn-over of Nestlé, for instance, doubles every three years and has reached Rs. 4 billion in 1996 ($100 million). Roche started in the 1980s and sees its sales growing. Novartis is very active in the field of pesticides. Electrical companies supply a large amount of equipment for the new power stations. Many textile factories are, at last, replacing obsolete machines with modern imported looms from Switzerland, and more recently from Japan.

Following the new investment policy in 1997, great hopes appeared of a large flow of foreign capital including more business in Central Asia for which Pakistan could attract joint ventures. Prominent were the negotiations between the Taliban, Pakistan and Unocal and some other companies for the building of a pipeline between Turkmenistan and

Pakistan across Afghanistan. In the first eight months of 1997/98, private foreign direct investments disbursed increased by 13 per cent, reaching $612 million.

By the middle of 1998, however, the situation changed. Rising disturbances in Karachi, the impact of sanctions following the nuclear tests, further deterioration of the financial situation, the freeze on foreign currency accounts, the impact of the controversies about the foreign electrical companies etc, all these factors put together had a discouraging effect on foreign enterprise. More than a dozen joint ventures have been suspended. Foreigners feel that the political future is uncertain, a feeling strengthened by the attempt of [former Prime Minister] Nawaz Sharif to push through an amendment in the Constitution on the Shariat and his pro-Taliban policy. Besides, foreign firms complain that possible local partners are slow to start or expand investments. The sad state of the stock exchange does not help either, as well as the lowering of Pakistan's credit rating by International Agencies.[11]

The prospects of Pakistan becoming a springboard to approach Central Asia are no less dim. Unocal has stopped negotiations with the Taliban. In addition, Pakistan's support of the government in Kabul is very unpopular with the Central Asian Republics which fear that the Taliban might interfere in their countries.

Standards of living and markets

Pakistan falls between South-East Asian countries and poorer countries of the continent. In 1947, it was more favoured than India in terms of population-resources ratio, with three-quarters of its crops under irrigation, lighter rural population densities, less landless labourers. Although the fast growth of population (higher than in India) is reducing these advantages, they have not yet disappeared. Remittances from expatriates are also comparatively much more important than in India. Then, black money may be more widespread than in India. Finally, the GDP growth rate, especially in the 1960s and 1980s has been quite high: around 5 to 6 per cent per year versus India's 3.5 per cent for 1950-1980 and 5.5 per cent during 1980-1990. Only in the 1990s has India moved faster than Pakistan.

One does come across destitute people, especially in Sindh or in some isolated mountain areas, but, on the whole, acute misery is less than in the poorest parts of India. Agricultural wages are, on the whole, higher.

Differences between India and Pakistan are no less striking when looking at posh urban colonies. The ones in New Delhi are less affluent than the ones in Karachi or Islamabad. In proportion, cars are more numerous in Pakistan. Even in the countryside one sees more of them than in Green Revolution villages of India. Semi-durable goods, televisions, refrigerators, and other consumer goods like cold drinks are more prominent in Pakistan, not only in towns but also in rural areas.

One lacks estimates on the number of people (middle and upper classes) who can afford goods beyond their basic needs. In India, one speaks of 200-250 million. In Pakistan, they could be between 35 and 45 million.

The global picture

As pointed out by V.A. Jafarey, former Governor of the State Bank, savings are too low, a trend which is not new: the rate of savings was 14 per cent of GDP in 1995/96, the rate of investment was 18 per cent, public savings 2.48 per cent, private households savings 11.7 per cent, private enterprises 1.38 per cent, whereas India's rate of savings amounts to around 25 per cent, and in the east Asian countries 30-35 per cent or more.[12]

For 1996/97, growth fell to 3 or 1.3 per cent, as later revised, versus the average of 4.8 per cent for the previous three years. In 1997/98, the economy picked up, particularly wheat and sugarcane and some industries. The growth rate is officially put at 5 per cent, which seems too high to some Pakistanis. The outlook for 1998/99 is not bright. Foreign trade and industry are sluggish, and financial constraints remain acute. In agriculture, even in the best hypothesis, cotton will remain below the peak year 1991/92. On the other hand, rice has done well. Finally, inflation is rising again.

It has been obvious for decades that the defects of the fiscal system and the low rate of savings and investment depend, to a major extent, on political leadership. Neither authoritarian regimes until 1988, nor the democratic regime have endeavoured to solve these issues. Politicians in power or in the opposition concentrate their energy on remaining in power or on reaching it.

There is no doubt that Pakistan has fallen into a number of dangerous, inter-linked traps, mainly due to external or internal politics, economic and social issues etc.

There is also no doubt that, at the root of the economic difficulties, lie political factors. Vested interests of politicians, feudal landlords, certain businessmen... prevent drastic reforms of the fiscal and banking systems and the curtailment of all kinds of leakage.

Towards a possible future

These lukewarm conclusions so often heard in Pakistan should not make us neglect the assets of the country and their possible better use. There is more money than is assumed when looking at the financial shortfalls of all types. A sound financial system with greater political stability could unleash many dynamic forces. The private sector would invest more in manufacturing and the State would be able to increase public investments and recurrent expenditures in infrastructure, in agriculture, health and education.

Such a scenario would be boosted by other factors. For the last ten years or so, one notices a new spirit (as also in India) among new generations of young entrepreneurs eager to modernize industries and to start new joint ventures. New industrial areas are growing away from the major centres of Karachi and Lahore. In villages, farmers, small and medium, are working hard and are keen to innovate, as shown with the fast progress of animal husbandry, fruit, poultry, flowers etc. The *waderas* (landlords in Sindh) who, for so long, sat

idle on their huge estates are becoming gentlemen-farmers
à la Punjabi.

Other assets are worth mentioning. In spite of the present
trouble in the power sector, Pakistan enjoys a surplus of
electricity. When industry moves upwards again, it will not
face the constraints faced in India, and to some extent too, in
China, where the lack of electricity is responsible for heavy
losses for the whole economy. Thus, in Pakistan the
manufacturing sector could quickly forge ahead.

As to transport, here again, although much remains to be
done, I am inclined to think that Pakistan is in a more
favourable position than China or India.

Then come all kinds of small changes and improvement in
economic and technical fields. They may escape the attention
of foreign newcomers or urban Pakistanis cut off from rural
life. For instance, since the early 1990s, you see an increasing
number of carts on tyres pulled by a donkey or a mule,
instead of the slow moving and costly bullocks. Locally made
machinery is growing in big villages and towns. The fast
growth of meat, milk, poultry are also evidence of the same
trends.

To sum up, Pakistan enjoys a number of assets, which
fully used, could lead to greater social and economic progress,
provided the necessary political changes do occur.

1998–2001: an update

Between the end of 1998 and January 2002, the economic
situation did not really improve. The shortcomings reviewed
above tended to worsen. The political situation, both internal
and external remained a matter of major concern, exacerbated by the latest events in Afghanistan and their consequences on Pakistan. The acute tension between India and
Pakistan in December 2001 also had an impact on the
economy.

In the medium- long term perspective there appears to be
hope. The government may move to reduce the influence of
the *madrasas* and extremist movements, five of which are
mentioned in the US list of 39 terrorist organizations.
Curbing these organizations as well as the *madrasas's*

activities would help in restoring greater political stability while creating a more favourable environment for economic growth.

The u-turn of Pakistan's policy *vis a vis* the Taliban has resulted in renewed links between Pakistan and rich donor countries, which has lead to substantial economic assistance. The IMF, the World Bank, and the Asian Development Bank are also ready to increase their aid.

If Afghanistan reaches a minimum level of stability, the massive reconstruction programme should benefit Pakistan. Most of the material aid should be channelled from Karachi to Kandahar or Kabul. For donor countries, it will also be cheaper to rely wherever possible on Pakistani goods, such as cement, chemical fertilisers, possibly cereals, various types of equipment like irrigation pumps which could further boost Pakistan's economy.

Provided peace becomes firmly established in Afghanistan, it would open the way to growing economic co-operation and integration between the Central Asian Republics, Afghanistan, Pakistan, and possibly India, which would benefit the whole region.

The immediate issues

Although GDP data are far from accurate, they at least indicate the basic trends of the economy. Never since the 1950s has Pakistan experienced such a deceleration of growth:

Average growth of GDP (% per year)

1960s (ten year period)	6.8
1970s	4.8
1980s	6.5
1990s	4.6

The situation has particularly deteriorated in the past few years:

Average Growth of GDP (%)
1998/99   4.2
1990/00   3.9
2001/01   2.6
2001/02   2.5–3 (as expected in December 2001)

Some factors beyond the will or the ability of the Pakistanis explain the latest record: an exceptionally severe drought in 2001/01, hitting agriculture and hydel power supply, a temporary increase in oil prices, the impact of the anti-Taliban war leading to a reduction of exports, new waves of refugees, and various other negative effects. Losses to the economy could amount to $2.5 billion according to tentative estimates by the Ministry of Finance. The slowing down of the US economy in 2001 has also brought down textile exports, 25% of which go to America. Foreign investments have for several years suffered from the political environment. In 2001/01, they dropped to their lowest level since many years: FDI and portfolio investments amounted to $182 million versus $480 million in the previous year.

In spite of these negative currents, the manufacturing sector did fairly well, with an overall growth of 7.8% in 2000/01 versus 0.1 in the previous year. But this was more than offset by a fall of 2.5% in agriculture which still accounts for 25% of GDP.

While the foreign debt has reached $38 billion, a substantial part of it should be rescheduled through greater assistance from international institutions and donor countries. Foreign exchange reserves had increased to $4 billion by the end of December 2001.

Thanks to better policies, the government of President Pervez Musharraf has brought down the fiscal deficit from 7% of GDP in the 1990s to 5.3% in 2001. Corruption and leakage have also been reduced. In spite of all these difficulties, imports have increased by 6% and exports by 7% in 2001/01, but it is feared that their performances may be lower in 2001-02.

How far is the overall standard of living being affected by this slow economic growth while population keeps increasing by around 2.5% per year? Can one follow the Asian Bank's estimates according to which the number of people below the poverty line rose to 32% in 1999 from 18% in the previous years? As we know, calculations on poverty are extremely dubious since it is particularly difficult to measure the income of the poor, and more so of the poorest. One should also bear in mind the share of the hidden or black economy which was estimated at 20% of GDP in 1973 versus 50% to 70% in 2000 following the latest estimates respectively of the World Bank and of the Pakistan Institute of Development Economics. However, it is fair to say that poor people on the whole benefit less from the black economy. As to foreign remittances, they only reach the relatively poor. Official remittances have fallen to about $1 billion per year, mainly from the Middle East, but remittances through the *hundi* system could amount to $4 billion a year.

Even if the figure of 32% below the poverty line may be overestimated, a number of danger signals have appeared in the past ten years. Unemployment and underemployment are rising. Private investments remain sluggish, and public savings and public investments available for development are wholly insufficient.

In spite of the present uncertainty, the final comments in my original study seem to remain valid. Pakistan enjoys enough human and material resources to overcome its present very serious difficulties. Initially, massive efforts should be devoted to the improvement of irrigation. The effects of the latest drought would not have been so severe if the canal system had been in better shape. Major efforts are also needed in agriculture. The industrial sector could show a greater resilience as done in the past, provided the private sector gets adequate support and the issue of the loss-making public sector enterprises is at last resolved.

Finally, we may surmise that the key issues are not so much economic but are more connected with internal and external political factors.

NOTES

1. Data, except when the source is specifically mentioned, come from the *Economic Survey* annual report published for the budget, and from the Five-Year Plan reports.
2. *Dawn*, 25 December 1997.
3. *Dawn*, 6 November 1998.
4. *Dawn*, 11 November 1998.
5. *Dawn*, 31 August 1998.
6. See Abdel Rahim Omran, *Family Planning and the Legacy of Islam*, London, Routledge, 1992.
7. *Dawn*, 20 May 1997.
8. IFPRI, 1997.
9. *Dawn*, 24 August 1998.
10. *Financial Times*, 5 August 1997.
11. See the comments of Sultan Ahmed, a leading economist, in *Dawn*, 6 and 16 November 1998 and also *The Economist*, 22 August 1998.
12. *Dawn*, 10 October 1997.

PART FIVE

THE CHALLENGE OF DEMOCRACY: THE LESSONS OF THE PAST

Democracy and Political Transformation in Pakistan

Pakistan, at fifty, is like a 'tale of two cities'; one a 'city of hope'—which has the potential for economic progress, growth, and democratic development; the other a 'city of impending economic disaster. Unfortunately, the prevailing mood in the country appears to be very negative.[1] We are warned that Pakistan could become another Afghanistan, Somalia or Sudan. The macroeconomic, social and political indicators— (i.e., corruption, over-population, fiscal imbalance, foreign debt, low literacy rate, low industrial productivity, inflation, unemployment, increase in violence, defence expenditure, uncontrollable domestic spending, limited tax base and the inability of the state to collect taxes, etc—all seem to reinforce this feeling.

It merits attention that among the Muslim states and the developing world, Pakistan is one of those few states where people have adopted a democratic parliamentary system and through popular mass movements demonstrated disapproval of military intervention and dictatorships. Recent developments such as the growth of the print media, assertion of the judiciary, curtailment of presidential powers, and most importantly, the rising level of political consciousness among the masses are some of the positive trends.[2]

In the past fifty years, Pakistan has undergone an enormous political transformation.[3] Civil society has expanded but has yet to stabilize. Non-governmental groups, formal associations, human rights organizations, autonomous bodies, even the size and scale of political parties have also increased.

A number of regional parties, for example, the Awami National Party (ANP) and the Baloch National Party (BNP) have gained representation in the federal structure and are better integrated. The democratic process has diffused separatist tendencies.

Post-1971 Pakistan bore the burden of prolonged military rule (1977-1988) which obliterated democratic norms and stifled democratic values, but aspirations for democracy continue to persist. For almost a decade (1988-1998) Pakistan had the longest period of civilian led regimes, although none of the elected governments have been able to complete their five-year term in power. It is encouraging to note that the principle of electoral competition has gained strength. Electoral procedures have acquired stability. Despite presidential interventions (1988, 1990, 1993 and 1996) and dissolution of assemblies, the democratic creed has survived. Local Bodies Elections in Punjab in 1998, despite violence and allegations of rigging, reflect a growing confidence in the electoral principle. Despite the frequency of electoral competition, political leaders have not been successful in promoting an environment that would encourage the growth of democratic norms and civility. Therefore, a strong tendency towards illiberal usage of democracy continues to threaten prospects of democratic consolidation. These contradictory processes are transforming the political landscape in Pakistan.

How can we analyse this relationship between democratic transition and political transformations? What are the forces of resistance and support to democracy? What is the role of political parties in promoting or hampering democratic development in Pakistan?

To respond to these questions I would like to identify, analyse and evaluate the processes of political transformation by focusing on six themes. (a) The democratic process and political transformation: the global context (b) The electoral process: establishing the supremacy of the political: the selected public official (c) Electoral competition: Politics and district administration (d) Behavioural patterns of political leadership (e) Socio-economic profile of parliamentarians and their inability to build parliamentary democracy (f) Political parties and challenges of democratic development.

The democratic process and political transformation: the global context

During the last quarter of this century, we have witnessed a major global trend towards democratization. It is estimated that between 1974-1994, about forty states have made the transition from various types of authoritarian regimes to a democratic order.[4] This transformation at the global level has roused considerable interest in democracy as a preferable system of government. It has generated debate on old issues and given birth to new formulations on the workings of democracy.[5]

For example, there is considerable literature that supports the contention that democratic development is a function of economic development.[6] That economic growth accelerates the development of the middle class which, in turn, helps in sustaining democracy. There are exceptions to this observation, for example India, which, despite low levels of economic development is able to sustain a 'flawed' democracy, while a number of rich, oil producing countries, despite a burgeoning middle class, continue to remain authoritarian. On the other side, a number of scholars also argue that democracy is a function of the historical context of a particular country and its cultural milieu. According to this perspective, democratic development is a function of the historical and institutional setting of a society rather than its level of economic development.[7] This debate has sharpened our focus on analysing the interplay of economic and cultural factors in hampering or promoting democracy.

This has also led some scholars to explain why in some cultures democracy is able to gain ground, while in others it continues to falter? More recently, scholars have drawn a distinction between the 'procedural' and 'substantive' aspects of democracy,[8] while others have drawn an analytical distinction between 'electoral' and 'liberal' dimensions of democracy.[9] A few have rung alarm bells stating that what we are witnessing in some states of Asia, Africa, Central Europe and Central Asia is an illusion and not democracy, because the outcome of the electoral process is 'illiberal democracy'.[10] They underscore that the electoral process alone is not sufficient to promote democratic norms, attitudes and institutions. The warning is timely and the observation is a grim reminder that in the 'new democracies' and the societies in transition, electoral competition could give birth to the tyranny of majority rule, encourage the growth of mafias and promote illiberal usage of freedom.

In this study, at the theoretical level, an argument would be developed that democracy is a system of governance and interest representation in which the supremacy of laws and procedures is a prerequisite. That the political leadership, the elite and powerful interest groups need to strive, not only to uphold the rule of law, but also to demonstrate respect for the law and seek observance and compliance from a wider segment of citizens.

Constructing and promoting democracy is not an easy task. It requires patience, time and most importantly, a consensus among the powerful groups and elite in a society on the desirability of the rule of law and governance through the consent of the people. The onus of responsibility for constructing democracy, promoting democratic norms, and institutionalizing democratic practices and principles is on the elite. However, it is equally important to co-ordinate and synchronize these democratic ideals at the popular level. A large number of people in a society have to accept and demonstrate faith in democratic principles. In societies where the gap between the elite and representatives of the people on professed principles of democracy, and their actual conduct, widens, people begin to lose faith in democracy. This aspect has not been given adequate attention in explaining the Pakistani experience with democracy.

Building democracy without democrats?

A number of studies recognize that in the case of Pakistan, democratic development has been constrained both by the historical/institutional setting and low levels of economic development.[11] My contention is that in explaining the democratic disabilities of Pakistan, the contribution of the historical/institutional setting and low levels of economic development is over-emphasized and the inability of political leaders and the elite to uphold the rule of law is not recognized. In this context it would be argued that the greatest stumbling block to democratic development has been the contradictory behaviour and attitude of Pakistani political leaders and elite. Despite struggling for the restoration of democracy, they have failed to build a legal framework, create a pro-democracy environment, and most importantly, develop a policy framework in which conflicts may be resolved through negotiations and by building consensus. Democracy cannot grow and function in the absence of a consensus among the elite. Political leaders and the elite, while struggling for democracy, reveal a democratic dispensation. However, upon assuming power, they change and demonstrate authoritarian tendencies. They pursue or adopt policies that strengthen authoritarian attitudes rather than promote democratic norms, flout the rule of law and defy tolerance of any political opposition.

In such conditions of endemic conflict between government-opposition groups, mafias and *Qabza* groups (usurpers of public land or property) begin to emerge. They take advantage of electoral principles, undermine democracy and promote conditions for 'illiberal democracy'. A negative outcome of electoral competition in Pakistan is the emergence of such groups—who defy the rule of law, encourage violence and distribute patronage by seeking control over the resources of the state. As a result of these tendencies, there is a growing scepticism about the sustainability of democracy. These conditions have also forced a number of small groups to raise their voice against these mafias and demand empowerment of the people.

The disappointment is not with democracy as a form of government but with the conduct and behaviour of parliamentarians and political parties who are expected to make democracy work. The parliamentarians have not been able to abide by the principles of liberal democracy—where respect for law, tolerance of dissent, minorities and opposition groups is a prerequisite and needs to be developed. The dominant political parties, i.e., the Pakistan Muslim League (PML) (N) and the Pakistan Peoples Party (PPP) and their leadership have failed to promote a pro-democracy environment—an environment in which plurality of views are encouraged and conflict of views and values can be resolved through non-violent means.

The foundations of democracy are built on acceptance of the rule of law among the wider number of members of civil society.[12] It is not to trivialize the significance of culture, social structure and level of economic development. Favourable disposition of these factors certainly brightens the prospect of democratic development. However, democracy thrives on competition and fairplay, and encourages merit. The spoil system or distribution of rewards—i.e., extension of patronage to supporters of a political party, is only one small aspect of the democratic process because in a democracy political parties compete to gain power to pursue and implement specific policies for the public good. The expectation is that a particular party will be in power for a certain period of time, therefore, in order to implement its policies, it advocates the groups that it represents, as it needs political activists and ideologues to achieve its goals. Thus, political parties, the patronage system and democracy grow side by side. On the other hand, the electoral process and political parties are not expected to obstruct merit, achievement orientation or the citizens right to compete, excel and advance their interests. In a number of developing countries like Pakistan, where aspirations for democracy are strong, but pro-democracy groups, and political parties are weak, retaining this distinction between the spoil system and the pursuit of merit becomes complicated. This complication rouses scepticism—about civil society's ability to respect the rule of law.

The electoral process: establishing the supremacy of the elected public official

Let me examine the relationship between the electoral process and the transformation of administrative structures.

Elections and the electoral process have brought about a change in the attitude of political parties and their leaders. Until the first general elections of 1970, political leaders and parties generally accepted the superiority and lawful authority of the bureaucratic elite. The colonial administrative structure, which established the supremacy of the bureaucratic elite, performed satisfactorily with minor irritations, until 1970. It did produce tensions whenever pro-democracy movements threatened the dominance of the bureaucratic elite (for example, the 1953 Ahmadi crisis, the mobilization efforts of the Muslim League in 1958, or the 1968 students movement). It has to be recognized that the British created an administrative structure which was not meant to be governed by elected public officials. The electoral process was confined to the Local Bodies and the local councillors were expected to accept the supremacy of the Administrative elite.[13] There were few instances of political leaders interfering in the functioning of administration; between 1947-1970, there were rarely any demands for posting and transfer of public officials. However, in the post 1970 period, particularly after the PPP, under the leadership of Zulfikar Ali Bhutto, assumed power in December 1971, elected public officials began to establish their supremacy on the non-elected public officials.

Through the 1973 administrative reforms, Bhutto sought to establish civilian supremacy over bureaucracy.[14] His goal was that at the macro level, the bureaucracy should accept the supremacy of the political leadership and representative institutions. He sought to alter the structural balance in favour of political leadership. He did not encourage interference in the workings of government at the micro level. The Bhutto government (1971-77) could be criticized for over enthusiasm in venturing to establish its dominance over state institutions (i.e. military and bureaucracy). However, Bhutto's approach gave a new sense of confidence to political parties and their leaders who, in subsequent years, began to aspire for civilian supremacy over the state institutions. General Zia's Martial Law (1977-1985) attempted to reverse this trend, by de-legitimizing politics at the national level, and by encouraging Local Bodies Elections. Thus, Zia attempted to restore the colonial model of politics, where local influentials could be co-opted to pursue political ambitions under the guidance and patronage of district administration, i.e., ensuring continuity of bureaucratic authority on policy and administrative matters. Party-less Local Bodies elections were held in 1979, 1983, and 1987. The regime's strategy was not only to initiate and promote new individuals and groups into the political arena, but also to de-legitimize the role and significance of leaders who had become members of parliament on the basis of affiliation with political parties. In pursuance of this objective, the Zia regime formulated a policy through which members of the Local Bodies were given developmental grants to improve health, education, and road networks in their constituencies. Thus, very much like colonial rule, the state extended patronage to build a new set of local influentials, who were willing to abandon party politics in favour of Local Bodies. He met with limited success but in the process facilitated the emergence of local influentials in the national political arena. As soon as the 1985 party-less elections gave birth to parliament and restored the democratic process, the elected public officials began to work for their preponderance with new zeal. The government of Prime Minister Mohammed Khan Junejo upgraded the same programme of allowing a developmental grant of Rs 50 *lakh* to each Member of the National Assembly. This development grant was funneled through the Public Works Department (PWD), Local Government, the Communication and Works Department (C&W), and the district administration. Thus emerged a new nexus of politician and administrator. In a number of instances, these grants were not properly utilized, funds were misappropriated and in some cases were usurped by politicians for personal advancement. At the popular level, democracy was seen as promoting corruption instead of development. Armed guards and Pajero's emerged as new symbols of power and authority in the rural setting. Thus, with each electoral contest, the candidates not only displayed new symbols of power, but the voters also began to demand more rewards. The contestants to the parliament came under pressure from their constituents to obtain jobs, resolve their problems and secure development. The voters also saw elections as an opportunity to advance their interests. Upon electoral victory, assembly members were expected to provide patronage to their constituents.

Electoral experiences in Pakistan 1985-1997, reveal a pattern; after each election (i.e. 1988, 1990, 1993, 1997) the political leaders not only secured greater autonomy, but were more vigorous in pursuing their supremacy. In the process, they were driven by the demands of their constituents and personal interest (i.e., providing jobs to members of their constituency, promoting developmental work through administrative help, seeking the removal of grievances of their voters and developing a personal connection with the public officials working in their sub-division or district). Interestingly, the electoral process has accentuated two trends, first, political interference in the administration has increased. Second, it has promoted demands for administrative decentralization, in return, paving the way for the creation of new districts and sub-divisions.[15]

These petty considerations have propelled members of parliament to seek postings and transfers of officers on whom they could rely for favourable administrative action. The democratic process manifested through electoral competition is an important contributory factor that has lead to the demand for the creation of new districts.

Electoral competition: politics and district administration

The impact of Local Bodies Elections was that local issues (i.e., caste, *biradri* rivalry, seeking patronage for develop-mental grants and schemes) acquired political salience. Thus, the military regime curbed politics at the national level but facilitated non-party electoral competition at the local level.

Therefore, the politicians and new entrants to politics began to work for creating greater autonomy for themselves and demanded the creation of new districts. In 1982, two new divisions, Faisalabad and Gujranwala, were created in the Punjab. Subsequently, (between 1982-1988) Rajanpur, Leiah, Bhakkar, Khanewal, Khushab, Toba Tek Singh, Okara and Chakwal were created as new districts. In the post 1988 period, Lodhran, Mandi Bahauddin, Pakpattan, Hafizabad, the Narowal were made new districts. Similarly, Gujrat was transferred from Rawalpindi Division to Gujranwala Division.[16]

In the rural setting and administrative structure of Pakistan, the district is the primary unit of administration. Since 70 per cent of the constituencies are rural, therefore political, economic and administrative activity revolves around the district. Consequently, local councillors and parliamentarians are obsessed with gaining control and influence in the district administration. These political imperatives prompt political leaders to influence postings and transfers at the lowest level of government. In the process, district administration is politicized and its ability to act judiciously and fairly is compromised.

The new districts (totalling thirteen) were created under political influence during the transition towards democracy. The local politicians were keen to establish effective administrative control over their districts. Since the state was regarded as the principal source of patronage, this patronage could be distributed only through administrative machinery over which the politicians had little control. Thus, the electoral process built a new bond between politicians and the district administration and local government institutions. Interestingly, it is not merely influence with the district administration that the politicians seek, but to consolidate their structural presence, they also start a scramble for securing appointments in the district administration. The local Councillors and Members of National and Provincial Assemblies (MNAs/MPAs) demand recruitment for relatives or supporters for the appointment of Tehsildars/Naib Tehsildars, Inspectors/Sub Inspectors of Police, school teachers, lady health visitors, and petty clerks.

In Punjab, between 1985-1990, an estimated 2000 Assistant Inspectors of Police, Tehsildars and Naib Tehsildars were recruited.[17] These appointments were made either on the recommendations of the Chief Minister or parliamentarians. This practice has continued, and its pace and scale has increased since 1990. As a result, democratization has strengthened the paternalistic model of administration. The [former] Punjab Chief Minister, Shahbaz Sharif brought about a change. He revived and reactivated the Punjab Public Service Commission (PPSC) for recruitments in the Punjab Police and Administration. In the provinces of Sindh, Balochistan and NWFP, similar practices of creating new districts and recruitment in the subordinate administrative class were pursued and continue to be in vogue. Through these devices, the political parties and their parliamentary leaders have built a structural presence in the provincial administration. The result is that the district administration has become highly politicized, coercive, and partisan and is perceived by the public as an instrument of oppression.

As a result, the office of the Deputy Commissioner, which was once the epitome of colonial glory and rule, but also imparted justice, promoted fairplay and provided effective governance has had its reputation tarnished, functioning underminded, and authority eroded. In this sense, democracy has considerably eroded the authority of administrative institutions. On the other hand, patronage has promoted corruption, and recruitment of the henchmen of politicians has strengthened the authoritarian streak in the existing feudal social order. Consequently, democratization has led to the development of illiberal tendencies, partisanship, lack of tolerance and distrust in the fairness of administration. These have been the negative fall out effects of democratization. Corrective measures can be adopted by restoring Local Bodies (Punjab has already done that), and by putting a limit on political appointees at the subordinate levels. Unless the principle of hierarchy of command and control by the senior administrators is strengthened, democratization would breed politicization, maladministration, impartiality, corruption and deepen the crisis of governance.

Here we must draw a distinction between social and electoral sources of power. Feudal power is rooted in the social order, while an elected public official draws authority on the basis of electoral competition. It is the legal framework that gives elected public officials the power to conduct the business of the state and promote the welfare of citizens. Instead of establishing the legal supremacy of elected officials on the state institutions, particularly the administrative structure, they have invariably resorted to using it as an instrument to pursue partisan goals. If this politicization was confined to the higher levels of bureaucracy, one could make a case for partnership between elected officials and public servants for promoting the policies of an elected government. In most democracies, such a partnership is recognized as legitimate, but in Pakistan what is alarming is that the state institutions have been politicized at the lowest level. Political leaders and parliamentarians demand postings and transfers of their choice at the lowest levels of government. Therefore, person and posting have become more important than efficiency and performance of a particular officer or office. Bureaucracies operate on the principle of hierarchy, merit, seniority and the rule of law.[18] When political parties and their functionaries demand placement of individuals at all administrative levels, this disrupts the smooth and efficient functioning of bureaucracy, undermines the authority of state institutions, violates respect for lawful rule and promotes corruption. This leads to erosion of governmental authority, promotes politicization and hampers the proper functioning of bureaucracy.

There is a growing perception in the public that state institutions collaborate with political leaders and the ruling political party more out of fear rather than shared interest and respect for each other's sphere of lawful authority. In the process, public welfare, justice for citizens and good governance is compromised. This mutual suspicion and distrust has become the defining principle of governance. Therefore, a political party, on assuming power indulges in purging civil servants (for example, Zulfiqar Ali Bhutto purged 1400 officials, Benazir Bhutto sidelined almost eighty officers in the first government and over thirty in the second government. Similarly Nawaz Sharif sidelined forty officials in the first government and eighty-seven officers were suspended in February 1997), followed by a massive reshuffle in the bureaucracy. Both at the policy-making and district level, those officers are appointed who are perceived to be loyal or are personally known to the political leaders. Pursuit of such goals has factionalized the bureaucracy, particularly at the provincial level. Each election and each regime change is preceded and followed by massive reshuffles in bureaucracy.

Behavioural pattern of political leadership

In a democratic system, the political leadership is expected to co-ordinate between the expectations and demands of its support groups and the groups that are not fully supportive of its leadership.[19] The task of the leadership is to establish a framework on the basis of which uniform and creditable principles of the political game may evolve. The Pakistani experience reveals a two-fold predicament. First, a growing tension between the political leadership's professed democratic creed and authoritarian policies and practices. This contradiction has considerably damaged the sustainability of democracy. Second, political leadership in Pakistan reveals a co-ordination dilemma. On the one hand they aspire and in some cases have struggled to restore democracy, espouse greater participation of the masses in the political process, promise to build constitutionalism, promote liberal democracy, uphold the rule of law, and yet in their conduct and behaviour, they portray an equally strong dispensation towards autocratic tendencies.

Let me exemplify some of these contradictions. The first Prime Minister of Pakistan, Liaquat Ali Khan (1947-51) aspired to move Pakistan towards constitutional rule, strengthen democratic processes, and stabilize the Muslim League as a party, yet he introduced PRODA (1949), which restricted both the emergence of representative leadership and the growth of political parties. Liaquat failed to translate democratic aspiration into reality, nor was he able to stabilize constitutional rule, promote the party system, and institutionalize dissent and dialogue.[20]

In the 1970s, Zulfiqar Ali Bhutto rose to political eminence portraying himself and perceived by the public as a democrat. He had been inducted into Ayub Khan's military regime, and remained associated with it from 1958-66. He subsequently disassociated himself from the regime and recreated an image for himself, and founded the Pakistan Peoples Party (PPP) in 1967. Through mass mobilization, socialist ideology and an organizational network, the PPP was developed into a national party. Bhutto did not encourage elections within the party, instead, he nominated leaders to the central executive committees at various levels—national, provincial, and local. The membership of the party expanded but the organizational structure was kept weak and under personal control.[21] On assuming power, Zulfiqar Ali Bhutto (1971-77) was successful in formulating a constitution for Pakistan through parliamentary consensus. His singular achievement was the making of the 1973 Constitution and its adoption by the National Assembly. However, his personal conduct and political style contributed little in promoting the rule of law. He could not curb his authoritarian propensities, when through a series of constitutional amendments he restricted the freedom of the judiciary, press, and even religion (i.e., in 1974 the Ahmedies were declared a non-Muslim minority). The attitude and behaviour of opposition political parties was equally hostile and confrontational. The government and opposition leaders demonstrated a co-ordination dilemma— they failed to iron out their differences on the functioning of parliamentary democracy. This encouraged the military to disrupt the fragile, quasi-democratic set up.

General Zia's rule, (1977-1988) further weakened civil society, and participatory processes, democratic norms and values were further mutilated. Political parties endured but were further weakened. The military rule, though harsh on civil and religious freedoms, could not suppress democratic aspirations among the public. Therefore, underneath his autocratic rule, tension between pro-democracy and anti-democracy forces persisted. General Ziaul Haq was skilful in encouraging and expanding the base of religious groups, trader merchants, and other right wing groups.[22] In 1981, political leaders with a feudal background and support base, along with urban professionals, launched a pro-democracy alliance—the Movement for the Restoration of Democracy (MRD). The MRD demanded the removal of martial law and called for holding of elections. These demands eventually paved the way for the restoration of democracy in 1985. Mohammed Khan Junejo, who was handpicked by Ziaul Haq as prime minister (1985-1988), revealed a democratic dispensation, and allowed the return of Benazir Bhutto to Pakistan. He also promoted an environment in which opposition political parties could function. Simultaneously, Junejo revealed a strong propensity to establish the dominance of the Muslim League. He introduced a scheme of granting developmental funds to the members of parliament for development and welfare purposes in their constituencies. He was modestly successful in creating a framework for government-opposition relationship. Before he could stabilize party rule and processes of democratic institution-building, he was dismissed by the military dictator, Ziaul Haq. Mohammed Khan Junejo is not given the credit that he deserves. Among Pakistani political leaders, he stands out as a prime minister who showed tolerance towards opposition political parties, respect for the rule of law and encouraged an environment conducive to the freedom of the press.

From 1988 to 1998, Benazir Bhutto and Nawaz Sharif, who in many ways represent a new generation of leaders, created an expectation for democratic rule.[23] In their own ways, both restored and reorganized their respective political parties, i.e., PPP and PML (N). Both aroused expectations about upholding the rule of law. As opposition leaders, in a limited way, they contributed towards an expansion of the democratic process. But both showed strong, autocratic tendencies as soon as they assumed power. Instead of upholding the rule of law, both flouted it, showed little respect for minority rights and views, suppressed dissent and restricted opposition.

This suggests that political leaders, since the restoration of democracy, have deepened the contradictions in Pakistani society. They have pursued policies that have led to an erosion of state authority, weakened democratic norms and values, and by default, encouraged the emergence of a number of non-governmental organizations, which are working for the protection of human rights, minorities, women's groups, other professional associations, farmer associations, etc. These new groups have grown because political parties have, by and large, accepted the legitimacy of the electoral process. Both the PPP and PML (N) continue to be the dominant political parties, and share almost 62 per cent of the total votes polled in various elections. (See Table I). Both have preferred to establish a dominant party system rather than encouraging the growth of a two-party system.

Table I
Party Share of Votes
All Pakistan National Assembly Elections

	1988		1990		1993		1997	
	% of Votes	No. of Seats	% of Votes	No. of Seats	% of Votes	No. of Seats	% of Votes	No. of Seats
PML (N)/IJI	30.16	54	37.37	106	39.86	72	45.88	134
PPP/PDA	38.52	93	36.83	44	37.85	86	21.80	18
MQM	5.37	13	5.54	15	–	–	3.55	12
JUI(F)	1.84	7	2.94	6	2.4	4	1.61	2
ANP	2.09	2	1.68	6	1.67	3	2.31	9
JWP/BNA	0.36	2	0.61	2	0.27	2	0.29	2
BNP	–	–	–	–	–	–	0.66	3
PKMA/PMAI	0.24	0	0.35	1	0.49	3	0.33	0
Others	1.92	6	4.38	5	12.46	21	9.2	2
Ind	19.50	27	10.30	22	7.40	15	14.99937	22
	100	204	100	207	100	202	100	204

Source: The *Herald*, March 1997

Socio-economic profile of parliamentarians and their inability to build Parliamentary Democracy

The dominant social class of Members of the National Assembly (MNA) is of landlords/tribal leaders. Data of five elections held between 1985-1997, reveals that the representation of various other classes and groups has shown some increase, but feudals/tribal leaders still continue to be the dominant class. Out of a total of 207 seats for the National Assembly (NA), they continue to retain, on an average, 125 seats. However, representation by professionals (i.e., lawyers, doctors, technocrats) is on the rise. This is a healthy trend. (See Table II).

Table II
Social Class Background of National Assembly Members

	1985	1988	1990	1993	1997
Landlords and Tribal Leaders	157	156	106	129	126
Businessmen/Industrialists	54	20	38	37	39
Urban Professionals	18	9	46	26	32
Religious Leaders	6	15	11	8	3
Retired Military Officers	–	7	3	5	2
Others	3	–	3	3	2
		207	207	207	207

Source: Compiled by Dr. Saeed Shafqat

Comprehensive data on the educational background of the members of the National Assembly is not available. Nine out of 207 Members of the National Assembly do not have formal schooling. A small number, about 10 per cent are proficient in English, Pakistan's official language while a large majority (i.e., 95 per cent) are only conversant with Urdu, the national language. However, I have been able to collect data on the composition of federal cabinets from 1985 to 1997. The data reveals that in the federal cabinet, feudals, lawyers/professionals and business groups continue to dominate the decision-making process. In the Junejo cabinet, feudals, lawyers/professionals and business groups were evenly spread. Therefore, in terms of social group representation, his cabinet could be considered most representative. While the first Benazir Bhutto cabinet (1988-1990) was dominated by feudals and lawyers/professionals, the second Benazir Bhutto cabinet (1993-1996) was overwhelmingly dominated by the feudals. It is interesting to note that the middle classes, which are not adequately represented in the NA, were equally under-represented in the Benazir cabinets. While Nawaz Sharif's cabinet (1990-1993) was dominated by business groups (9), lawyers/professionals (12) and feudals (12) were significantly represented. The second Nawaz Sharif cabinet (1997-98) is extremely narrow-based. It is overwhelmingly dominated by professionals and business groups, and the number of feudals is significant. However, representation of the middle classes has remained marginal in all the federal government cabinets from 1985-1998. (See Table III).

Table III
Composition of Cabinets 1985–1998
Federal Ministries

	Feudals	Business	Lawyers /Professionals	Generals	Women	Ulema	Minorities	Unidentified	Total
M.K. Junejo 1985–88	12	3	8	2	1	1	–	–	27
Benazir Bhutto 1988–90	15	1	14	3	4	–	1	6	44
Nawaz Sharif 1990–93	12	9	12	1	1	1	2	2	39
Benazir Bhutto 1993–96	17	3	13	2	1	–	1	2	39
Nawaz Sharif 1997	8	6	8	1	2	–	–	1	26

Source: Several Gazette Notifications, Government of Pakistan, compiled by Dr. Saeed Shafqat.

National Assembly: Expectations and Performance

Between 1950-1970, proceedings and debates in the Constituent and National Assemblies were primarily conducted in English. In the post-1985 period, this has changed significantly, and a large number of parliamentarians in the National Assembly prefer to speak in the national language—a positive trend toward indigenousization.[24] However, the quality of debate has considerably deteriorated because the MNA's have either little or no knowledge about national issues: in fact, the quality of debate among the MNAs of the 1970s was far superior to that heard in the 1990s. Parliamentarians are inadequately informed about the rules and procedures of parliamentary practice. They pay little attention to developing the National Assembly into a forum for debating national issues and formulation of legislation. Parliamentary parties and their leadership have paid little attention towards developing their position on specific issues.

During thirteen years of parliamentary democracy from 1985 to 1997, the NA held very few sessions and legislative performance was also weak. During the first Benazir Bhutto government only eleven meetings were held, while during her second tenure there were thirty-one sessions. During Nawaz Sharif's first term, the NA held seventeen sessions, while during his second term only twenty sessions were held. The duration of these sessions was short. This clearly suggests that either the NA did too little or had no legislative work. During Junejo's government, parliament had longer sessions, indicating that it met for debate and also did some legislative work. (See Table IV).

Table IV
A comparative study of the duration of
National Assembly sessions

Parliamentary Government 1985–1998	National Assembly Sessions	Total Days	Average Duration (Days)
Mohammad Khan Junejo P.M. 1985–88	15	545	36
Benazir Bhutto P.M. 1988–90	11	218	20
Nawaz Sharif P.M. 1990–93	17	417	25
Benazir Bhutto P.M. 1993–96	31	525	17
Nawaz Sharif P.M. Feb. 1997 – March 1998	20	140	7

Source: Secretary National Assembly, Islamabad, compiled by Dr. Saeed Shafqat

The NA has not been able to develop into a forum which may inform, educate and reflect the opinions of citizens or representative interest groups. Little effort has been made to develop consensus on important legislation. Invariably, it is through Ordinances, rather than through debate that legislation, if any, has been adopted. Parliamentarians and political parties have not been able to bring conflicting interests and issues for debate and resolution into the NA. Therefore, extra-parliamentary tactics continue to dominate Pakistani politics. Major national issues are debated and managed outside parliament (over the years, no meaningful discussion on Kashmir, the sectarian problem or India's nuclear explosion etc has taken place in the NA). Thus, the NA has not been able to develop as an institution that could promote and strengthen democratic norms and practices. If parliamentary democracy has to succeed, more sessions of the assembly, greater debate and legislative work needs to be created to enhance the capacity of the NA.

The political parties remain instruments of patronage and mass mobilization and they have yet to acquire the skills of interest representation in parliament. Given mass mobilization orientation, the political leadership uses political parties for street demonstrations and politics of agitation. Thus, political parties have developed into effective tools for extra-parliamentary politics, but they continue to have limited utility for promoting democratic norms and performing legislative/rule-making functions in parliament. The challenge for the party leadership in Pakistan is to transform the character of their particular political party from an instrument of mass mobilization to interest representation in parliament. They must build a party system that would reduce tension and conflict and promote prospects of bipartisan consensus. The mobilizational parties, by their nature and origin are confrontational. Therefore, even when these political parties assume office through electoral contest and form governments, their style of governance remains combative and confrontational. They treat state institutions in a combative manner instead of promoting partnership and harmony with other organs of the state, political leadership perpetuates conflict.

Political Parties and challenges of democratic development

Political parties and parliamentarians have unconsciously undermined their power by not developing the National Assembly into a forum for national debate and primary source for legislation, therefore, most of the time the NA has adopted Ordinances or acts, and has remained a rubber stamp for adopting these ordinances. In one year, the PML (N) (1997-98) got forty-six Bills passed from the Assembly, as compared to forty-four Bills passed by the PPP in three years. The PPP issued 346 Ordinances during three years, while the PML (N) has so far issued ten.[25]

An outstanding feature of party politics in Pakistan has been the making and breaking of alliances and coalitions outside parliament. However, coalition building within the parliament has remained weak and inconsistent. Bi-partisan or multi-party consensus on a particular issue has rarely developed. (Recently, political parties have demonstrated consensus on two occasions first, on removing the 8th Amendment and passing the 13th Amendment. Second, while adopting a Bill enhancing the salary and pay structure of the MNAs). The party in power invariably seeks to exclude the opposition parties and attempts to establish dominance, while the opposition parties, by making extra-parliamentary alliances, resort to street protest and mobilize the masses. Their basic aim is to dislodge the government rather than engage in dialogue. For example, the Democratic Action Committee (DAC) 1968, the Pakistan National Alliance (PNA) 1983, Islami Jamhuri Ittehad (IJI) 1988, and the Pakistan Awami Tehrik (PAT) 1998 coalitions that were built because the opposition political parties were inadequately represented in the NA, so they had little stake in parliament, and pressurized the government or the president to dissolve the assembly.

Since the restoration of democracy, the protesting political parties have sought to put pressure on the judiciary, the president, or the military to dissolve respective governments. However, since 1988 (i.e., removal of the Junejo government), there is evidence to suggest that the military and the president acted in concert to dislodge elected governments in 1990 and 1993. In 1996, the president and the judiciary played a vital role in the dismissal of the Benazir government.

Despite struggling for the restoration of democracy, political leaders, the elite and interest groups have failed to build a legal framework, create a pro-democracy environment, and most importantly, develop a policy framework in which conflicts may be resolved inside the parliament, through negotiations, by making bargains, by seeking accommodation and by building consensus. Democracy cannot grow and function in the absence of elite consensus. The critical question is, why even pro-democracy elite, upon assuming power, continue to reveal authoritarian tendencies? Why do they pursue or adopt policies that strengthen authoritarian attitudes rather than promote democratic norms, respect for the law or tolerance of any political opposition? For example,

Zulfikar Ali Bhutto, who led a pro-democracy movement, upon assuming power in December 1971 imposed restrictions on freedom of the press, dealt with opposition in an authoritarian manner and passed legislation to restrict the authority and independence of the judiciary. Similarly, the current Nawaz Sharif government has passed legislation in haste that curtailed the powers of the president, and passed an anti-defection clause that bound members to party discipline. Further, the PML (N) party leadership did not discourage its supporters from attacking the Supreme Court building in November 1997. The formation of Khidmat Committees, the Ehtsab Cell and Open *Kutcheries* are some of the methods that show authoritarian tendencies and weaken the position of representative institutions.

Conclusion

From the foregoing analysis it is evident that the results of Pakistan's experimentation with parliamentary democracy, (particularly during 1985-98) are mixed. Several contradictory trends are noteworthy. First, political leaders continue to reveal a lack of commitment to the principles of democracy, and above all, have found it difficult to develop the National Assembly as the primary forum for national debate, dialogue and legislation. To make parliamentary democracy succeed, parliamentarians need to strengthen the parliament. Confidence in electoral competition has to be matched by parliamentary performance. The challenge for parliamentarians is to enhance the legislative and consensus building capacity of the NA.

Second, electoral competition has integrated a number of regional parties, like the Awami National Party (ANP), the Baloch National Party (BNP), the Mohajir Quami Movement (MQM), and the Jamhoori Watan Party (JWP) within the national political system. This has diffused separatist tendencies and encouraged confidence in the democratic process. The smaller provinces are assertive in their desire to expand their share in the federal structure. The transition to democracy has strengthened the federal character of the

Pakistani state. This has given a boost to the devolution of administrative authority. The electoral process has accelerated the pace for such a change at the provincial level, where after each election the structural presence of elected officials has gained ground. The negative fall-out effect is that partisanship has compromised the neutrality and fairness of administrative machinery.

Third, there is a growing awareness among the public that the dynastic character of the political parties is an obstacle for the development of democracy and the party system. In recent years, some muted voices of reform from within the political parties have appeared, though with little effect. The challenge for the leadership both in the government and the opposition is to reform and democratize the structures of political parties. Reformed and democratized political parties are the best guarantee for the continuity and stability of democracy in Pakistan.

Fourth, the global trend towards democratization has restricted the possibility of direct military intervention, although the military will continue to monitor and influence the direction of the political process from a distance. Therefore, in the foreseeable future, Pakistan's transition to democracy should endure albeit with pain, occasional violence, conflict and corruption.

Finally, democracy has become an expensive form of government. The 1985 election cost the government of Pakistan around 17 *crore* rupees (170 million), in 1993 the cost had risen to 41 *crore* rupees (410 million). In 1988, on an average a candidate contesting for the National Assembly seat spent around Rs. 5 *lakh* (0.5 million). In 1997, the election cost of an NA seat had risen to Rs. 50 *lakh* (5 million). This suggests that only big landlords, businessmen and in a few cases urban professionals could contest elections. In order to sustain and consolidate democracy, and encourage the representation of the middle classes, the cost of electoral competition needs to be lowered. There are signs of revolt among the middle classes in the urban centres, where

[Editor's Note: The writer adds 'Predictions are difficult to make. Writing this paper in early 1998, I did not anticipate that the military will return to power in 1999.']

resentment is growing against the ineffectiveness of democratically elected government to provide justice and security to citizens. Failure to meet this challenge could deepen the crisis of governance and cause social upheaval, anarchy and mass agitation.

NOTES

1. Several writings in Pakistani newspapers reflect this trend. For some recent comments and analysis see for example, Sheikh Manzoor Ahmad, 'Bisquieting Portents', *Dawn*, Lahore, 20 April 1998. Dr Maleeha Lodhi, 'Power and Authority', *The News*, Islamabad, 15 April 1998. Kunwar Idris, 'Prime Minister and SHOs', *Dawn*, Lahore 15 April 1998.
2. Leo E. Rose and D. Hugh Evans, 'Pakistan's Enduring Experiment', *Journal of Democracy*, Vol. 1, January 1997. pp. 961; also see for highly perceptive analysis on the subject, Inayatullah, Sarah Inayatullah and Sohail Inayatullah, 'The Futures of Democracy in Pakistan—A Liberal Perspective', *Futures*, Vol. 29, No. 10, 1997. pp. 955-970.
3. For a detailed analysis on this point see, David Taylor, 'Political Parties Elections and Democracy in Pakistan', *Journal of Commonwealth and Comparative Politics*, Vol. 30, No. 1, March 1992. pp. 96-115. Ainslie Embree, 'Statehood in South Asia', *Journal of International Affairs*, Vol. 51, No. 1, Summer 1997. pp. 10-15 (pp. 1-18); also see Mohammad Waseem, *Politics and the State in Pakistan*, Lahore, Progressive Publishers, 1989. pp. 44-60.
4. Samuel P. Huntington, 'What Price Freedom', *Harvard International Review*, Winter 1992-1993. pp. 3-7; also see, *The Economist*, London, 27 August 1994. pp. 15-17.
5. For a concise and comprehensive analysis on the nature of this debate, see, Samuel P. Huntington, 'After Twenty Years: The Future of the Third Wave', *Journal of Democracy*, Vol. 8, No. 4, October 1997. pp. 3-12.
6. For an updated and improvised interpretation on Seymour Martin Lipset's classic work, *Political Man: The Social Bases of Politics*, New York, Double Day, 1960. See, Larry Diamond, 'Economic Development and Democracy Reconsidered' in *Re-examining Democracy: Essays in Honor of Seymour Martin Lipset*, Garey Marks/Larry Diamond (ed) Newbury Park, Sage Publications, 1992. pp. 93-139.

7. See, John B. Londregan and Keith T. Poole, 'Does High Income Promote Democracy?' *World Politics*, No. 49, October 1996. pp. 1-30.

8. See for example, Juan J. Linz, 'Transition to Democracy', *The Washington Quarterly*, Summer 1990. pp. 143-164; also see Ayesha Jalal, *Democracy and Authoritarianism in South Asia: A Comparative and Historical Perspective*, Lahore, Sang-e-Meel Publications, 1995. pp. 1-8.

9. For a perceptive and insightful conceptual differentiation on this point see, Larry Diamond, 'Is the Third Wave Over', *Journal of Democracy*, Vol. 7, No. 3, July 1996. pp. 20-39.

10. For an incisive survey and analysis of problems of democracy and growing illiberal trends in new democracies, see, Fareed Zakariya, 'The Rise of Illiberal Democracy', *Foreign Affairs*, November/December, Vol. 76, No. 6, 1997. pp. 22-43.

11. Hasan Gardezi and Jamil Rashid (ed) *Pakistan: The Roots of Dictatorship*, London, Zed Press, 1983; also see, Ayesha Jalal. pp. 9-25 and 48-62.

12. For a detailed review of literature on this point see, Barry A. Weingast, 'The Political Foundations of Democracy and the Rule of Law', *American Political Science Review*, Vol. 91, No. 2, June 1997. pp. 245-263.

13. For an analysis and history see, Ayesha Jalal. pp. 18-20.

14. For detailed study of 1973 Reforms, see, Charles Kennedy, *Bureaucracy in Pakistan*, Karachi, Oxford, 1987. pp. 54-87.

15. Interviews.

16. Interviews.

17. See editorial comment *The Friday Times*, Lahore, 22-28 August 1997, also *The Nation*, Lahore, 4 July 1994.

18. For theoretical and conceptual foundations of bureaucracy, see, Max Weber, *The Theory of Social and Economic Organization*, (Ed., Tallcot Persons) New York, The Free Press, 1947. pp. 329-341.

19. For a general discussion on co-ordination dilemmas of political leadership in a democracy, see, Barry R. Weingast, pp. 246 and 261-262.

20. For an informative analysis on Liaquat's rule, see, Allen McGrath, *The Destruction of Pakistan's Democracy*, Karachi, Oxford University Press, 1997, Chapter 3. pp. 52-78.

21. For a detailed discussion on organization of the PPP see, Anwar H. Syed, *The Discourse and Politics of Zulfikar Ali Bhutto*, London, MacMillan, 1992. pp. 205-230.

22. For a detailed analysis of Zia's Policies, see, Saeed Shafqat, *Civil-Military Relations in Pakistan*, Boulder, Westview, 1997. pp. 189-219.

23. Ibid. pp. 225-254.

24. Several Issues of *Debates: The National Assembly of Pakistan*, Karachi, The Manager Publications. These official reports are published regularly and are obtainable from the Government of Pakistan from 1980 to 1997.

25. These figures were given by Mushahid Hussain, Minister of Information and Broadcasting, Government of Pakistan, *Dawn*, Lahore.

Political Parties in Pakistan: Role and Limitations

Any observer of Pakistan's political life in 1998 can but be baffled at the contrast between the apparent abundance of democratic institutions including political parties, (a notorious perquisite for a normally active and evolutive political life), and the atmosphere of permanent crisis, with some peaks of violence, which prevail in the country. One of the questions which, therefore, arises is the very adequacy of existing political parties to a normal expression of public opinion's trends, including hopes and disappointments, through regular polling, and the role these parties actually play in the Pakistani democratic set-up.

The first sight

At first sight, the country's polity seems to be organized around two main poles which benefit from almost equal support among the voters and manage to attract smaller political forces in the framework of electoral or parliamentary alliances.

One of the poles is openly devoted to 'caring' and tries to respond in its programmes to the need for improved social welfare. It is embodied essentially in the Pakistan Peoples Party (PPP) and some of its long standing allies such as the Pakistan Muslim League (PML) (J) (which is now in a very weak position).

This major component of Pakistan's polity seems chiefly led by what could be called an educated and heavily landed gentry whose aim is to preserve its social position through a long term strategy consisting in gaining sustainable popular support. This requires some attention to the most urgent needs of the poorest, especially the villagers and rural workers, so as to soothe them through some improvement in their living conditions and thereby reinforce their allegiance to their traditional rural elite. This means that social inequalities in the countryside are not totally rejected as such but rather made bearable as a means of progress in daily life.

The same political force endeavours to win some popularity in the townships and cities through implemented or just promised measures aimed at improving the working classes' standard of living to the detriment of industrial or commercial firms' profit margins.

Generally speaking, the PPP and its allies seem prone to feed the state budget or address the problems of the destitute by taxing the 'urban rich' rather than the landlords whose influence and help seem vital for the parties concerned.

For a long time one of the main items of their programmes was curbing unemployment and poverty through state intervention. Such a tendency has shown its limitations since any emerging industrial sector can hardly be competitive if loaded with too heavy a fiscal or social burden. On the other hand, state intervention has been, for the last decade, outdated by the new trends of world economy. In any case, the budget of Pakistan being largely absorbed in debt servicing and military expenditures, any sizeable social action programme has to be handed over to international organizations.

Nevertheless, the spirit of 'social caring' still prevails in these parties, especially the PPP, and can help in conceiving new policies whenever harsh liberalism does not bear the expected fruits and some kind of social welfare becomes badly needed.

The other pole would lay the stress on 'steering' rather than 'caring', and leave the society to address its own problems provided the macro economy is kept on the right direction by the State. The main political force which represents such a trend is the Pakistan Muslim League (Nawaz) (PML-N). Its leaders generally belong to the entrepreneurial set. They usually hold, at least, important shares in banks or firms. The strong points of this party's programmes are modernization and economic growth thanks to the bold intervention of local and foreign investors. When in government, its supporters would tentatively reduce customs duties and taxes on industrial production with a view to boost all kinds of creative investment. To feed the state budget they might be tempted to increase taxation on real estate, and in the framework of provincial legislation, on profits derived from agriculture as well as some downstream activities stemming from it. Their strategy is centred on employment growth through industrial expansion and export of a rising number of manufactured goods.

A party like the PML(N), with its strong stand in favour of privatization and de-regulation can normally rely on international moneylender's support. It, can therefore, arise some expectations in the electorate.

The difference in nature between the ruling elite of the two main parties may not be so clear-cut as appears at first sight. In fact, and according to common observation, business people tend to purchase real estate and farming properties not only as long term investments but also in order to join the 'gentry' and gain influence in rural areas. On the other hand, PPP or PML(J) landlords might evince some taste in business and buy shares in banking and industry. Moreover, the educational background is much the same at the top level of the main political poles. However, the two described trends do persist and remain clearly differentiated. Besides the prevalent political topics, a conversation with a PPP member would normally concentrate on agricultural output and market opportunities for mangoes, rice and raw cotton. Much of their immediate prospects have apparently much to do with the quality of the monsoon and the state of the dams and irrigation canals. On the other hand, a PML(N) stalwart would rather speak about investment profitability in the urban sector such as industry, housing and hotels. While PPP supporters seem more especially concerned with raw cotton and yarn exports, PML members would rather focus their comments on downstream textile activities involving sizeable value added (as, for instance, fabrics and ready-made garments).

Such a bipolar configuration makes sense and is not unlike what is witnessed in many a democratic country. Indeed, one could assume that the average parliamentarian is a man of property with a strong ambition of keeping aloof from the populace. Many Pakistani analysts deplore the absence of any real 'House of Commons' in their country, the parliament consisting only, according to them, 'in a House of Lords and a Senate'. In other words, little chance is supposedly given to the middle classes to be fairly represented in spite of the importance that any successful development policy is bound to give them sooner or later. Still, some elbow-room should normally be granted to their politicians within the framework of the two leading parties or in smaller and even new ones. Besides, and in view of the gradual and necessary social changes, the two 'poles' seem obliged for the very stability of their function to encourage debate, invention and creativity among their own militants and so adjust to local and international realities. This means that they are bound to accommodate the demands of the middle classes in their election strategies. Under these conditions, the main parties, when in government, should normally deliver at least a part of what they had pledged to do in their election campaigns.

As a matter of fact, it does happen that the man in the street expects some result from their competition for power. In 1993, for instance, it was commonly heard that Nawaz Sharif's policy having been unsuccessful at curbing inflation and unemployment, it was Benazir Bhutto's turn to try. Anyway, democracy seems deeply rooted in Pakistan since it was in practice at the very time of the country's inception as a state. The leaders of that time managed, thanks to their high prestige, to transmit some of the Aligarh heritage in terms of mindframe and relationship with religious belief. Worthy of note is the fact that 'Democracy' is translated into Urdu by a word of Arab origin as if it were a religious concept.

No wonder that in 1993, a superficial observer would have believed that, after all, alternance was likely to be fruitful provided the game remained fair. Such a hope found some ground in the possible arbitration of the President (under the army's supervision), and in the presence of a powerful judiciary. The only point was to properly organize the balance between the different powers which the 1973 Constitution, with its many amendments, could not really offer as was shown in the legal intricacies of the 1993 crisis. Reaching such a goal through some remodelling of the constitution could be seen as a reasonable prospect.

A deceitful reality

In fact, the subsequent years seemed to show how difficult, say impossible, an alternance system was, and still is. Each and every act of government has had as a first motive neither a gain in popularity nor any social or economic achievement. Success is not really the aim but appears, at the utmost, as a tool. What is at stake is less being a reliable political force among others than eliminating these very others, be they parties or diverse public institutions. A craving for majority absolutism is apparently hidden under the garb of democracy. Opposition is branded as illegitimate and its claim of defending the people's rights as a hoax.

In such conditions one may wonder whether such a ruthless antagonism between parties which affect to have contempt for each other, really fits in any real democratic system relying first and foremost on respect of opposition, not only within the polity at large but also within each party. Pretending to save the country from the grip of a dishonest and over ambitious oppositional force is tantamount to a plea for dictatorship in the roman sense. We also know that such a dictatorship means, in view of exceptional circumstances, a limitation of public liberties 'for their own sake' which more often than not happens in Pakistan under majority rule.

Therefore, democracy appears in the country as an aspiration, a longing, but not an actual practice in spite of all the speeches which underscore the democratic character of Pakistan's public life.

Moreover, reliance on strictly legal, open and honest means against dishonest 'would be dictators' appears dangerously naive. 'Why do you keep undermining your main opponent's wealth?' was asked of one of the chief leaders. 'For fear of "horse trading" which is his favourite trick' was the answer.

In such a permanent meddle there is no end to drifting away from established and recognized norms of behaviour. 'If they rig elections whenever they can, why won't we do the same in our turn?' was another private statement by a politician.

An obvious fact was that, in 1993, because the army had retrieved some credentials as an impartial body, it was entrusted with the organization of free and fair elections which meant that neither the political parties nor the bureaucracy were able to join hands in what should otherwise have been so simple a task.

Historical drawbacks and possible evolutions

To account for this paradoxical situation of parties using illegal tricks to save democracy and thus feeding each other's accusations of being undemocratic, it is tempting to resort to historical explanations.

It is true that the PPP was created at a time when leadership was seen as the key to social and economic progress in developing countries and as an ultimate protection against subservience to any of the two 'blocks'. Non-alignment was hardly thinkable without the strong will of a charismatic statesman. To survive independently and eventually emerge as a power, a country should then have its own Nasser or Soekarno. Instances of take over or small-scale revolutions then abounded which showed how vivid the trend was. Colonel Gaddhafi in Libya and Sardar Daud in Afghanistan forced their way to power to meet the supposed requirements of the time. It is, therefore, hard to deny that the PPP was conceived as a leader's party and the 1973 Constitution as the appropriate framework for the rule of a powerful prime minister. One can trace back to the very inception of the PPP its culture of leadership and power hoarding. On the other hand, the PML, and more especially PML(N), are often seen as an offspring of General Zia's martial law administration, an origin which would mean a tradition of highly controlled freedom and a concept of disciplinarian say, narrowly-guided democracy. In both cases, street power is likely to protect some basic rights whenever one of the parties is victimized and also to stifle any strong criticism.

The fact remains that both parties accepted from 1988 onwards to co-exist within a reborn democratic set-up. They even gave visible signs of their readiness to co-operate whenever vital national interests seemed at stake. One could, therefore, hope that their references to entirely antinomic leaders such as Zulfikar Ali Bhutto and General Zia would gradually decline in significance, more especially as the voters were seemingly expecting governments to 'deliver' and not to take revenge.

If the basic dislike between the two opposing parties was still strongly felt, many a sensible politician still hoped that an appropriate reshuffling of the Constitution with some reliable set of checks and balances would gradually dismiss the misgivings and fears, and de-dramatize the prospects of alternance in government.

However, nothing of this kind ever happened. Neither of the two political parties adjusted to the very existence of the other. As for the minor parties which might have upheld the expected alternance through the role they could have played in threatening to disrupt any political alliance whenever the government indulged in extreme partisanship, they were gradually and sometimes brutally marginalized. Attempts at creating new parties aborted and the exclusive character of bi-polarization not only persisted but increased.

Possible reasons for failure

One may wonder why party politics failed to pave the way for an open public debate on competing ideas and pro-grammes, and why they obstinately remained a sort of ruthless strife for life.

The beginning of an answer could be found in some expressions which are often used in political discussions, that is: 'vote bank', 'constituency', 'horse-trading' and 'floor crossing'. When carefully analysed, in the case of Pakistan and of other developing countries, these very notions suggest that any successful politician must be able to secure, in any case, a sizeable number of votes in his favour (the vote bank), that these votes are linked to a definite area (the constituency) which is, to a large extent, geographic but reflects also a certain number of connections with various decision makers, that such a politician is in a position to change at will his political allegiances without being sanctioned by his electorate (floor crossing) and that such an initiative may, at times, be a response to certain financial offers (horse-trading). Although these practices are often criticized and even forbidden by provisions of parliamentary law, the very fact that they can and do take place suggests that political loyalties tend to follow quite other lines than convictions and social visions. If so, the links between party leaders, stalwarts and supporters might heavily rely on interests rather than militancy.

The networks

In fact, something specific is operating which can be described as networks of solidarity. Observation of state life and the criticism expressed about it by the press, neutral political observers or even by the political parties themselves, in their frequent exchanges of accusations, seems to reveal that most of the public life, from policy to economy, is largely influenced by a system of networks with a rationale of its own, far from the proclaimed objectives of the major institutions, including political parties.

What are these networks up to? Apparently, they tend to preserve and protect a certain amount of incomes and social positions from the odds of life and all upheavals created by changes in the economic fabric of the country.

These solidarity groups rely on a combination of 'natural loyalties' (which means traditional, cultural, religious and ethnic proximities) and 'functional loyalties' which means privileged relationships say, exchange of services with a number of bureaucratic and economic actors. In such a way, networks are built which secure, through a set of mutually beneficial complicities, a rather stable income and the unequal distribution of it within the groups where one or several leaders appear as the wealthy benefactors of the other members.

Such a solidarity system offers the advantage of preserving a social status and also the means of sustaining it, even for those who would otherwise lead a very precarious life. For instance, everybody agrees that a modest civil servant, such as a policeman, can hardly rely on his meagre salary to sustain his family's livelihood in a decent way. Lending services to some powerful network and so becoming part of it would keep him above the poverty level. In a way, a parallel economy is created which is a safety net as against the failures and discrepancies of the more visible one.

The question which arises is: how are the networks of patronage which seem to play a growing role in political life financially fed?

One of the core elements seems to be the income deriving from hereditary wealth. In this respect, landed property is likely to play a leading role according to some Pakistani observers. Still, it seems that industrial or commercial firms also take part in the building up of networks.

Obviously, these traditional means of patronage do not seem enough to make the networking sustainable. Therefore, other sources of income are sought. One is offered by 'banking facilities' which in many cases end up, as is repeated in the press and appears in judiciary cases, in loan defaulting. Another is tax evasion, which requires a fair amount of complicities within the bureaucracy.

More respectable is apparently the attraction of oil money from neighbouring Arab countries. It can be invested in joint ventures of diverse categories such as industry, trade, banking and real estate.

In particular, there is also a large influx of this oil-generated wealth in religious organizations such as schools of different Muslim denominations and levels, universities, and also teaching, preaching or highly militant organizations (*madrasas*). Such a regular cash flow is important for political life in as much as it fosters an active solidarity between different kinds of people ranging from the scholar to the zealot who share the same hope of pervading the society with ultra-orthodox tenets of creed. It also generates all kinds of economic activities from which dependency networks may stem.

The last main source of income to be mentioned is trafficking, a concept which encompasses not only what could be called benign smuggling but also speculative hoarding of basic commodities, and last but not least, drug trading along a number of routes connecting the poppy fields of Afghanistan and some northern heroin refineries with the main sea ports or some clandestine anchorages.

It is amazing how these sources of income and activity can combine, in spite of their disparities, to strengthen the existing networks. Such underground organizations, the complexity of which can sometimes outwit their very initiators and beneficiaries, seem to act in a relatively peaceful way. Only networks which overtly or covertly aim at intimidating the state or the society resort to violence, such as was apparently the case with the MQM which, after gathering more or less voluntary tributes from Mohajir industrialists and tradesmen, managed to build up a militant wing and challenge State authority in urban Sindh. The goal of such violent action which claimed many lives was to restore the political and social influence of a well-defined category of people (Urdu speaking migrants from Uttar Pradesh in India), and when negotiations replaced confrontation the violence abated. Another instance of networking ending up in killing is given by certain religious extremist movements which pledge to eradicate heresy and impiety by all means, including assassination. Beside these notable exceptions which gave way to a turmoil akin to civil war in Karachi for the first one, and to sectarian killing in Punjab and Sindh (a phenomenon which still persists) for the second one, there is nothing which could be interpreted as warfare on behalf of networks or as a violent confrontation between themselves, despite their confirmed tendency to indulge in extra-legal, say, criminal activities of the Mafia type. There apparently is a 'gentleman's agreement' not to let the country sink into a chaos which could be detrimental to all the beneficiaries of

the networking. Nevertheless, one can but be impressed by
the number of bodyguards surrounding some political leaders
'just in case'.

Running into debt

One may wonder why such an agreement cannot be extended
to the political and judiciary fields and why political parties
remain so determined to eliminate each other legally instead
of sharing the power which networking gives them.

The supposition which comes to the mind of anyone who
tries to scrutinize the social evolutions of Pakistan is
summarized in one word: indebtedness. Obviously, the
networks get short of fulfilling all their promises. To avoid
collapsing or petering out they are bound to seek more and
more power and income. As a matter of fact, their solidarity
rules consist in a set of duties that most of the actors can
hardly perform. Responding, from the very time of their
inception in the mid-1980s, to the financial perplexities of
their members, the networks seem doomed to expand on an
inflation pattern.

This suggests their high degree of fragility. If one of the
sources of income happens to dry up, even partially, like in
the case of bad crops, slumps in oil or cotton prices or in
demand of commodities on the Asian markets, or even
setbacks in drug trafficking, then the networking won't be
able to uphold the political patronage anymore. In other
words, Pakistan can probably withstand any major crisis in
its visible macro economy thanks to its parallel economy, but
if the latter collapses, the political and probably social fabric
of the country might experience an unprecedented disruption.

Prospects

Some Pakistani analysts who equate the networks leaders
with the traditional feudal lords predict for their own country
an experience which might resemble the French Revolution
in which an indebted nobility was disqualified for having

become a burden. Still, we know that in France the alliance between a part of the gentry (of the 'Mirabeau' type), and a powerful middle class of small landholders, urban entrepreneurs and lawyers, was able to overthrow the remnants of the feudal system. Is such a middle class in Pakistan strong enough to assert itself and find its own spokesmen? One must for the moment doubt it. The middle class itself is now dependant on the patronage networking and is hardly able to create any new political force. All attempts made in this sense, such as Imran Khan's endeavours to form a party of his own, or the Muttahida Qaumi Movement's (MQM) recently voiced ambition to represent also a non-Mohajir middle class electorate have been hitherto unsuccessful.

Therefore, the prospect of a revolution or a social sea change is rather unlikely. The only way towards a normalization of political life can be sought in a set of reforms which might encompass the Constitution, the judiciary, banking and the bureaucracy at large, which includes police and customs. What forces could exert enough pressure to impose such reforms? The only ones which could really challenge the pervasive influence of networks are the civil society and the Army. The former includes associations, solidarity councils at community level, 'non-aligned' religious organizations like Sufi Brotherhoods, charity foundations, and more generally, all that can enhance the independence of the citizens. A special stress should be laid on traditional communities such as villages and districts. In spite of all that makes Pakistan different from India, the former has the same characteristics as the latter in terms of the ability of small communities (*panchayat*) to meet the challenges of political instability, as was long observed by many foreign analysts including the founder of French political science, Alexis de Tocqueville. By the way, networks seem to feel the threat in as much as many attempts at addressing social issues at community levels are hindered by so called 'political interference' which means attempts at replacing consensual spokesmen with networks members. Above all, the last recourse for the implementation of the necessary reforms remains the Army, but after several bitter experiences of martial law and for fear of international disapproval, the Army has probably to wait for the present set up (with its visible form of party politics and its hidden one of networks) to collapse and put the country on the brink of a major disarray, before intervening once again.

PART SIX

REGIONAL GEOPOLITICS: THE QUESTION OF NATIONAL INTERESTS

Pakistan's Afghan Policy

With the invasion of Afghanistan on 27 December 1979, Pakistan was confronted for the first time with a direct threat on its western border. Even if an armed invasion was a remote possibility, there was a real concern that Moscow would help separatist movements in Balochistan and the North West Frontier Province (NWFP). In fact, there were some training camps for Baloch separatists in the South of Afghanistan in 1978. The powerful chief of the Baloch Marri tribe, who had resisted the Pakistani State between 1973 and 1977, and Khan Abdul Ghaffar Khan, the leader of the Khuda-i Khidmatgaran (Servants of God), a Pathan movement opposed to the central Pakistani government, were welcomed in Kabul.[1] Besides, the Afghan secret service, the KHAD, in co-operation with the KGB, was extremely active in Pakistan and is generally held responsible for some of the numerous bombings and killings in the NWFP during the 1980s.

But, if the Afghan war was an obvious threat for Pakistan, it was also a resource for the regime of Ziaul Haq. After the hanging of Zulfikar Ali Bhutto, Zia's martial law regime, severely criticized by the international community, was quite isolated and would not have lasted so long without the Afghan war. The military regime gained a new credibility after the Soviet invasion of Afghanistan, and becoming a front-line state for the United States, Pakistan received in 1981 a $1.6 billion credit from the IMF (the largest credit ever given to a developing country at that time), and secured a 3.2 billion dollar military aid programme from the USA. In total, Pakistan obtained more than $7.2 billion from the USA during the 1980s.[2] Even if the presence of the Afghan refugees was a burden for Pakistan as a whole (due to ecological problems in this overpopulated country), a large part of the aid aimed at the Afghan refugees was retained by the Pakistani administration, and for both Afghans and Pakistanis, the common frontier became a major economic resource with a spectacular increase in smuggling.[3]

Pakistan's role in the Afghan war cannot be overestimated. Pakistan became a place of settlement for 3.2 million Afghan refugees after 1979, and the Pakistani administration had also an essential part in channelling arms and money to the Afghan resistance (approximately six billion dollars in the 1980s). In consequence, the attitude of Pakistani officials was decisive for the Afghan political parties that were created in 1978-79. For example, the Pakistani government decided to stop the process of segmentation in the resistance, and limit the number of Afghan (Sunni) political parties to seven.[4] On the diplomatic scene, Pakistan had represented the *mujahiddin* who were not allowed to participate directly in any negotiations.[5] In the same way, throughout the war, a Pakistani general attended all the meetings between the Afghan parties, and Islamabad played a vital part in the definition of the strategy of the *mujahiddin*. Thus, the attempt to take the city of Jalalabad in 1989 was directly organized by the ISI (Inter-Service Intelligence), with a number of Pakistani officers on the field to co-ordinate the *mujahiddin*. To enforce its strategy and protect its interests, Pakistan established a network of clients with preferred Afghan commanders and parties. The Hezb-i Islami, for the most part of the war, and the Taliban after 1994, were the most favoured allies of Pakistan.

The relationship between the Hezb-i Islami and the ISI can be traced back to the beginning of the 1970s, when the leaders of the Islamist movement in Afghanistan went into exile in Pakistan because of Daud's repressive policies.[6] In 1975, when some young Islamist militants attempted a coup against President Daud, Hekmatyar, the future leader of the Hezb-i Islami, was in charge of the contacts with the ISI. Since that time, he benefited from the constant support of the Pakistani intelligence services and the Hezb-i Islami is said to have received around 40 per cent of the foreign supplied arms (much more than in proportion to his influence among the people of Afghanistan). Besides that, the Hezb-i Islami was also connected with the Pakistani refugee administration, and in consequence, was able to use part of the funds aimed at the refugees for its own purposes. Until 1994, Pakistan never questioned its support to the Hezb-i Islami, even when this party maintained a very ambiguous relationship with the Kabul regime. After the Soviet withdrawal, the strategy imposed on the Afghan parties aimed to put the Hezb-i Islami in power. More specifically, the Jalalabad campaign in the spring of 1989 was a clear initiative aimed at opening the road to Kabul for Hekmatyar and at marginalizing his arch enemy, Masud. The progressive isolation of Hekmatyar and the lack of support from the population didn't deter the Pakistanis from supporting their client, at least until 1994 when they chose the Taliban as their new client.

The emergence of the Taliban in the summer of 1994 dramatically changed the course of the Afghan civil war and regional politics.[7] The initial nucleus of the Taliban were trained and armed in ISI military camps on the Afghan-Pakistan border in the summer of 1994. The spectacular success of the Taliban surprised even its ISI sponsors, who decided to shift their support from the declining Hezb-i Islami to this new, promising movement. The assistance provided by the Pakistan government to the Taliban is well documented and the building of such an efficient military force is totally unexplainable without the support of the ISI. Pakistani officers have fought along with the Taliban on different occasions, and Pakistani logistic support has been essential in very crucial moments. For example, during the advance of Ismail Khan towards Kandahar in the spring of 1995, the logistic support provided by the ISI was decisive, allowing the Taliban to resist and counter-attack successfully. The point here is not to single out Pakistan for helping an Afghan faction, but to notice that Pakistan's support was much broader and more effective than that of India and Russia for Masud or Iran for Hezb-é Wahdat. Since we have described the deep involvement of Pakistan in the Afghan war, we can now centre our analysis on two questions: a) the logic of Pakistan's policy, and b) its consequences for the diplomacy and internal equilibrium of Pakistan.

The logic of Pakistan's policy

The logic of Pakistan's policy is intricate, not necessarily consistent, and largely produced by ideological or cultural (mis)perceptions. In this perspective, the Afghan policy of Pakistan could become a classical counter-example for the Realist theory in International Relations: the State is not a united actor but a network of institutions maintaining no monopoly on the foreign policy and the very concept of 'national interest' is irrelevant. The Pakistani State or, more precisely, a configuration of state administrations (ISI, Army, Foreign Affairs ministry etc) and private groups have been involved in the Afghan crisis.

Due to the need for covert operations, the ISI was the main actor in charge of the implementation of the Afghan policy in the 1980s, under General Akhtar until 1987, then under Hamid Gul until 1989.[8] The growing influence of the ISI in this period is due both to its role as an arms conduit for the *mujahiddin* in Afghanistan and to the political preferences of Ziaul Haq, who saw the army as a political institution in charge of maintaining an Islamic ideology in Pakistani society. In comparison, the Ministry of Foreign Affairs was reduced to a very figurative role. Even though Benazir Bhutto dismissed General Hamid Gul in May 1989, after the failure of the campaign for Jalalabad, she did not successfully challenge the control of the ISI vis-á-vis the Afghan policy. Yet, she was able to give a new orientation at a very crucial point. Originally, support for the Taliban came from the government of Benazir Bhutto, with the limited goal to secure the road from Pakistan to Turkmenistan. The Interior Minister, Major-General Naseerullah Babar, himself a Durrani Pushtun and former governor of the NWFP, was directly involved in the Afghan policy and had decided to clear the road of the war lords and commanders who were robbing and killing travellers. After a few months of confusion during which Pakistan helped both the Taliban and the Hezb-i Islami, the deliquescence of the latter drove Pakistan logically towards full support for the Taliban.

In addition to the state institutions already mentioned, some private political or religious groups also influenced Afghan policy. For the Islamist or fundamentalist movements, the Afghan *jihad* was a unique opportunity to put Islam on the political agenda and mobilize its militants. The Jamaat-i-Islami[9] inspired the Afghan Islamist movement in the 1970s and was deeply involved in the making of Pakistani policy as a pro-Hezb-i-Islami lobby. The Jamaat-i-Islami was a staunch support of the Hezb-i-Islami until the fall of Kabul to the Taliban in September 1996, when there were contacts between the Taliban leadership and the *amir* of the Jamaat-i-Islami Qazi Hussein Ahmed, who proposed a peace-mission between Iran and Afghanistan. The Jamaat-i Islami, which was close to the Hezb-i-Islami, seemed to desire a rapprochement with the Taliban. The Taliban relied on the Jamiat-i-ulema-i-Islam,[10] and more generally, on the Deobandi fundamentalist *ulema* in Pakistan. Maulana Fazlur Rahman, leader of the main branch of the Jamiat-i-ulema-i-Islam, used to be Chairman of the Foreign Affairs Commission of the Parliament and close to Benazir Bhutto. This didn't leave much room to manoeuvre for the government since these religio-political movements, even if they never obtained any noticeable success in the elections, have enough power of disturbance to oblige any government to be cautious. The last category of actors influencing the policy of the State was, and is, linked to economic interests. Moreover, the Taliban, like the Hezb-i-Islami before them, were also part of the smuggling economy of the NWFP and Balochistan and had close contacts with the provincial governments. Peshawar developed tremendously in the last two decades, due to NGO money and smuggling. The corruption of some Pakistani officials is well known and there is a lobby protecting special interests (keeping the border open, protecting some Afghan partners in the drugs trade, etc).

Studying the Afghan policy of Pakistan, we can examine the rationality of this policy on different grounds. Most of the time, Pakistan's policy towards Afghanistan has been linked to 'geopolitical factors', that is the Kabul-New Delhi alliance and the Durand line question. This could be true for the discourse of the State or of the institutions, but the concrete involvement of Pakistan in the Afghan war is better explained with the addition of two other dimensions: first, an ideological commitment to some Islamist or fundamentalist parties to the detriment of the internal balance of power in Afghanistan, and second, a perception of Afghanistan as a big Pushtun tribal area on the NWFP model.

For Ziaul Haq, and this idea was never to be challenged after him, the Afghan war was an opportunity to put an end to the alliance between India, Afghanistan and the USSR. The strategic goals of Pakistan were then to push the Soviets out of Afghanistan and to obtain, in the long term, the de-colonization of Central Asia and a friendly government in Kabul. The emergence of a large Sunni Muslim area meant practically reinforcement for Pakistan vis-à-vis India, and also new economic opportunities. That is why the ISI tried to extend the Afghan war by smuggling Coran to the other side of the Amu Daria, and supporting small skirmishes in Soviet territory.[11] The Afghan Islamist parties were equally prone to denounce Central Asia as a Russian colony open to *jihad* as shown in some maps displayed in the office of the Jamaat-i-Islami in Peshawar. In this perspective, the Afghan Islamists were favoured by Pakistan to the detriment of the traditional conservative parties which were inclined to favour the return of Zahir Shah, the deposed king of Afghanistan. Despite strong support in the refugee camps, they were not given sufficient help on the ground as it was feared that they would be likely to return to a neutral or pro-India policy. On the other hand, Hekmatyar publicly took a position in favour of a confederation between Afghanistan and Pakistan. For example, the call to traditional elite to convene a *Loya Jirga* (Great Assembly) in the early days of 1980, triggered a successful campaign by the ISI against the traditional conservative parties (which were anyway deeply undermined by nepotism and corruption).

The pro-fundamentalist or Islamist bias in the Pakistani policy is obvious and could be explained as a consequence of the strategic goals of Pakistan or, in a more convincing manner, as the product of the activism of the fundamentalist parties who were encouraged by Ziaul Haq. After the coup of 5 July 1977, Ziaul Haq, himself from a middle-class and fundamentalist background,[12] legitimized his power through the Islamization of Pakistani society. Inside the ISI, and more generally, within the army, the fundamentalist trend continued to grow during the 1980s, favouring co-operation with the Islamist movement.

However, the most pertinent factor in understanding the functioning of Pakistani policy is to look at the way this policy was put into effect. The fact that the ISI was in charge of Pakistan's Afghan policy was not without consequence on the conception of the war itself, and the means actually used by the ISI were not necessarily consistent with the strategic goals defined by Ziaul Haq. The ISI had been formed mostly of officers who tended to reproduce the model they had learned from the British vis-à-vis the Pathan (Pushtun) tribes, and in fact, the Pakistani policy towards Afghanistan was mostly a British-inspired tribal policy with a strong pro-Pushtun bias. Afghanistan has traditionally been dominated by the Pushtun (around 40 per cent of the population), even if the war has given more autonomy to other groups who, historically had bad relationships with the central State, like the Hazaras.[13] This pro-Pushtun policy could also be due to the fact that the Pathan community is important in the NWFP, Balochistan (and today also in Karachi), in the army and in some political parties. For example, the Interior Minister Naseerullah Babar, the leader of the Jamaat-i-Islami, Qazi Hussein Ahmad, the leader of the Jamiat-i-ulema-i-Islam, Fazlur Rahman etc are of Pushtun descent. The ISI (Pushtun dominated) has been instrumental in developing support for the Taliban, in spite of the more balanced views of Nawaz Sharif and the Army Chief of Staff General Jehangir Karamat (both Punjabis).

On the field, the Pakistani policy was to divide and rule to keep control of the Pushtun area on the borderland with Pakistan. This is probably why the ISI helped *mawlawi* Khâles to secede from the Hezb-i Islami in 1979, and was playing one commander against another to avoid the emergence of a strong regional or political power (except in places like Herat, far from the Pakistani border and close to Iran, where Pakistan preferred a united front of the *mujahiddin*). Basically, Afghanistan was perceived in the Pakistani political class as a kind of protectorate in the continuum of the tribal area of the NWFP. In 1996, the project to repair the Chaman-Thoghundi road (from Pakistan to Turkmenistan) was perceived as a further step in the integration of Afghanistan into a greater Pakistan, and even if this plan was later abandoned, the building of a network of economic interests, partly linked to the smuggling of drugs, and common infrastructures is reinforcing this fading of the frontier.

These three dynamics (geopolitics, political Islam, tribal policy) are to some extent contradictory and that explains the confusion we observe at times in Pakistan's policy. The argument that the Islamist parties were less likely to make a deal with India and return to the traditional '*alliance de revers*' is not quite convincing since, for example, Masud (who was undoubtedly an Islamist) has nevertheless received help from India since the fall of the communist regime in 1992. To choose the Hezb-i-Islami as an ally, and at the same time, to conduct a tribal policy was also deeply contradictory in terms. More specifically, the 'divide and rule' policy was preventing the concentration of military or political power as the Hezb-i-Islami did not have enough support in Afghan society to impose itself on the other parties. This explains the failure of Pakistan's policy until 1994. Subsequently, even the victory of the Taliban was not a clear cut benefit for Pakistan because it prevented Pakistan from gaining any political or economic advantage in Central Asia. Since the new post-USSR Central Asia is made of former *apparatchiks* strongly opposed to political Islam, Pakistan's policy was in contradiction with its stated objective of a Muslim alliance against India. Finally, the perception of Afghanistan as a tribal area is both misleading and dangerous because Afghan identity and nationalism is, in fact, far from non-existent, and because the feedback from the Afghan war in Pakistan is more and more felt.

The consequences of the Taliban victory for Pakistan

The Taliban were by no means ISI puppets and Pakistan was actually facing difficulty in controlling the activities of its client. The Taliban, in a very revolutionary move, were imposing a new political/religious order, unknown in Afghanistan and maybe in the recent history of Muslim countries.[14] They had their own agenda in foreign policy and it was a revolutionary one. As any new revolutionary regime, they were willing to export their ideology like, in some respects, the Iranian regime after 1979. The Taliban were actually engaged in a confrontation with the West, conservative Arab countries and the Central Asian States.

The United States had ruled out any kind of dialogue with the Taliban since they refused to act against Osama Bin Laden. On 22 September 1998, the Taliban officially announced that they were closing the Osama bin Laden case because the US administration had failed to provide any evidence showing his involvement in terrorist activities. This meant that the Taliban were ready to pay a high diplomatic (no recognition from the United States) and economic price (no oil and gas pipe-line from Central Asia) for ideological reasons. On the other hand, Saudi Arabia (one of the three States, with Pakistan and the United Arab Emirates, to recognize the Taliban government) expelled the Taliban diplomatic representative in reprisal for the Taliban's continued harbouring of Osama bin Laden. Saudi Arabia was also said to have reduced its aid to the Taliban since the autumn of 1998 and was coming to a rapprochement with Iran. In September 1998, Tehran requested Saudi assistance in connection with the killing of Iranian diplomats in Afghanistan, and Saudi newspapers became frequently critical of the Taliban, although staying neutral in the crisis between Afghanistan and Iran. The killing of the Iranian diplomats during the fall of Mazar-i Sharif in the summer of 1998 was the immediate cause of the tension between Iran and the Taliban. The build-up of a military force on the Iran-Afghanistan border made it seem that Iran was on the verge of launching an attack on Afghanistan. But, since the beginning of 1999, a progressive détente between Afghanistan and Iran became perceptible, due to the willingness of the Taliban to isolate Masud from his foreign support, and to the evolution of the Iranian regime which had apparently renounced the idea of playing an active part in Afghan internal politics.

The Taliban also had political ambitions directed against the post-communist regimes established after the collapse of the USSR. Thus, the Tâjik civil war has a growing Afghan dimension. The Tâjik refugees (about 40,000) who came into Afghanistan were, for a time, under the control of different Afghan political parties. When the Taliban gained control of the northern province of Kunduz, they helped the Tâjik refugees by sending arms and volunteers to fight in the name of *jihad*. We can roughly assess their number to a few hundred.[15]

This brief description of the Taliban's 'foreign policy' may lead many to ask if support for the Taliban was really consistent with the official goals of Pakistan's policy—all the more since the Taliban were becoming directly or indirectly part of the internal dynamics of Pakistan. We can distinguish three different factors: 1) the growing difficulties for Pakistan with Western countries and its traditional allies 2) the failure of Pakistan's policy towards Central Asia, and 3) the destabilization of Pakistan by fundamentalist movements.

1) Support for the Taliban created tensions between Pakistan and its allies and neighbours. The diplomatic cost was high for Pakistan and the unpredictable dynamics of a revolutionary movement could have lead Pakistan into a difficult situation. Pakistan's relationship with the United States was damaged by its support to the Taliban. Furthermore, the US strikes on Afghanistan in 1998 (against Osama bin Laden) were also, to a certain extent, a signal for the Pakistan government since it was a camp of the Harkat ul Ansar that had been targeted. The missile attack on 20 August 1998, on alleged terrorist bases in Zhawar (Paktia) may then have marked a turning point in US policy towards Afghanistan and Pakistan. In addition, the killing of Iranian diplomats in Mazar-i Sharif compromised Pakistan's

rapprochement with Iran, which was very supportive of Pakistan during the nuclear test crisis.

2) There was a contradiction in Pakistan's Central Asian policy. If Afghanistan was supposed to be the means to open Central Asia to Pakistan, its support for the Taliban alienated all forms of co-operation with former communist regimes dominated by governments that were extremely worried about fundamentalist destabilization. Following the advance of the Taliban in the North in the summer of 1998, the Defence Ministers from the Central Asian States met in Tashkent and Moscow to push for reinforcement of the security system on the Amu Daria. In others words, it meant that the Taliban regime in Afghanistan was an obstacle to Pakistani projects in Central Asia.

3) The legitimization and reinforcement of fundamentalist parties linked with the Afghan *jihad* and the Taliban, was potentially destabilizing for Pakistan. The Taliban had well-known connections with the Jamiat-i-ulema-i-Islam that had built up real support among the Durrani tribes in the NWFP and Balochistan during the 1990s. The Jamiat-i-ulema-i-Islam, a fundamentalist movement inspired by the Deoband school of thought, organized a network of *madrasas* in the NWFP with the support of the Pakistani government in the 1980s, and thousands of Afghans were trained there. According to some sources, 80 per cent of the students in the *madrasas* established along the Afghan border were Afghans.[16] Thus, the Dar ulum Haqqania *madrasa* led by Maulana Sami ul Haq (leader of a branch of the Jamiat-i-ulema-i-Islam) provided hundreds of recruits for the Afghan *jihad*. The emergence of the Taliban was then a by-product of this educational project, and the links between the Taliban and the Deobandi movement were strong.

This broad set of links between the Taliban and a section of Pakistani society brings us to another question: were the Taliban a Pakistani as well as an Afghan movement? Firstly, most of the Taliban came initially from the refugee camps in Pakistan and a lot of them had Pakistani identity cards because they were refugees in Pakistan for years, but the 'real' nationality is sometimes difficult to appreciate. Anyway, a number of Pakistani citizens (outside the ISI officers) had participated in the fighting alongwith the Taliban, especially for the conquest of Jalalabad and Kabul. But the Taliban's leadership was exclusively Afghan and the movement had no claim on the Pathan side of the border. What we know about the nature of the Taliban seems to show that a direct involvement of the Taliban on the Pakistani side of the border was not likely. Still, according to a report released in the press, one hundred *madrasas* have given military training to the Taliban.[17] The presence on Pakistani soil of thousands of Pakistani militants, who are now back in Pakistan after having been trained in Afghanistan, will be a real challenge for the security of the country. It has been difficult for the government to react to this situation since the fundamentalist movements are justifying themselves by their support for the national cause, the Kashmir issue. Moreover, the growing influence of the Taliban has also been a source of sectarian tensions. With some reason, the Shia minority in Pakistan saw the Taliban as extremely anti-Shia, even if the real (as opposed to perceived) situation in Afghanistan was much more complex.[18]

Conclusion

Pakistan's policy vis-á-vis Afghanistan has been a result of the interaction and the relationship between Afghan and Pakistani political parties, geopolitical strategy and local economic interests. This explains the complexity and sometimes the contradictions in Pakistan's Afghan policy. The consequences for Pakistan have been negative in the sense that Pakistan isolated itself from its Arab allies and Western countries, not to mention the degradation of its relationship with Iran. This diplomatic cost was not balanced by the certainty of a friendly government in Kabul in the long-term since the interests of the two countries were likely to diverge. More dangerous, the 'encapsulating' strategy towards Afghanistan tended to erase the differences between the Pakistani tribal area and Afghanistan. That, combined with a loss of control by the Pakistani State in the NWFP, since the period of Ziaul Haq, could be a real threat to the stability of the country.

NOTES

1. Duprée, Louis, *Afghanistan*, Princeton, Princeton University Press, p. 492. Abdul Ghaffar Khan was granted political asylum in Kabul for some time and was buried in Jalalabad in January 1988, in the presence of Najibullah, the then Afghan President.

2. Dikshit, P., '1993: Afghanistan Policy', *Strategic Analysis*, Nov, vol. XVI, no 8, p.1073. For the background to Pakistan's foreign policy see Burke S. M. and Ziring L., *Pakistan's Foreign Policy. An Historical Analysis*, Oxford, Oxford University Press, 1990.

3. On the economic situation in the NWFP during the Afghan war see Rashid, Ahmed, 'Nothing to declare', *Far Eastern Economic Review*, May 11, 1995.

4. The elimination of the secularist or non-religious political parties, like the Maoist and nationalist parties, was due in part to the policies of the Pakistan government. The situation for Shia parties was different due to Iran's patronage, but one of the most effective Shia parties in the field, the Harkat-i Islami, was receiving help from Pakistan and was based in Islamabad, due to its bad relationship with the Iranian regime.

5. Cordovez D. and Harrison S. S., *Out of Afghanistan. The inside Story of Soviet Withdrawal*, Oxford, Oxford University Press, 1995.

6. Tahir Amin evaluates the number of Islamist militant victims of Daud to 600, 'Afghan Resistance: Past, Present and Future', *Asian Survey*, vol: XXIV, no. 4, April, 1984. See also Roy, Olivier, 'The origins of the Islamist movement in Afghanistan', *Central Asian Survey*, vol. 3, no. 3, 1984.

7. Maley, William (ed.), *Fundamentalism reborn? Afghanistan and the Taliban*, London, Hurst and Company, 1998, and Matinuddin, Kamal, *The Taliban Phenomenon, Afghanistan 1994-1997*, Oxford, Oxford University Press, 1999.

8. For a presentation of the strategy of the ISI see Yousaf, Mohammad, *Silent Soldier. The man Behind the Afghan Jihad*, Jang Publishers, Lahore, Pakistan, 1991 and *The Bear trap*, Jang Publishers, Lahore, Pakistan, 1992.

9. See Gaborieau, Marc, 'Le néo-fondamentalisme au Pakistan: Madudi et la Jama'at-i Islami' in Olivier Carré (ed), *Radicalismes Islamiques*, Paris, L'Harmattan, 1986 and Bahadur, Kalim, *The Jama'at-i Islami of Pakistan*, Lahore, Progressive Books, 1978.

10. Metcalf, Barbara D., *Islamic Revival in British India: Deoband, 1860-1900*, Princeton, Princeton University Press, 1982.

11. Maj. Abdul Rahman Bilal, *Islamic Military Resurgence*, Feroz Sons, Karachi, 1991.

12. General Akhtar Abdul Rahman and General Ziaul Haq were both *refugees* from Jullundur, India and very committed to the Islamic ideal of Pakistan.

13. On Pushtun domination of Afghanistan see Poullada, Leon, *The Pushtun role in the Afghan political System*, New York, Afghanistan Council of the Asia Study, 1970.

14. Marsden, Peter, *The Taliban: War, Religion and the New Order in Afghanistan*, London, Zed Books, 1998.

15. Interviews with some Taliban *mujahiddin* coming from Tâjikistan in Ghazni, January 1997.

16. Matinuddin, Kamal, *The Taliban Phenomenon, Afghanistan 1994-1997*, Oxford University Press, 1999 page 14.

17. Matinuddin, op. cit., p. 20

18. See Mariam Abou Zahab's contribution in this volume. As Sunni fundamentalists, the Taliban should have had a conflicting relationship with the Shias, all the more so since they were Pushtun with an old tradition of feud with the Hazaras (80 per cent of the Shia community are Hazaras). But, surprisingly, the Taliban had been noticeably conciliatory with the Shia minority during their advance in Uruzgan and Ghazni province, even if the killings in Mazar-i Sharif in March 1995 destroyed this first attempt to establish a good relationship with the Shias. However, in the part of the country they controlled, the Taliban stopped the armed-robberies against the Shia Hazaras that were quite common, especially in Ghazni province, and the Hazaras living there had come to an understanding with the Taliban. In spite of this, after the fall of Mazar-i Sharif in August 1998, thousands of Hazaras were slaughtered by the victorious Taliban, avenging the killings of the year before. However, in November of that year, Akbari, a key figure of the Hezb-i Wahdat, defected to the Taliban, offering co-operation and asking for some kind of role in the government. The reason for this rallying, besides the fact that the military situation was desperate for the Hezb-i wahdat, was the hope that Shia *ulema* could find a place in a clerical State, even if dominated by the Sunnis. What was also at stake here was the Taliban's ability to enlarge the government to include *ulema* from different ethnic backgrounds.

Bibliography

Akram, Assem. 1996. *Histoire de la guerre d'Afghanistan*. Paris: Balland.

Dorronsoro, Gilles. 1995. "The present situation in Afghanistan', *Current History*, vol. 94, no. 588. 37-40.

———. 1997. "Réseaux et territoires en Afghanistan." *Hérodote*, no. 84. 217-237.

———. 1997. "Désordre et crise du politique: le cas des Taliban en Afghanistan." *Cultures et Conflits*. no. 24-25. 135-159.

Grare, Frédéric. 1997. *Le Pakistan face au conflit afghan (1979-1985): Au tournant de la guerre froide*, Paris: L'Harmattan.

Maley, William (ed.). 1998. *Fundamentalism Reborn? Afghanistan and the Taliban*, London: C. Hurst and Company.

Marsden, Peter. 1998. *The Taliban: War, Religion and the New Order in Afghanistan*. London: Zed Books.

Matinuddin, Kamal. 1999. *The Taliban Phenomenon, Afghanistan 1994-1997*. Karachi: Oxford University Press.

Olesen, Asta. 1995. *Islam and Politics in Afghanistan*. London: Curzon Press.

Rubin, Barnett R. 1995. *The Search for Peace in Afghanistan. From Buffer State to Failed State*. New Haven and London: Yale University Press.

Rubin, Barnett, R. 1998. *Testimony on the Situation in Afghanistan*, United States Senate Committee on Foreign Relations. 8 October.

Normalization of Relations between Pakistan and India: Possibilities and Impediments

Ever since their emergence as independent entities in 1947, India and Pakistan have dealt with each other as enemies. In the short span of fifty years, this mutual antagonism has caused three wars between them in 1948, 1965 and 1971, two near-war situations with nuclear overtones in 1987 and 1990, and following the Bhartia Janata Party's rise to power in India in March 1998, is once again threatening to push them towards the nuclear abyss. The Indian nuclear test explosions of 11 and 13 May 1998, and Pakistan's rival nuclear tests two weeks later have unleashed a new strategic dynamic which has grave implications for the cause of peace and stability in South Asia.

How does one account for the Pakistan-India rivalry, its intensity and persistence? Scholarly literature offers a number of explanations for the enduring character of this conflictual relationship, some of which are briefly examined below.

According to S.M. Burke, the roots of the Pakistan-India confrontation pre-date their emergence as independent states and the dynamics of their rivalry stem from the two diametrically opposed philosophies of Hinduism and Islam. As he writes: 'Centuries of dedication to such diametrically opposed systems as Islam and Hinduism could not but nurture an utterly different outlook on the outside world among their respective followers. That Pakistan has consistently sought a special relationship with other Muslim countries....while India has uniformly professed non-alignment is a perfectly logical consequence of each wishing to advance her national interests within the climate of her own special ideological preferences.'[2]

As opposed to this ideological explanation of Pakistan-India hostility, W. Howard Wriggins has located its dynamics in the requirements of a 'balancing process' which a larger power imposes on its weaker neighbour. He observes: '[A] more general element in Indo-Pakistan relations derives from the simple fact of size and strategic and economic asymmetry...However unjustified Indian leaders may have thought it, Pakistan's over-riding concern vis-à-vis India was fear, fear of India's size, the size of its army...and fear compounded out of not infrequent public statements by prominent Indians regretting the tragedy of partition and reiterating the inherent unity of the subcontinent.'[3] How balance-of-power considerations motivate smaller Pakistan to constantly challenge its larger neighbour, India, thereby creating a situation of a 'persistent Cold War' between them is also pointed out by Rajesh Basrur.[4] Viewing the discord between the two countries from the perspective of structural realism,[5] Basrur argues that in the South Asia system, India is the 'hegemonic' power while Pakistan is the challenger, resisting Indian domination. Thus 'India tends to play the role of the regional security manager...feeling the necessity of maintaining regional power balance to its advantage' while Pakistan 'seeks to strengthen itself by obtaining strategic support from outside the system...'[6]

Drawing upon insights of modern social-psychology, Richard Sisson and Leo Rose have traced the roots of the 'troubled and hostile relationship' between Pakistan and India to a 'legacy of misperception' and 'culture of distrust' which the Indian National Congress and Muslim League had spawned among their respective followers before and after Independence. They argue:

> One critical factor in the hostile relationship between India and Pakistan has been the pre-partition heritage of the two movements. Most of the political and social concepts that

dominated the ideology and psychology of the narrow elites that controlled these two movements survived into the independence period and have not disappeared. This has been particularly true of their intensely negative perceptions of each other.[7]

This social-psychological explanation of enmity between Pakistan and India derived from 'misperceptions' and 'enemy images' has also been articulated by some Indian analysts. Navnita Chadha, for instance, has argued that Pakistan-India 'enemy images are embedded in the history and politics of the Subcontinent.' She points out the 'most fundamental aspect of Pakistan's enemy image of India is that New Delhi is unreconciled to Pakistan's independent existence,' while 'India views Pakistan as a recalcitrant neighbour that has refused consistently to accept regional power realities.'[8]

And finally, scholarly attention has also been focused on the unresolved issue of Kashmir as the fundamental and continuing cause of tensions between Pakistan and India. Ever since Pakistan and India emerged as sovereign states in 1947, Kashmir has been a focus of dispute. As a Muslim-majority state that was contiguous to Pakistan, Kashmir was not allowed to become part of Pakistan. The Hindu ruler of Kashmir chose instead to join India. Pakistan contested the legality of this decision following which the two countries fought a brief war in 1948 which led to the division of Kashmir between the contending states. Pakistan and India fought another war over Kashmir in 1965, and since then both countries have continued to challenge each other in Kashmir short of engaging in a full-scale war.[9] Since India and Pakistan have adopted diametrically opposed views on Kashmir and both countries seem unable to work out a peace settlement, analysts argue, the 'possibility of its escalation into a fourth international war cannot be discounted.'[10]

As this brief survey of scholarly literature on the sources of Pakistan-India rivalry suggests, the forces underpinning and sustaining their adversarial relationship are embedded deep in history, or what Norman D. Palmer calls the 'pre-independence'[11] factors, incompatible belief systems, rival claims concerning Kashmir, and above all Pakistani fears of a hegemonic India. Because of these overwhelmingly negative influences, it is hardly surprising that Pakistan and India have not been able to chart a path to peace for themselves. To the contrary, both countries have pursued their security policies within the framework of unilateral security. The intended gains for one side were supposed to result in an equivalent loss for the other side. Yet, over time the situation as a whole has become a negative-sum game in which both are losing on net (that is, compared to their situation if they were not playing). There are several important reasons as to why this pursuit of unilateral security by each side has become a negative-sum game. The first reason is related to the fact that all zero-sum games in the international political system tend to generate what economists call 'transaction costs.' That is, the transfer of an 'asset' does not occur 'free of charge' in terms of the actual mechanics of play. To varying degrees, both Pakistan and India have incurred enormous 'transaction costs' as a consequence of their efforts to seek third party alignments in their bilateral conflicts. Deep involvement of external powers in their domestic politics, increasing outside political manipulation and cultural penetration of their key decision-making areas have been some important aspects of these varied transaction costs. Second, zero-sum games also have 'policy effects' for each side, whereby each constantly carries out policies, which have costs, to position itself for future plays. Third, these zero-sum games in the context of the arms race lead one side to counterbalance the other's prior gain, or to gain itself, while both pay the costs of new weapons. According to one estimate, India and Pakistan have already spent over $60 billion on the purchase of conventional weapons systems that have either become dysfunctional or totally obsolete as effective war-weapons due to changes in war technology and military strategy. A fourth reason why a series of zero-sum games played by India and Pakistan has yielded a negative-sum game over time involves stability. The continuing arms race has repeatedly threatened to create, and sometimes, as in the case of the Indian exercise known as 'brasstacks' in 1987, created a less stable relationship than existed previously between strategic forces of the two sides. It is a known fact that destabilization in the arms race does prove time-consuming, and is difficult and costly to correct; and while they exist they may significantly and dangerously alter strategic perceptions, increasing the shared risk of war. The risk of war is never zero as 'playing the game' is never a neutral activity. It is a disposition that is constantly imposing some chance of catastrophe on both sides, and in that sense a negative-sum activity. As the foregoing suggests, due to a combination of both security risks and security costs, neither side is capable of cumulatively winning the series of zero-sum games. As a consequence, inter-state wars, continued tension, ethnic turbulence and an intense arms race have been the hallmarks of their contemporary politics. Because of these factors, South Asia has often been described as the 'danger zone' and the probable theatre of nuclear conflict.[12]

However, with the nuclearization of South Asia, Pakistan and India have been left with no option except to wage peace with each other. Luckily, their emergence as nuclear enemies coincides with a new global trend towards 'rethinking security.' I would now like to discuss several elements of 'co-operative security' which Pakistan and India can adopt as a relevant framework for normalizing relations. I have resisted the temptation to make specific policy recommendations for either country, mainly because I feel that without a 'thought revolution' or a *Gestalt* switch in the way they think about security, no amount of policy prescription will suffice.[13]

Co-operative Security: A Way Out

The traditional concept of national security which viewed security as a 'function of the successful pursuit of interstate power competition' has been supplanted by a broader conception of 'human' and 'environmental' security in which social and economic aspects play the central role.[14] Informed by a liberal tradition of thinking on international relations, this broader view of security often entails the normative objective of replacing coercion, conflict, and war in the international system with co-operation, bargaining, and peaceful change. These attempts at re-defining security have spawned a new genre of scholarly literature on 'co-operative' and 'mutual security.'[15]

The notion of 'co-operative security' has been defined as a 'broad approach to security which is multi-dimensional in scope and gradualist in temperament; emphasizes reassurance rather than deterrence; is inclusive rather than exclusive; favours multi-lateralism over bilateralism; does not privilege military solutions over non-military ones; assumes that states are the principal actors in the security system, but accepts that non-state actors may have an important role to play; does not require the creation of formal security institutions, but does not reject them either; and which above all, stresses the values of habits of dialogue 'on a multilateral basis.'[16]

Co-operative security also embraces the ideas both of 'common security (that a nation's best protective option is to seek to achieve security with others, not against them), and collective security (the idea of states renouncing force among themselves, and agreeing to assist any member under attack).[17]

At the most general level, mutual security means that the two sides, presently in a state of some mutual insecurity, can take actions that create a 'positive sum game', in which both win by improving their respective security together. Unlike actions for 'unilateral security' which are intended to enhance the security of only one side, actions intended to develop mutual security create a situation where both sides gain in security. A well-known image of what illustrates the idea of mutual security or an interactive security relationship is the 'image of two men in one boat. One of them cannot make his end of the boat safe by trying to rock the other end of the boat. If the boat rocks, it rocks for both.'

There are three broad conceptions of mutual security, each of which generates a viewpoint on what kind of policy can and should be undertaken to achieve its own form of mutual security. These are: the technical conception; the threat reduction conception; and the supportive conception. The technical conception focuses chiefly on what has come to be called the danger of 'inadvertent escalation', the danger that a developing crisis will escalate to levels that neither side wants. In this conception, the basic and continuing systems of interactions between the two sides cannot be changed much by design; but it is possible to make technical adjustments around the margins of those interactions, sometimes in ways that may be very useful. According to the threat reduction conception of mutual security, not only must the dangers of inadvertent conflict be staved off but these moves must be accompanied by efforts to reduce and minimize all forms of deliberate threats between the two sides.

The supportive conception of mutual security, instead of exclusively focusing upon military and military-political dangers or threats that both sides face, holds that achieving real mutual security also requires each side to forestall dangers to the other that have their origins outside that relationship. These dangers too, by reducing one side's security, inevitably reduce the other side's security. What is common to all these differing conceptions of security is the idea that the best approach to national security, within an interactive relationship, can be found most completely when it is found in the form of mutual security. And achieving adequate mutual security, in that relationship, requires that each side give its chief emphasis not to other goals for power but to national security.

Co-operative security, while recognizing the fact that states have differing interests and that they organize their security autonomously, assumes that 'states are interested in developing processes aimed at furthering co-operation and removing or ameliorating sources of antagonism and conflict.'[18]

Confidence and security building measures are posited as devices that 'can be useful in managing the transition from autonomous to co-operative security.'[19] Defined as 'management instruments' that seek to multiply the disincentives to the threat or use of force and thereby reduce the chance for military conflict or escalation, confidence-and security-building measures serve four principal functions:[20]

1) Provide assurances of non-aggressive intentions— introduce predictability in military exercises and movements by subjecting them to prior notification, observation,

information exchange and verifications, thus essentially removing these types of (otherwise potentially threatening) activities from contention between the states concerned.

2) Reduce the scope of the threat or use of force or political intimidation—advance notification of military activities takes away the option of staging troop movements, on short notice, for purposes of military intimidation, and such intimidation is made more difficult by the acceptance of inspection on request and observers at military exercises of agreed levels.

3) Enhance crisis stability by reducing the possibility of inadvertent escalation—advance notification of military activities, together with observation and inspection enables states to provide reassurance of non-aggressive intentions in a time of crisis, and further, serve to extend peacetime patterns of behaviour to raise the crisis threshold.

4) Facilitate arms control and disarmament measures—increased transparency and predictability prepare the ground for developing mutual confidence, which in turn serve to curb arms race dynamics, and help achieve arms control and disarmament.

NOTES

1. The author teaches international relations at Quaid-i-Azam University, Islamabad. Pakistan.
2. S.B. Burke, *Mainsprings of Indian and Pakistani Foreign Policies* Oxford University Press, Karachi 1975, p. 22.
3. W. Howard Wriggins, The Balancing Process in Pakistan's Foreign Policy, in Lawrence Ziring et al; eds. *Pakistan: The Long View* Duke University Press, Durham, N.C. 1977, pp. 303-4.
4. Rajesh Basrur, 'South Asia's Persistence Cold War,' *ACDIS Occasional Paper* (University of Illinois, Urbana-Champaign 1996), 1-8.
5. Realism holds that broad patterns of state behavior can be best understood in terms of the structure of international systems, which is defined as the outcome of anarchy among states and the distribution of power among them. Anarchy makes states self-centred and power-seeking, thereby limiting the scope for co-operation. Power distribution determines state preferences

in balancing, alliance making, distancing, and other state strategies. For a seminal 'realist' argument see Kenneth N. Waltz, *Theory of International Politics* (Addison-Wesley Reading, Mass., 1979).

6. Basrur, *op.cit.,* pp. 2-3.

7. Richard Sisson and Leo E. Rose, *War And Secession: Pakistan, India, And the Creation of Bangladesh* (Oxford University Press, Karachi 1992), p. 35.

8. Navnita Chadha, 'Enemy Images: The Media and Indo-Pakistan Tensions,' in Michael Krepon and Amit Sevak, ed., *Crisis Prevention, Confidence Building, and Reconciliation in South Asia* (St. Martin Press, New York 1995), p. 172.

9. For a detailed study of the genesis and evolution of the Kashmir dispute, see Robert G.. Wirsing, *India, Pakistan and the Kashmir Dispute* (St. Martin Press, New York 1994). Josef Korbel, *Danger in Kashmir* (Princeton University Press, New Jersey 1954). Mushtaqur Rahman, *Divided Kashmir: Old Problems, New Opportunities for India, Pakistan, and the Kashmiri Problems* (Lynne Rienner, Boulder, London 1996). Summit Ganguly, *The Crisis in Kashmir: Portents of War, Hopes of Peace* (Cambridge University Press, Cambridge 1997); Sumantra Bose, *The Challenge in Kashmir: Democracy, Self-Determination and Just Peace* (Sage Publications, New Delhi 1997).

10. *1947-1997 The Kashmir Dispute At Fifty: Charting Paths to Peace* (Kashmir Study Group, U.S.A. 1997), p. 57.

11. For India these pre-independence factors are: Hindu traditions and values; the conditioning of the Indian mind during the struggle for freedom and the influence of Mahatama Gandhi on India's national outlook. For Pakistan they are: the influence of Islam upon Pakistan's foreign policy; the course of Muslim nationalism, particularly the impact of the two-nation-theory and the events leading to the demand for a separate state of Pakistan. For a detailed discussion of the influence of these background factors on the foreign policy outlook of India and Pakistan see Norman D. Palmer, *South Asia and United States Policy* (Houghton Mifflin Company, New York 1966), Ch. 7 especially pp. 1162-66.

12. Taking a gloomy view, Robert Galluci has predicted that if there is any detonation of a nuclear weapon in anger in the next five years or so, the most likely place for it to happen would be South Asia. Quoted in *Arms Control Today* (April 1994), p. 14.

13. For an eminently sensible policy prescription on how to resolve the differences between Pakistan and India relating to the

thorny issue of Kashmir see Maleeha Lodhi, 'Still a Cold War,' *The World Today* (May 1998), pp. 133-137. Lodhi argues that while agreeing to address 'the sovereignty' at a later stage, Pakistan and India should take the following 'first steps' to promote a 'genuine political solution' to the Kashmir dispute. They are: the de-escalation of violence; reduction of Indian troop numbers; allowing people-to-people contact and trade across the Line of Control; a genuinely free election in Indian controlled Kashmir under international supervision; the involvement of 'elected Kashmiri representatives' on on-going Indo-Pakistan negotiations.

14. Gareth Porter, 'Environmental Security as a National Security Issue,' *Current History* (May 1995), pp. 216-222.

15. See Janne E. Nolan (Ed.) *Global Engagement: Co-operation and Security in the 21st Century* (The Brookings Institution, Washington, D.C. 1994), Ch. 1.

16. Gareth Evans, *Co-operating for Peace: The Global Agenda for the 1990s* (Allen and Unwin, Sydney 1991), p. 4.

17. Tariq Rauf, *Track Two Diplomacy: A Framework For a Co-operative Security Dialogue in South Asia* (Canadian Centre for Global Security, Ottawa 1994), p. 3.

18. Tariq Rauf, 'Regional Approaches to Curbing Nuclear Proliferation in the Middle East and South Asia,' *Aurora Papers* No. 16 (The Canadian Centre For Global Security, Ottawa 1992), p. 96.

19. Ibid.

20. Sverre Lodgaard, 'A Critical Appraisal of CSBMS by Category,' in Disarmament Tropical Papers 7 (United Nations, New York 1991), pp. 17-19.

LIST OF CONTRIBUTORS

MANZOOR AHMED–former Vice Chancellor of Hamdard University, Karachi.

IMRAN ALI–Professor, and Dean, Lahore University of Management Sciences, Lahore.

GILLES DORRONSORO–Professor, Institute of Political Studies, Rennes.

GILBERT ETIENNE–Emeritus Professor Graduate Institute of International Studies, Geneva.

MARC GABORIEAU–Director, Centre for the Study of India and South Asia, EHESS-CNRS, Paris.

RIFAAT HUSSAIN–Chair Department of Defence and Strategic Studies, Quaid-i-Azam University, Islamabad.

NIGHAT SAID KHAN–Dean, Institute of Women's Studies. Ms Khan also heads the ASR Resource Centre, Lahore.

PIERRE LAFRANCE–Ambassador of France to Pakistan in the 1990s.

CLAUDE MARKOVITS–Senior Fellow, Centre for the Study of India and South Asia, EHESS-CNRS, Paris.

SOOFIA MUMTAZ–Chief of Research, Pakistan Institute of Development Economics, Islamabad.

JEAN-LUC RACINE–Senior Fellow, Centre for the Study of India and South Asia, EHESS-CNRS, Paris, and Director, South Asia Programme, Maison des Sciences de l'Homme, Paris.

SAEED SHAFQAT–Director of Studies, Civil Service Academy, Lahore.

MARIAM ABOU ZAHAB–National Institute of Oriental Languages and Civilizations, Paris.

ARSHAD ZAMAN–Chairman, Arshad Zaman Associates, Karachi. Formerly Chief Economist, Planning Commission, Islamabad.